364.6
AMN

HV 8593 A44 1975

Amnesty International.
Report on torture.

AUDREY COHEN COLLEGE
Y0-DLZ-398

DATE DUE

DEMCO

COLLEGE FOR HUMAN SERVICES LIBRARY
201 VARICK ST., N.Y.C. 10014

Amnesty International

REPORT ON TORTURE

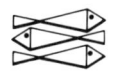

Farrar, Straus and Giroux · New York

© 1973, 1975 Amnesty International

"Special Report on Chile" by Rose Styron copyright © 1975
  by Farrar, Straus and Giroux, Inc.

All rights reserved
First American edition, 1975
Printed in the United States of America

Library of Congress Cataloging in Publication Data

Amnesty International.
  Report on torture.

  Bibliography: p.
  1. Torture. 2. Torture—History. I. Title.
HV8593.A44   1974   364.6'7   74-10569

COLLEGE FOR HUMAN SERVICES
LIBRARY
345 HUDSON STREET
NEW YORK, N.Y. 10014

CONTENTS

PREFACE TO THE AMERICAN EDITION 7

INTRODUCTION 13
Historical aspects of torture 27
The problem of legal definition 33

1 MEDICAL AND PSYCHOLOGICAL ASPECTS OF TORTURE 39
Torture as a stress 41
Manipulation and resistance 49
Pharmacological torture 55
Injury and long-term effects 58
Torturers: psychological aspects 63
The difficulty of investigation 68

2 LEGAL REMEDIES 70
International governmental organisations 71
Regional organisations 74
Non-governmental organisations 76
Case Study A: The UN and occupied territories of the Middle East 77
Case Study B: Regional and international response to the use of torture in Greece, 1967-1973 79
Case Study C: The UK government and Northern Ireland 105

3 WORLD SURVEY OF TORTURE 114
The nature of the evidence 114

Africa 117
  Burundi 118
  Cameroun 119
  Ethiopia 120
  Ghana 121
  Malawi 123
  Morocco 124
  Rhodesia 126
  South Africa 128
  Namibia 133
  Tanzania 137
  Togo 139
  Tunisia 140
  Uganda 141
  Zambia 144

Asia   145
  India   149
  Korea   151
  Indonesia   152
  Pakistan   156
  Philippines   157
  Sri Lanka   158
  Vietnam   160

Western Europe   168
  Belgium   169
  Portugal (and territories)   172
  Spain   176
  Turkey   179

Eastern Europe and the Soviet Union   184
  Albania, Hungary, Poland and Czechoslovakia   185
  German Democratic Republic   185
  Romania   186
  USSR   187

The Americas   191
  The United States   193
  Argentina   195
  Bolivia   196
  Brazil   198
  Colombia   201
  Chile   202
  Cuba   210
  Dominican Republic   211
  Ecuador   212
  Mexico   213
  Paraguay   214
  Peru   215
  Uruguay   217
  Venezuela   219
  Costa Rica   220
  El Salvador   221
  Honduras   221
  Panama   221
  Guatemala   221
  Nicaragua   222
  Haiti   223

The Middle East   224
  Bahrain   226
  Egypt   226
  Iran   227
  Iraq   230
  Israel   231
  Oman   234
  Yemen   235
  Syria   238

CONCLUSIONS   240
APPENDIX: SPECIAL REPORT ON CHILE BY ROSE STYRON   243
SELECT BIBLIOGRAPHY   283

PREFACE TO THE AMERICAN EDITION

In the following pages Amnesty International presents the first international review of the use of torture. During the last few years the press has featured stories of torture in South Africa or the U.S.S.R. or Brazil and for a few days the world has been horrified by the account of the brutalities which one group of human beings, under the protection of the state, has inflicted on another. But this very process of concentrating first on this country and then on that has disguised the most significant feature of the situation: that torture has virtually become a world-wide phenomenon and that the torturing of citizens regardless of sex, age, or state of health in an effort to retain political power is a practice encouraged by some governments and tolerated by others in an increasingly large number of countries.

In short, what for the last two or three hundred years has been no more than a historical curiosity has suddenly developed a life of its own and become a social cancer. To describe torture as a malignant growth on the body politic is, however, not simply to employ a figure of speech but to announce a program of action to remove it.

This is Amnesty's purpose. This Report on Torture represents one facet of Amnesty International's commitment to the continuing Campaign for the Abolition of Torture that was initiated in December 1972. The first year of the campaign was successful in publicizing the widespread use of torture, in collecting more than a million signatures from all over the world in support of an anti-torture resolution in the United Nations, and in obtaining the unanimous passage of that resolution, General Assembly Resolution 3059 (XXVIII), which calls on all governments "to become parties to existing international instruments which contain provisions relating to the prohibition of torture and other inhuman or degrading treatment or punishment."

The culmination of the first year's activities was the Conference for the Abolition of Torture that opened in Paris on December 10, 1973, the twenty-fifth anniversary of the

Universal Declaration of Human Rights. Approximately three hundred participants, including many internationally distinguished figures, representing governments and international non-governmental organizations as well as AI's own national sections, discussed various aspects of torture and actions to abolish it.

Four commissions were convened at the conference to discuss different problems: (1) the collecting and collating of information about the identity of torturers and of institutions where torture occurs; (2) the socio-economic and political factors affecting torture; (3) international, regional, and national legal factors affecting the practice of torture; (4) the short- and long-term psychological and medical effects of torture on the victim.

Discussion of these problems led to several recommendations: the establishment within AI of a central clearing house for information about specific incidents of torture; the formulation of codes of ethical conduct related to torture for medical, police, and military personnel; the cooperation among clergy, educators, lawyers, doctors, artists, trade unionists, and the like through their respective organizations on behalf of victims of torture; the strengthening of international and national laws that should govern the protection of the accused against torture; the promotion of research into the medical and psychological effects of torture; and the setting up of a register of health professionals to undertake missions to investigate allegations of torture in specific countries.

Immediately after the conference, AI's International Executive Committee, in accordance with the recommendations made, decided to establish a new division within the International Secretariat to work exclusively on the continuing Campaign for the Abolition of Torture. The campaign department, which began its full operation in the spring of 1974, signifies the continuing determination of Amnesty International to oppose and eradicate torture throughout the world.

Since the publication of the first British edition of this report in 1973 (before the Paris Conference), Amnesty International has continued to receive information to indicate that torture is indeed a world-wide phenomenon that does not belong solely to one political ideology or to one economic system. This information as well as decisive new events require that this Report on Torture be brought up to date for this first American edition.

The surveys of the historical, medical, and legal aspects of torture that were presented in the first British edition are still valid, and these sections have been retained in their entirety. Time has conspicuously overtaken the information about some countries, however, and those sections have accordingly been updated. One principle for revision has been that if new information is now available about torture in a country that was not mentioned in the first edition, a section has been added to deal with that country: whereas Saudi Arabia and Cyprus were not given attention before, this edition summarizes the material that has been received in the past year. A corollary of this principle is that, if new evidence has confirmed previous inferences, we have stated the case more strongly: incidents of torture in South Korea, for example, are not so difficult to substantiate today as they were a year ago.

The other governing principle for the revisions has been that wherever a change in governmental policy regarding torture has been radical, the section on that country has been rewritten. Circumstantial differences, however, have not been noted: no changes have been made in the sections that deal with such countries as Indonesia, where the victims may change but the political structure and the institutionalized use of certain methods of torture remain unabridged. The policies regarding the detention and treatment of prisoners in Chile, on the other hand, have severely changed since the military coup in September 1973, which occurred after the report had gone to press. The visit to Chile by an Amnesty International team of investigators shortly after the coup makes it possible to comment with relative precision on the use of torture by the Chilean junta. In addition to expanding the discussion of Chile on pages 202–210, the American edition contains a special appendix on Chile, written by Rose Styron, for conditions in Chile have been the subject of important and perhaps far-reaching debate in the United States.

Likewise, during the past year the governmental policies regarding torture have changed sharply for the worse in Namibia (formerly known as South-West Africa): during the autumn of 1973 the South African government, in cooperation with local tribal authorities, reintroduced public flogging as a tool of political repression.

There have been favorable changes of policy in Portugal, Turkey, and Greece. An amnesty granted by the new civilian government emptied Turkish jails of political prisoners in July 1974, and the April 1974 military coup in Portugal had a similar effect there. When the military government of Greece resigned in favor of a civilian administration, Greek political prisoners were also freed. In each of these cases, the outgoing government had denied for many years that it had practiced torture. It is now possible to prove beyond any doubt that those denials were false.

This report, the conference in Paris, and the programs of national and international action now underway all have the purpose of arousing public opinion to the danger which threatens the citizens of every country, however long its tradition of civilized conduct. For nothing is clearer from the record which follows than that once one group of citizens has been set on one side as licensed to torture, and another as a group so far beyond consideration as human beings that any brutality can be inflicted on them, the fatal step has been taken. The group of victims is rapidly enlarged while at the same time the apparatus of the state moves in to protect the torturers from punishment or even from inquiry.

In the face of so much that is deliberately brutal, Amnesty reasserts the principle which has guided it from the beginning: that every man, woman, and child is of value, that none should be made to suffer for holding or expressing his own opinions, and that, in consequence, torture must be recognized for the evil that it is, the public mobilized, and international and domestic machinery set up to bring it to an end.

The publication of the Report on Torture in several languages will help to further these aims. The report has already been published in a Dutch translation; German, French, and Japanese editions are scheduled for publication in the autumn of 1974. Under consideration are translations into Spanish, Turkish, Italian, Portuguese, and Urdu.

The report was constructed with the help of Mr. James Becket, Mrs. Elise Smith, Dr. Henry Oakeley, and the Research Department of Amnesty International, in addition to the many people who supplied Amnesty with the material upon which the report is based.

August 1974   Amnesty International

INTRODUCTION

Name: Ayse Semra Eker
Place and date of birth: Ismir, Turkey 1949
Date of arrest: 18 May 1972

On 18 April 1972, I was attacked by several people in the street. My eyes were covered by a special black band and I was forced into a minibus. The vehicle did not move for a few minutes. During this time I noticed that the people around me were addressing each other with expressions like 'my colonel' 'my major'. They started asking me questions from the first moment they put me into the minibus. When I did not answer, they started threatening me in the following manner. 'You don't talk now,' they would say; 'in a few minutes, when our hands will start roaming in between your legs, you will be singing like a nightingale.' The vehicle travelled for quite a long time before it stopped before a building I could not recognise. When I got off the minibus, I realised that I was in a relatively high open space. I was then taken into the basement of the building before which we had stopped, and then into a rather spacious room. I was surrounded by people whom I guessed to be military officers from the ways they addressed each other. They asked me questions and kept on saying that unless I spoke it would be quite bad for me and that we would have to do 'collective training' together. After a short while they forced me to take off my skirt and stockings and laid me down on the ground and tied my hands and feet to pegs. A person by the name of Umit Erdal beat the soles of my feet for about half an hour. As he beat my soles he kept on saying, 'We made everybody talk here, you think we shall not succeed with you?' and insulting me. Later, they attached wires to my fingers and toes and passed electric current through my body. At the same time they kept beating my naked thighs with truncheons. Many people were assisting Umit Erdal in this. One was a rather large man, tall, with curly hair and a relatively dark skin. A second was a small man with a relatively dark skin, black hair and a moustache. The third was a young man with a fair skin, dark hair and a moustache. The fourth was rather elderly, of middle stature, and of a dark complexion. He constantly wore dark glasses. The fifth was rather old, fat, of middle stature and with blue eyes and grey hair. At the same time, during the tortures, a grey-haired, stout and elderly colonel, and a grey-haired, blue-eyed, tall and well-built officer would frequently come in and give directives. After a while, they disconnected the wire from my finger and connected it to my ear. They immediately gave a high dose of electricity. My whole body and head shook in a terrible way. My front teeth started breaking. At the same time my torturers would hold a mirror to my face and say: 'Look what is happening to your lovely green eyes. Soon you will not be able to see at all. You will lose your mind. You see, you have already started bleeding in your mouth.' When they finished with electric shocks, they lifted me up to my feet and several of those I mentioned above started beating me with truncheons. After a while I felt dizzy and could not see very well. Then I fainted. When I came to myself, I found out I was lying half-naked in a pool of dirty water. They tried to force me to stand up and run. At the same time they kept beating me with truncheons, kicking me and pushing me against the walls. They then held my hand and hit me with truncheons in my palms and on my hands, each one taking turns. After all this my whole body was swollen and red and I could not stand on my feet. As if all this was not enough, Umit Erdal attacked me and forced me to the ground. I fell on my face. He stood on my back and with the assistance of somebody else forced a truncheon into my anus. As I struggled to stand he kept on saying 'You whore! See what else we will do to you. First tell us how many people did you go to bed with? You won't be able to do it any more. We shall next destroy your womanhood.' They next made me lie on my back and tied my arms and legs to pegs. They attached an electric wire to the small toe of my right foot and another to the end of a truncheon. They tried to penetrate my feminine organ with the truncheon. As I resisted they hit my body and legs with a large axe handle. They soon succeeded in penetrating my sexual organ with the truncheon with the electric wire on, and passed current. I fainted. A little later, the soldiers outside brought in a machine used for pumping air into people and said they would kill me. Then they untied me, brought me to my feet and took me out of the room. With a leather strap, they hanged me from my wrists on to a pipe in the corridor. As I hung half-naked, several people beat me with truncheons. I fainted again. When I woke, I found myself in the same room on a bed. They brought in a doctor to examine me. They tried to force me to take medicines and eat. I was bleeding a dark, thick blood. Some time later they brought in Nuri Colakoglu, who was in the same building as myself, to put more pressure on me. They wanted to show me into what state they had put him. I saw that the nails of his right hand were covered with pus. I realised that they had burned him with cigarette butts. They themselves later confirmed this. The sole of one of his feet was completely black and badly broken. The same night we were transferred to Istanbul together with Nuri Colakoglu. The next morning, the colonel I have already described came into my cell (I do not know where the cell was). He beat me and threatened me. 'Tonight I shall take you where your dead are. I shall have the corpses of all of you burnt. I will have you hanging from the ceiling and apply salt to your cut soles.' When he did not like the answers I gave him, he beat me again; then he had my eyes tied and sent me to another building. I was brought into a small room with my eyes tied. I was tied on the ground to pegs from my arms and ankles and electricity was passed through my right hand and foot. They then administered falanga. During the whole time I was in Istanbul, my hands were tied to chains. Because of this and because my tongue had split, I could not eat. A doctor would occasionally come to look at me and suggest first aid. One night I heard the sound of a gun and the sound of a man fall and die on the ground very close to me. I cried out: 'Whom have you killed?' They answered: 'It is none of your business. We kill whomever we want and bury him into a hole in the ground. Who would know if we did the same to you?' As I knew already, there was no security for my life.

During the ten days I stayed at MIT (the Turkish Secret Service) the same torture, insults, threats and pressure continued. On 28 April I was sent to the house of detention. Despite the fact that I went to the doctor at the house of detention and explained that I was badly tortured, that my right hand did not hold and that I had other physical complaints including the fact that I had no menstruation for four months in the following period, I was given no treatment. Some of my physical complaints still continue.

Signed here and at every page
6 February 1973*   Semra

Name: Vladimir Lvovich Gershuni
Place and date of birth: USSR, 1930
Date of arrest: 17 October 1969

Vladimir Lvovich Gershuni, born in 1930, is the nephew of one of the founders of the Socialist-Revolutionary Party, G.A. Gershuni. In 1949, Vladimir Gershuni was arrested and sentenced by decision of a Special Conference (i.e. the Security Police), to 10 years in special camps for his part in an anti-Stalin youth group. He was released in 1959 from a labour camp.

After his release, Gershuni, working as a bricklayer, became active in the civil rights movement in the USSR, taking part in numerous protests, signing appeals by the Action Group for the Defence of Human Rights to the United Nations in 1969 and writing pamphlets. He has been described as '... a man with an unusually highly developed

---

* See the section below on Turkey for a discussion of the changes in the treatment of prisoners in the past year.

instinct for justice. For him struggle against lies and violence is not a part of life, but the whole of it. He cannot reconcile himself with any manifestations of Stalinism' (*Chronicle of Current Events* No. 11, 1969).

On 17 October 1969, Gershuni was arrested in Moscow after various typewritten articles had been taken from him. These articles were *samizdat* documents, typewritten manuscripts circulating unofficially in the Soviet Union, and in this case considered illegal. The articles in Gershuni's possession dealt with the oppression of civil liberties within the Soviet Union. The following day further material was confiscated from his flat. Gershuni was put in Butyrka prison, and a week later was transferred to the Serbsky Institute for psychiatric examination and diagnosis. He was declared of unsound mind. He was then sent back to Butyrka prison to await trial.

The trial of Vladimir Gershuni was held on 13 March 1970 in a Moscow city court. He was charged under Article 190-1, referring to 'the distribution of deliberately false fabrications discrediting the Soviet social and political system'. This carries a maximum sentence of 3 years' imprisonment. Witnesses testified that Gershuni had condemned the use of Soviet armed forces in Czechoslovakia, and that he was critical of the Soviet leadership's policies on Czechoslovakia. He was charged with having in his possession 20 copies of a leaflet in defence of Major-General Grigorenko, a well-known dissident detained in a mental hospital since 1969. His signing of an appeal to the UN on behalf of civil liberties in the Soviet Union was seen as a discredit to the Soviet state. All witnesses denied that Vladimir Gershuni was mentally ill and emphasised his good character and performance at work.

Having been diagnosed by psychiatrists as being of unsound mind, Gershuni was not allowed to attend his trial. The court concluded in his absence that he should be sent to a psychiatric hospital of a 'special type'.

In Butyrka prison, in a cell together with criminals, Gershuni announced a hunger strike timed for 10 December (Human Rights Day). Explaining the causes and aims of the hunger-strike in a statement to the USSR Supreme Court, Gershuni included in his demands the return of letters and telegrams confiscated from him. On New Year's Eve he was sent to a newly instituted prison hospital in Oryol, an old

Russian city lying 170 miles south of Moscow.

Gershuni discontinued his hunger-strike on 31 January 1971, after a period of 55 days. In March Gershuni wrote notes on his treatment in the Oryol hospital which later reached the West. According to his diary, on the 43rd day of his hunger strike (17 January) a warder struck him on the face, which caused a great deal of damage to his teeth and gums because of their poor condition due to the hunger-strike. The official account of the incident was that Gershuni, in a fit of insanity, smashed a pane of glass with his head, cutting his mouth and breaking his jaw at the same time. He was given no medical or dental treatment for his injuries.

During the hunger-strike, Gershuni was forcibly fed and was also given injections of aminazine in large doses. He describes this treatment and its effects:

During rounds, just by way of an experiment, I complained about feeling poorly after a dose of haloperidol, and asked that the dose be reduced. This led to my being prescribed even more aminazine than I was already receiving... During a hunger-strike in January (I had been given aminazine ever since my arrival), I felt steadily worse and worse, and after making a complaint, I began to get aminazine injections in the maximum dose, or very close to it (approximately 6 cc). I couldn't sleep at all; yet the same dose was administered to me for twelve days in a row, until they became convinced that I was still not sleeping, and that the injections had not made me give up my hunger strike. I was given two injections a day, from 7 to 18 January, and from 19 January onwards, I have been given two tablets of haloperidol twice daily, that is four tablets in all (and XX assures me that this will go on for a long time). This medicine makes me feel more awful than anything I have experienced before; you no sooner lie down than you want to get up, you no sooner take a step than you're longing to sit down, and if you sit down, you want to walk again — and there's nowhere to walk...'

As of July 1973, Vladimir Gershuni is still being detained in Oryol Special Psychiatric Hospital.

Name: Maria Dina Roggerone de Greco
Country: Uruguay

On 21 April this year at approximately 11 o'clock I went to the Unidad

Militar Batallon de Infanteria No. 8, accompanied by my husband, because I had heard that the combined forces had been at my home looking for me. I talked to an officer who told me that there was a warrant for my arrest and that I would stay there for four days to be interrogated about the irregularities of the Mayor's Office. I told him that I had nothing against this. I was then blindfolded, and this official gave orders that I be taken to the *sala de disciplina* (interrogation room). The *'sala'* was a cell. There they made me stand with legs and arms akimbo and hands against the wall. I stood like that all of that day without eating; I was given water on three occasions, and at about 1 o'clock in the morning a soldier came and said to me, 'Lie down on the bunk'. It was only a mattress. As it was cold and I was wearing very light clothes I asked him for something to cover myself with, and he answered that I would have to put up with it. The whole of that first day I kept asking them to allow me to take off my contact lenses which were hurting my eyes because of the pressure of the blindfold. They didn't let me take them off. The following day about 7 o'clock, I was standing like that until the afternoon when they took me to make my statement. I crossed a patio, and they took me to a room where there were several people. They repeated again that the interrogation was about the irregularities of the Mayor's Office. They told me that I should specify all the people who had stolen, especially what the mayor and I had stolen. Without giving me time to answer, another person said to me: 'What do you know about Raffaglio, de Mellero and Traico?' I said that before answering I requested that a lawyer be called. Then the second gentleman who had spoken to me said: 'We will show you that we are lawyers, prosecutors and judges...' One of them slapped me several times, and they punched me in the head and used bandages to tie my hands behind my back. Placing themselves on either side of me, two soldiers took me by the legs and arms and submerged me into a barrel of water which covered my head and up to the middle of my chest. Without asking me any new questions they told the soldier to put me back in the same position in my cell, expressing their hope that with this my memory would be refreshed.

When I came back to the cell, I told the policewoman that I was pregnant; then came a soldier who insulted me in all sorts of ways and said to me that 'that was the pretext of all whores...' At any rate I again stood in the position against the wall until night-time, and they gave me water three times. In the afternoon Dr Burgel examined me in the infirmary but I was forbidden to speak to him. I was again taken and put in the same position in the cell and the policewoman gave me a large glass of water because they had to make a urine analysis. I was never told the result of this analysis although I asked for it several times. That night, like the previous night, they let me lie down for a while and the following morning they again took me to make a statement. They questioned me again about Raffaglio, De Mellero and Traico. I answered what I knew, but this didn't suit them because they then beat me repeatedly in the face and on the head. They then submerged me again in the same way as on the previous day in a barrel of water four or five times before they took me out almost drowned. I was told to go on thinking, and they put me back in the same position of discipline, as they called it. At this point they stopped even giving me the water, and since coming there I hadn't eaten anything. In the evening at what must have been about 9 pm, shortly after the guard had been changed, I felt ill with strong pain in the groin. I was seen by the male nurse who immediately called for Dr Burgel. Burgel told me that the pain was caused by the hours I had been standing and the lack of food but that he wasn't in a position to allow me to lie down, that he was going to talk to some superior, but that it was very difficult because I had to stay all night like that. The doctor went away, and after a little while the policewoman came and told me that they had given permission for me to lie down; she transferred me to another cell and brought me another cape, of the kind that soldiers use, to cover myself with.

The new cell to which they transferred me was full of red ants and because of them I couldn't sleep; I spent all my time killing ants. The following day when they took me to make my statement I showed them how I was bitten all over by the ants and one of them answered: 'You wanted to play us a trick ... but we had you bitten by ants and fleas so you couldn't sleep.' They interrogated me again and plunged me so many times into the tank full of ice cold water that I must have fainted, for I woke up in the infirmary.

On 1 May — I remember this because it was a very special day in the barracks — they took me to the interrogation room, gagged me, handcuffed me (with my hands behind my back) and one of the soldiers said to me: 'Now you're for it.' They brought another person whom they started to ill-treat and when they started to maltreat him, I was held up by two soldiers gripping my legs and I heard the blows they dealt to my husband; when they put him into the water he himself wept and shouted. Then they asked him to say everything that I, Garrasino and he had stolen, until in the end Greco said anything. They took Greco away, and they removed my gag and submerged me into the water saying: 'Confess, confess!' They also directed electricity to my hands and beat me. One of them lifted up my sweater and asked the other one to turn electricity on to my stomach, then the problem of the pregnancy would be done with and they could do anything to me. They held me like this all day taking me out several times, the last time was very early in the morning and I was wrapped in a towel, which the policewoman had helped me to sew because all my clothes were wet through. By now I said everything they wanted because I couldn't take any more. As a result of these soakings, I still have a sort of bronchitis for which Dr Burgel began to treat me. In the barracks I have the medicines they gave me. My whole body, except my face, hands and feet, came up in spots. They told me it was a nervous allergy — I wasn't allowed to talk to the doctor — and they gave me intra-muscular injections of something like 'Clorotrimetrol'. I heard them comment on it. I had a temperature, and despite my spots they continued to soak me as before. They didn't allow me to stay in bed and I had to go to the prison wall in the 'position of discipline'. The only day they allowed me to stay in bed was when I came to make the first declaration to the judge. I said to the soldier who came to fetch me that I didn't feel fit to go there and he said, 'Don't play act,' and that we deserved a treatment worse than animals. I got up and they brought me clothes, allowed me to drink a glass of water before I left and another glass which I took here before the tribunal. I arrived at 10 o'clock and left at 5 pm. Before I came to the judge's office they had subjected me to an interrogation where the answer was written down without consulting me. When it was finished, they gave it to me to read; I started to read it and I said there were a few things I didn't agree with. Then they said to me: 'Well then, don't read it. Sign or we'll start all over again.' Then I signed.

This testimony was first published in the Uruguayan weekly newspaper *Marcha* on 30 June 1973. It was the last copy of the periodical to appear before its suspension.

> No one shall be subjected to torture or to cruel, inhuman, or degrading treatment or punishment.
>
> Article 5, Universal Declaration of Human Rights

Can what happened to Ayse Eker be justified? There are those who must think it can. The country-by-country survey in this report indicates that many states in the world today deliberately use torture. Policemen, soldiers, doctors, scientists, judges, civil servants, politicians are involved in torture, whether in direct beating, examining victims, inventing new devices and techniques, sentencing prisoners on extorted false confessions, officially denying the existence of torture, or using torture as a means of maintaining their power. And torture is not simply an indigenous activity, it is international; foreign experts are sent from one country to another, schools of torture explain and demonstrate methods, and modern torture equipment used in torture is exported from one country to another.

It is commonplace to view our age as one of 'ultra-violence'. Much of the mass of information we are exposed to in the West reports catastrophes, atrocities, and horrors of every description. Torture is one of these horrors, but even in an age of violence, torture stands out as a special horror for most people. Pain is a common human denominator, and while few know what it is to be shot, to be burned by napalm, or even to starve, all know pain. Within every human being is the knowledge and fear of pain, the fear of helplessness before unrestrained cruelty. The deliberate infliction of pain by one human being on another to break him is a special horror. It is significant that torture is the one form of violence today that a state will always deny and never justify. The state may justify mass murder and glorify those that kill as killers, but it never justifies torture nor glorifies those that torture as torturers.

And yet the use of torture has by all indications increased over the last few years. The continual limited wars of our time – civil wars, colonial wars, and territorial wars – account for part of this, but an increasing proportion is accounted for by states who use torture as a means of governing. Torture in those countries plays an integral role in the political system itself. Its function is not only to generate confessions and information from citizens believed to oppose the government; it is used to deter others from expressing opposition. For those who govern without the consent of the governed this has proved to be an effective method of maintaining power. To set torture as the price of dissent is to be assured that only a small minority will act. With the majority neutralised by fear, the well-equipped forces of repression can concentrate on an isolated minority.

Torture today is essentially a state activity. While the state hardly has a monopoly on the use of violence in today's world, and the increase in criminal violence and political terrorism bears witness to this, the preconditions for torture make it almost the exclusive province of the state. Torture requires that the victim be kept under the physical control of the torturer. The criminal or the insurgent does not have the same facilities for detention as the state, and he uses other means of violence, not because he is less violent necessarily, but because the techniques of torture are normally not available to him. As one approaches a situation of developed insurgency and civil war, the possibilities for torture by the anti-government forces grow.

The widespread use of torture is alarming in itself, but what is especially alarming is that the consensus against torture is being weakened not only by its constant violation but by the attitude of people in general. Many people are indifferent, and some even appear ready to accept the practice, and to say so in public. General Massu, a former Commander-in-Chief of the French Army, recently wrote how he ordered torture and commended its use during the Algerian War. This fact had always been officially denied. The open justification by an important personality caused considerable reaction in France, though since World War II justifications for torture have appeared in print, generally in military literature dealing with counter-insurgency. An example is provided by the French theoretician Trinquier, who incorporates torture into his system of modern warfare. Trinquier, a French Colonel, is quite explicit in his book *Modern Warfare*, first published in 1961. He writes that the terrorist 'must be made to realise that when he is captured he cannot be treated as an ordinary criminal, nor like a prisoner taken on the battlefield . . . No lawyer is present for such an interrogation. If the prisoner gives the information requested, the examination is quickly terminated; if not, specialists must force his secret from him. Then, as a soldier, he must face the suffering and perhaps the death he has heretofore managed to avoid. The terrorist must accept this as a condition inherent in his trade . . .' These justifications never use the word 'torture'. Torture is of course forbidden by the Geneva Conventions.

It is apparent today that much of state torture is carried out by the military forces, usually elite or special units, who displace the civil police in matters of political security. Their military training and their exposure to post-World War II theories about 'unconventional war' make them particularly apt for the practice and enable them to apply the concept of 'war' to any situation of civil political conflict no matter how mild.

Those who consciously justify torture, and are not candid enough to state that they use it to defend their own power and privilege, rely essentially on the philosophic argument of a lesser evil for a greater good. They reinforce this with an appeal to the doctrine of necessity — the existential situation forces them to make a choice between two evils. Only the sadist, and there are obviously many sadists directly involved in torture, would celebrate the act of torture for itself. The non-sadist must view it as a necessary means to a desirable end. The usual justification posits a situation where the 'good' people and the 'good' values are being threatened by persons who do not respect 'the rules of the game', but use ruthless, barbaric, and illegal means to achieve their 'evil' ends. Only similar means will be effective enough to defeat the evil purposes of these persons beyond the pale. This argument has had a broad appeal and continues to have it: Stalin had to use torture since the bourgoisie use it and it gives them an unfair advantage; the only way to defeat the Tupamaros in Uruguay — or any other urban guerillas — is by making them talk; it is the only way to deal with Communists/Fascists/Catholics/etc.

The most effective presentation of the argument justifying torture today is given in the form of a concrete dilemma. The classic case is the French general in Algiers who greeted visiting dignitaries from the metropolis with: 'Gentlemen, we have in our hands a man who has planted a bomb somewhere out in that city. It will go off within four hours. Would you not use every means to save the lives of innocent people?' An updated version would be a jumbo jet with a bomb aboard and only the man in your custody can tell you how to disarm it – if he will speak. What if you could bring utopia to earth by just torturing one man? The thrust of this argumentation is that if one places a value on human life, indeed the highest value, one is really obliged to hurt one person to save many lives. In real life cases do not present themselves this sharply, but for the sake of argument it does take the issue and push it to its most extreme possibility.

The prohibition of torture as a *universal value* is a recent achievement. The abolition of slavery was achieved only in the last century, and its prohibition is a universal value, though it continues to be practised in some regions in violation of this prohibition. The prohibition on torture is based on man's long experience as a social and moral being who developed increasingly humane standards out of his belief in the dignity and integrity of each human being. The prohibition finds support in the teachings of the world's religions, the writings of philosophers, and the development over the last three centuries of a concept of inalienable human rights.

One argument that has been presented in the past and is often heard today is that torture is inefficient. This addresses itself to two points. One is that if you produce false confessions and wrong information it is an inefficient means of attaining the goals of punishing the guilty and uncovering mischief. The other is that there are more efficient ways to get information, and clever methods of interrogation get better results, another way of saying that torture is not necessary. The line of argumentation based on inefficiency is totally inadmissible. To place the debate on such grounds is to give the argument away; in effect it means that if it can be shown to be efficient it is permissible. It might well be that there are more efficient methods to obtain information than torture, but this does not mean torture cannot also be efficient. In a country without trained interrogators it might indeed be relatively efficient. Furthermore, this argument tends to disregard its major use today, which is to deter others from action, and the evidence is that torture is quite efficient in this respect.

The main arguments for the abolition of torture have based themselves on its inhumanity and injustice. In a classic work first published in 1764, *On Crime and Punishment*, the Italian Beccaria wrote: 'The strength of the muscles and the sensitivity of the nerves of an innocent person being known factors, the problem is to find the level of suffering necessary to make him confess to any given crime.' The argument that innocent persons were being forced to confess and were being executed is as valid today as it was in the eighteenth century. The injustice of torture is found also in the fact that it offends the notion of just punishment which is based on a fixed term of imprisonment for a specific offence. The duration of torture is completely open-ended and often has nothing to do with a specific offence.

No act is more a contradiction of our humanity than the deliberate infliction of pain by one human being on another, the deliberate attempt over a period of time to kill a man without his dying. The thorough degradation and debasement of those involved is well described by a victim of torture:

> I have experienced the fate of a victim. I have seen the torturer's face at close quarters. It was in a worse condition than my own bleeding, livid face. The torturer's was distorted by a kind of twitching that had nothing human about it. He was in such a state of tension that he had an expression very similar to those we see on Chinese masks; I am not exaggerating. It is not an easy thing to torture people. It requires inner participation. In this situation, I turned out to be the lucky one. I was humiliated. I did not humiliate others. I was simply bearing a profoundly unhappy humanity in my aching entrails. Whereas the men who humiliate you must first humiliate the notion of humanity within themselves. Never mind if they strut around in their uniforms, swollen with the knowledge that they can control the suffering, sleeplessness, hunger and despair of their fellow human beings, intoxicated with the power in their hands. Their intoxication is nothing other than the degradation of humanity. The ultimate degradation. They have had to pay

dearly for my torments. I wasn't the one in the worst position. I was simply a man who moaned because he was in great pain. I prefer that. At this moment I am deprived of the joy of seeing children going to school or playing in the park. Whereas they have to look their own children in the face. (Geo Mangakis, 'Letter to Europeans', *Index*, vol. 1, no. 1).

The arguments against torture rest essentially on moral grounds. And yet man's historical experience provides a very practical argument. Nowhere is the argument that the means corrupt the end more true. History shows that torture is never limited to 'just once': 'just once' becomes once again — becomes a practice and finally an institution. As soon as its use is permitted once, as for example in one of the extreme circumstances like a bomb, it is logical to use it on people who might plant bombs, or on people who might think of planting bombs, or on people who defend the kind of person who might think of planting bombs. The example of Algeria is a classic case. Torture began under certain restraints and then it spread into an indiscriminate orgy of brutality, the victims first limited to 'natives', then finally spreading to France itself. It was effective as a weapon in the struggle, and the French won the military battles, but they lost the war. Cancer is an apt metaphor for torture and its spread through the social organism. The act of torture cannot be separated from the rest of society; it has its consequences, it degrades those who use it, those who benefit from it, and it is the most flagrant contradiction of justice, the very ideal on which the state wishes to base its authority. It can be argued that torture could produce short-term benefits for those in power, but it is a basic principle of law and civilisation that many short-run expediencies are prohibited to preserve a greater value, a value on which society itself is based. The illegal obtaining of evidence is an example. It might produce the conviction of a criminal in one case, but the greater value of protecting every citizen from arbitrary and illegal searches is a higher value than one conviction. So also with torture. History has shown that a system can function well without illegal evidence and without torture, and it also shows that once these are permitted the temptation to use 'easy' methods is unavoidable. Just as states say that to give in to terrorism is to invite the loss of many more lives, so to give in to the use of torture is to invite its spread and the eventual debasement of the whole society. Torture is never justified.

The absolute prohibition on torture is the only acceptable policy. The system that uses it only mocks any noble ends it might profess. If the use of torture occurs, and abuses occur in every system, it must be dealt with by an impartial tribunal, a tribunal that would take into account the circumstances as it would for other crimes such as homicide. Man with his innate aggression has learned to place limits on his capacity for excess. He has learned to place limits on the exercise of the power by the few to protect the many and ultimately to protect everyone. Torture is the most flagrant denial of man's humanity, it is the ultimate human corruption. For this reason man has prohibited it. This human achievement must be defended.

Historical aspects of torture

Every nation has practised torture at one time or another in its history. Looking back over the history of mankind it is difficult to contest this generalisation, a generalisation based not on mere incidents of excess but on an established practice. The historical record implies that the capacity to torture is a potential common to man, or at least to some men in every human group:

Torture has been common in the Western experience in time of war and social stress, while in less troubled times the declared values of Western societies toward their own citizens have followed cycles of legalisation of torture and its abolition. When legalised, torture has served to produce confessions and information for the judicial system. The demerits and merits of the practice have been the subject of debate among the learned in the West throughout the centuries.

Ancient Greece and Rome, from which the West traces much of its liberal and humanist tradition, forbade torture of the citizen. However, in Athens a slave's testimony was not considered reliable unless he had been tortured. In Republican Rome the same double standard applied, but under the increasingly despotic regimes of the Empire, the free man was subject to torture for an ever-widening range of offences. The 'Question' (*Quaestio*) first acquired its fear-inspiring meaning. The torture of the early Christians went beyond the simple extortion of confessions, the 'putting of the question', and was used to force the faithful to renounce their faith — a use of torture that would echo into the future. (This use raised the opposition of certain Roman jurists who considered it an abuse of the proper use of torture!) With the triumph of Christianity, the practice fell into relative disuse in the West as the Church was opposed to torture.

Torture reappeared at the end of the eleventh century, and the relevant Roman laws *de quaestionibus* were resurrected. By the thirteenth century the practice was in full renaissance. Torture was considered to produce *probatio probatissimi*, 'the proof of all proofs', and its practice was meticulously regulated and codified with all of man's genius for institutionalising and sanctifying his inhumanity to his fellow man. The 'question' was divided into different degrees, ordinary, extraordinary, preparatory, and preliminary, and torture was administered in a special chamber by a civil servant, who also served as the public executioner. Magistrates sat comfortably amidst the various paraphernalia, duly noting the time, the weights and the measures of various tortures, and then recording the confessions, which, not surprisingly, were generally forthcoming.

The Roman Catholic Church, fearful of growing heresy, soon entered the field with the power of investigation, *Inquisitio*. The infamous Inquisition was launched. History demonstrates that once man accepts the possibility of torture, he constructs a highly logical framework of argument justifying it. For example, there is indeed a logic in holding that a slave will always support his master and only torture will produce the truth. Those justifying the use of torture by the Church argued that the mob was burning and torturing heretics and the Church should bring it under control and thus minimise the use of torture. Furthermore, if the state could torture the common criminal, why should the more serious crime of heresy escape detection just because St Augustine had said that the heretic would suffer spiritual punishment? As has continually happened in history, once torture was permitted, the supposed limits of regulation were easily bypassed, and new chapters added to the annals of human cruelty and suffering.

Though even in the Middle Ages there were voices raised against torture, the abolitionist current gained real force only during the eighteenth century and the Enlightenment which propounded reason and human progress. In France, the Declaration of the Rights of Man, which was to have such a wide influence on a new age, abolished torture 'forever'. The right not to be subject to torture was thought of not as a political right that could be granted, but as a 'natural, inalienable, and sacred right'. The French Revolution, which guillotined thousands without discrimination as to rank or station, has few cases of torture on its record. The French Penal Code, in proscribing torture, placed the torturer in the same category as the murderer by making it a capital offence.

With some lapses, abolition carried the day in nineteenth-century Europe. Liberal and humanitarian ideas espoused by the ascendent bourgeoisie flourished in the wake of the Industrial Revolution. The economically obsolete institution of slavery, as well as practices like mutilation, branding, and many corporal punishments, were abolished. By the 1920s a European scholar could write that torture was a distant relic of a barbarous past, a practice forever left behind on man's journey to progress. This was essentially a European vision of Europe. European domination of the world reached its apogee before World War I, and the five centuries of European expansion had been accompanied by crimes including torture and genocide. There is evidence that torture diminished in the colonies in the nineteenth century. And one of the justifications for the imperialism of the nineteenth century was to stop the barbarous practices of certain peoples. The scholar of the 1920s cannot really be accused of blind optimism, for the trend looked at from that period seemed to be away from the barbarism of past epochs. Within a few years Europe was plunging toward the holocaust, a global war. The first extermination camps in Nazi Germany, like Dachau, began their history as detention camps for German political prisoners. From the beginning there were torture chambers installed, and later there were ovens. Once again torture would take on a quasi-legal status as permission to torture was written in orders from superiors in Nazi Germany.

Out of the agony and wreckage of World War II came a new resolve of 'never again'. The winners of the war saw themselves as representatives of the best in Western civilisation with its principles of equality and freedom, while they saw their fascist enemies as the representatives of the dark side of the European soul, its racism and oppression. One of the shared values of the humanist tradition was the abolition of torture. This principle found its way into the post-war declarations on human rights and laws of war without any dissent or debate.

A new balance of power also emerged from World War II. It was again to be Eurocentric, with two continental superpowers confronting each other in the centre of Europe. Extended Europe would continue to be the centre of the international system in political, economic, cultural, and communications terms. While the conflict of this confrontation, the Cold War, would cause considerable tension, it did result in political stability in the centre. The periphery, or what came to be called the 'Third World', would become the unstable region, as peoples sought to throw off the yoke of European colonialism, and the superpowers extended the Cold War to these areas. Torture was to be part of political struggle in these areas, used either by the colonial power as a weapon against national liberation forces, or by local governments against domestic opposition. No ideology has had a monopoly on the use of torture during this period, but those who have used it have generally used the labels of the Cold War to establish that their enemies are beyond the human pale.

Just as wealth and power were still concentrated in the extended Europe area, so the developing system of the protection of human rights was also centred in Europe, more specifically in the West. It was here that international organisations, both governmental and non-governmental, were based. It was here that the media were most active and influential and that public opinion had a meaningful and independent existence. And it was here at the political centre that pressure groups had the greatest chance of success. This consciousness and action for the international protection of human rights was part of the historical continuity of the great European contradiction: on the one hand the aggressive expansion of Europe, and, on the other, its tolerant humanism and defence of liberal ideals.

The war and post-war years have also been marked by a seeming paradox. Never has there been a stronger or more universal consensus on the total inadmissability of the practice of torture: at the same time the practice of torture has reached epidemic proportions.

There has been a consistent link in the past between the use of torture and crimes against the sovereign or the state. While its use is often much broader, it is what we today call 'political offences' that have tended to be the first for which torture was legalised and the last for which it was abolished. In Ancient Rome torture against the free man was first introduced in cases of *crimen majestatis* or *lèse majesté*; torture came to be considered a legitimate defence by the sovereign power against those who acted against them. Restricted at first, it expanded as the despotic nature of the sovereign's power expanded, until the smallest slight to the ruler was reason for torture. In 1740 in Prussia under the strong abolitionist pressure of German jurists, Frederick II abolished legal torture with three exceptions: murder, treason, and *lèse majesté*. There is a close connection between absolutist power and the use of torture. The aphorism about 'absolute power tending to corrupt absolutely' is relevant, as torture seems to be inevitably part of that corruption. As Pierre Vidal Naquet has written: '*Torture d'état* is in effect nothing other than the most direct and most immediate form of the domination of one man over another, which is the very essence of politics.'

Man is capable of torturing fellow human beings, but he also feels the need to justify what he is doing. It seems to be a pre-condition for torture that the torturer have a world view, no matter how crude, that divides man into the torturable and the non-torturable. This distinction can be based on any of the manifold ways of distinguishing one man from another: it can be race, colour, nationality, class, or differing beliefs, usually political or religious. The torturer represents, and by the act of torture is defending, the 'good' values. The victim is not 'chosen', he is not human.

Those that are believed to threaten the established order are placed in a category that puts them beyond the pale. It is no accident that slaves have been torturable. Class has always played a role in the use of torture, just as punishment has followed class lines, reserving the greatest cruelty and severity for the lower classes and for 'traitors' to the ruling class. It is interesting to note that the actual act of torturing is normally not a ruling-class activity. The task itself is left to someone of lower station, as it has never been particularly reputable work. In the military it is 'sergeant's work'. This is not to say that those of higher station are not above ordering it and witnessing it and above all gaining from it.

A related feature is the use of torture as an element in the process of exorcising evil from a society. A community under stress needs a scapegoat to confess responsibility for the evils besetting the society. While the 'witch hunts' of the past might seem today like collective madness, especially as the 'crimes' are irrational crimes, the need for this process of exorcism is most contemporary — the purge trials in the Soviet Union provide one of many examples.

It is the doctrine of equality that is profoundly opposed to those attitudes that permit torture. While the signers of the American Declaration of Independence did not really mean that negro slaves and Indians were 'created equal', the idea that 'all men are created equal' had been espoused. By the middle of the twentieth century this idea was universally accepted as a principle, though it was evident that 'some were more equal than others' and that the use of torture continued to be based psychologically on a denial of equality to the despised group.

It is very difficult to compare the past with the present, as too little is known about either to enable judgments of 'more' or 'worse' to be made. When the practice is legalised, there is no doubt it is used, and there is documentary evidence. When it is outlawed it is difficult to know the real extent of its use. There is the further problem that facts enter into history only when the articulate and the literate are concerned. There is evidence to suggest today that the increased knowledge about the incidence of the practice results from the fact that it is increasingly being used on the literate classes of society. Today modern communications also help in bringing together information about the practice. One can only speculate about whether or not there was more or worse torture a hundred years ago, or five hundred years ago. One can state with some assurance that the practice is both more widespread and more intense today than it was fifteen years ago.

In a comparison of the past and present, however, there is evidence of a definite development of techniques of torture. While many primitive methods based on physical force remain common, modern technology, most notably the use of electricity, has made its contributions. Part of the reason for this is that when the practice is illegal, every effort is made not to leave marks. Modern psychology and pharmacology have co-operated in developing techniques in sensory deprivation and new drugs that have primarily psychological effects. One major difference lies in the fact that the modern use of torture is hidden. A third character has been added to the drama of torturer and victim: the state official who denies it. The debate in the past was an open one between those advocating abolition and those advocating legalisation. The debate today is between, it has been said, 'abolitionists and liars'.

The problem of legal definition

Everyone has an idea of what torture is; yet no one has produced a definition which covers every possible case. There is good reason why the concept of torture resists precise and scientific definition; it describes human behaviour, and each human being is unique, with his own pain threshold, his own psychological make-up, his own cultural conditioning. Furthermore, torture is a concept involving degree on a continuum ranging from discomfort to ill treatment to intolerable pain and death, and a definition must resort in part to qualitative terms which are both relative and subjective. Despite these difficulties it is important to try to be as precise as possible in order to eliminate ambiguity, especially in that 'grey area' in which the modern state and modern technology are anxious to operate. Also, torture, like other words, has an evaluative as well as a descriptive content. Given that the word 'torture' conveys an idea repugnant to humanity, there is a strong tendency by torturers to call it by another name, such as 'interrogation in depth' or 'civic therapy' and a tendency of victims to use the word too broadly.

There are certain essential elements which give torture its particular meaning and which should be incorporated in any comprehensive definition. In the first place the nature of torture assumes the *involvement of at least two persons*, the torturer and the victim, and it carries the further implication that the victim is under the physical control of the torturer. The second element is the basic one of the *infliction of acute pain and suffering*. It is the means used by the torturer on the victim and the element that distinguishes him from the interrogator. Pain is a subjective concept, internally felt, but is no less real for being subjective. Definitions that would limit torture to physical assaults on the body exclude 'mental' and 'psychological' torture which undeniably causes acute pain and suffering, and must be incorporated in any definition. The concept of torture does imply a strong degree of suffering which is 'severe' or 'acute'. One blow is considered by most to be 'ill-treatment' rather than 'torture', while continued beatings over 48 hours would be 'torture'. Intensity and degree are factors to be considered in judging degrees.

Thirdly, there is implicit in the notion of torture the effort by the torturer, through the infliction of pain, to make the victim submit, to 'break him'. The *breaking of the victim's will* is intended to destroy his humanity, and the reaction to the horror of this finds expression in various human rights instruments in such phrases as 'respect for the inherent dignity of the human person'.

Finally, torture implies a *systematic activity with a rational purpose*. The unwitting, and thus accidental, infliction of pain, is not torture. Torture is the deliberate infliction of pain, and it cannot occur without the specific intent of the torturer. Inherent in this element of purpose are the goals or motives for employing torture, and while torture can be used for a variety of purposes, it is most generally used to obtain confessions or information, for punishment, and for the intimidation of the victim and third persons. The first two motives relate directly to the victim, while the purpose of intimidation, in wide use today as a political weapon, is intended to be a deterrent to others as well as the victim.

The definition of torture adopted here is: 'Torture is the systematic and deliberate infliction of acute pain in any form by one person on another, or on a third person, in order to accomplish the purpose of the former against the will of the latter.'

There is little jurisprudence or legal writing defining torture. Pictet's *Commentary on the Geneva Conventions*, which makes frequent reference to torture, states: 'The word torture refers here above all to suffering inflicted on a person to obtain from him or a third person confessions or information' (First Geneva Convention 1949, Art. 12(2); Second Geneva Convention 1949, Art. 12(2); Third Geneva Convention 1949, Art. 13; Fourth Geneva Convention 1949, Art. 32). This definition limits itself to two purposes, includes the case of the torture of one person to break the will of a third person, but leaves the matter of degree quite open with an unqualified 'suffering'. The European Commission of Human Rights give a definition of torture in the Greek Case which is of particular interest as it was developed for the one case where an international judicial body found a state guilty of using torture as an administrative practice. The definition is therefore of more than academic interest, especially as there are cases pending before the Commission which again raise the issue of torture. The Commission stated: 'The word "torture" is often used to describe inhuman treatment, which has a purpose, such as the obtaining of information or confessions, or the infliction of punishment, and it is generally an aggravated form of inhuman treatment. The notion of inhuman treatment covers at least such treatment as deliberately causes severe suffering, mental or physical, which in the particular situation is unjustifiable'. (Council of Europe, European Commission of Human Rights, *The Greek Case: Report of the Commission*, vol. 2, part 1, page 1). The definition, while it includes the idea of deliberately inflicted 'severe' suffering and gives some purposes, also adds the new element of 'justifiability'. This clause leaves the Commission's definition open to the interpretation that if *A* beats and uses electricity on *B* over three months for a 'good' purpose or a 'justifiable' purpose, it is not torture. This appears not only faulty as a definition but dangerous as a policy. While all definitions must include the mental states of intent, pain, and purpose, these elements can still be determined with some objectivity. But 'justifiability' is a value judgment, and to introduce a value judgment into the definition is to render it scarcely operative. As a policy it would leave the door open to abuse, for the prohibition on torture could be circumvented by judging the most heinous acts to be 'justifiable', and thus not torture.

The question arises whether or not what constitutes torture is culturally determined and can vary from culture to culture. On this issue the distinction may usefully be made between 'physical' and 'mental' torture. The physiology of the human nervous system is the same for all human beings regardless of race, climate or culture. In general the effect of physical torture such as beating, electro-shock, near-drowning, sleep deprivation and drugs will be the same on any human system. Although cultural conditioning can have remarkable effects on resistance to pain, as for example in the case of religious firewalkers, the result of the infliction of pain against the victim's will would seem to be universal at the physiological level. Mental or psychological torture, on the other hand, can be different, for it usually depends on the value system of the victim for its effect. Some values, such as the protection of children, might be universal for reasons deeper than culture, but values like religion are culturally determined. To make a Moslem fall to his knees and kiss the cross can be a humiliation and torture for him, while the same act for a Christian would not be. What is universal is the prohibition of torture; the means of infliction of pain might vary from culture to culture, the prohibition of torture is universal.

An area of legal controversy which bears directly on the problem of definition involves the so-called doctrine of the 'sliding scale'. This doctrine essentially holds that the state should have the right to escalate its means of interrogation the greater the threat to its security. This has a particular attraction to governments facing an 'urban guerrilla' or political terrorism. The proponents of this doctrine do not advocate 'torture' as described in the cases which introduce this Report, but rather methods that occupy the 'grey area', the area of 'ill-treatment', 'degrading' or 'inhuman' treatment. It is in the 'grey area' that the definition of torture is particularly weak. The definition developed here is essentially inductive, derived from the way the word is used. It is an attempt to develop an agreed core of meaning, but it depends on a subjective qualification of degree with the adjective 'acute'. The question of degree relates to the problem of where society 'draws the line' in its interrogation methods, a problem which every society must face whether it is dealing with an emergency or not. Where a government rules with the consent of the governed and permits pluralistic expression, a number of groups are generally struggling over where to draw the line, and ideally this process would balance fairly competing interests within the limits set by basic human rights guarantees. The danger comes when this balancing of interests is no longer permitted and the state's interest is the only one to determine where the line is to be drawn. There is no support in the legal texts for the proposition that the state has the right to move the line toward the torture and ill-treatment end of the scale when the state perceives a threat. The European Convention recognises the possibility of this threat, the situation of a public emergency or state of war, and under Article 15 it permits the suspension of most of the basic human rights. However, it specifically forbids the suspension of Article 3, which categorically holds that 'no one shall be subjected to torture or to inhuman or degrading treatment or punishment'. Nothing in the Convention would allow this to be qualified. The doctrine of the 'sliding scale' risks being the doctrine of the slippery slope. The state already has abundant legal means to meet an emergency, including such means as suspending *habeas corpus*, freedom of association and speech. When these rights are suspended and that is coupled with the right to escalate the means of interrogation, this combination leaves the door wide open to abuse. The prohibition must be left sacrosanct and any attempt to move the line toward the torture end of the scale must be resisted.

Although there may be grey areas in defining those acts that constitute torture, there can be no misunderstanding about its unlawfulness. Under every relevant international legal document torture is prohibited.

In time of war, or other international armed conflict, all combatants, those placed *hors de combat* and other protected persons, are, under the Geneva Conventions of 12 August 1949, forbidden to be tortured. Common Article 3 of the same Conventions also prohibits the use of torture in the case of armed conflict not of an international nature. Thus, in cases of civil war, no claim or domestic jurisdiction can be invoked by the parties to the conflict to deny the international illegality of the use of torture.

Similarly, the Universal Declaration of Human Rights (Art. 5), the American Declaration on the Rights and Duties of Man (Art. 26), and the Declaration of the Citizen's Rights in the Arab States and Countries (Art. 5), all prohibit the use of torture in time of peace. So do the International Covenant on Civil and Political Rights (Art. 7), the European Convention on Human Rights (Art. 3), and the American Convention on Human Rights (Art. 5). Furthermore, even though the latter treaties permit derogations from some of the rights protected in case of extreme threats to the internal order of the state, the right not to be subjected to torture is one from which no derogation is permissible (Covenant, Art. 4; European Convention, Art. 15; America Convention, Art. 27).

It can safely be stated, accordingly, that under all circumstances, regardless of the context in which it is used, torture is outlawed under the common law of mankind. This being so, its use may properly be considered to be a crime against humanity.

1 Medical and Psychological Aspects of Torture

An analysis of the effect of torture inevitably involves a study of human tolerance to pain or stress. This raises two preliminary difficulties of a theoretical as well as a practical nature. First, pain or stress produces biological responses in man which are best understood in terms of a combination of mental and physical processes. Secondly, it is virtually impossible to discuss isolated torture methods and their effects without reference to the context in which the torture is being administered. This second difficulty is particularly relevant to the problem of relating results from laboratory stress situations to actual torture environments themselves.

The first difficulty, particularly that of discussing experiences of pain, arises from the traditional and convenient habit of considering the 'body' and the 'mind' as discrete entities. This theoretical separation has been, by and large, axiomatic in cultures with religious and philosophical roots as diverse as the Judaeo-Christian and the Hindu. But, however appropriate this concept of a mind-body dichotomy may appear to be in the development of moral and behavioural norms, it poses severe obstacles to a proper understanding of certain human phenomena such as pain. In spite of the research which yet needs to be done in this field, it is nevertheless significant for the purposes of this report that contemporary pain studies, as well as research into psychosomatic illnesses and stress, point to increasing acceptance of a synthetic (i.e. unified) concept of the body/mind relationship. It has become unacceptable to insist upon a division between 'physical' and 'mental' experiences of pain. This development prevents one from cataloguing torture methods and effects according to discrete categories of the physical and psychological.

It is generally held, of course, that there is a very real distinction between 'third degree methods' (physical assault such as the falanga) and 'fourth degree methods' (psychological disorientation such as sensory deprivation). But they are both at points on a single physical-psychological continuum. Yet differences based on technical factors do not necessarily reflect rigidly corresponding distinctions in the character of distress experienced. The anxieties, susceptibilities and tolerances of each person are variables — what will 'break' one victim may be 'only a scratch' to another. Torture is a positive feed-back process and cannot be explained in terms limited by a passion for classification. Indeed, in the light of *contemporary stress studies and conditioning theories*, it is more profitable to give secondary importance to the matter of 'techniques' and concentrate on the overall character of the torture situation as well as the short- and long-term impact on the participants.

Furthermore, evidence does not indicate that actual torture is generally subjected to the kind of military discipline which would be conducive to assessment of fine distinctions in technique. In fact, the order which is usually held to 'authorise' torture is a directive to collect intelligence 'by all means available'. It is impossible, both in theory and in practice, to define a torture situation which does not combine inextricably, elements of 'third' and 'fourth degree' torture methods. The adverse pressures can include the discomfort of the prison conditions (cramped quarters, inadequate toilet facilities), brutality (rough handling), assault (beatings, kickings), social deprivation (separation of families, cultural indecencies), injustice (violation of legal rights), and sleep deprivation.

It is naturally possible to isolate some aspects of the impact of such a situation on a victim. It is also possible to establish the probability of injuries resulting from specific insults and determine whether these require medical or psychiatric treatment. But at a time when much clinical and theoretical study exhibits the influence of mechanistic concepts of human behaviour and motivation, it is important to exercise analytical caution. The implications of the statement 'I was kicked in the stomach' go far beyond the possibilities of rupture and internal haemorrhaging.

It is these factors that have dictated the approach to this subject. What follows is: first, a consideration of torture in terms of the erosion of human tolerance of stress; secondly, an account of studies of the manipulation of human behaviour in stressful situations; thirdly, a consideration of the impact of torture on the victims and practitioners.

Torture as a stress

In human terms a stress is any event which changes or threatens to change the stability of one's environmental, physical or mental well-being. The majority of the stresses applied to an individual are easily dealt with by inherited and acquired defence processes. Just as a physical assault may be warded off by a movement of the forearm, so a verbal assault may be dismissed by a laugh or a contemptuous reply. These defence factors which enable us to survive stress are keenly studied and cultivated by the military establishment in the training of soldiers, and they are studied with equal keenness by torture technicians and by torture resistance training groups. In order to understand the nature and function of these stress-survival factors, it will be necessary to outline briefly the characteristics of stress itself.

Stresses are customarily divided into three categories: the acute (short-lived), the sub-acute (medium-term) and the chronic (long-standing). The response to each stress type differs accordingly. In 'acute' stress a sudden reflex, primitive, 'fight or flight' response occurs. The brain becomes alert, the heart beats faster, the blood vessels to the skin constrict to divert more blood to the brain and muscles, the adrenal glands secrete adrenalin and corticosteroids into the blood stream. A state of maximal arousal results. If the acute stress is intolerable, a paradoxical situation may result: in such circumstances the subject may vomit, become 'paralysed by fear', faint or even fall asleep.

The 'sub-acute' response is a reaction to a more prolonged stress, marked by anxiety or excitement (i.e. moderate cerebral arousal) with noticeable alterations in sleep, appetite and libido. However, the subject retains confidence in his ability to cope and maintain his integrity and morale. Even if the stress includes the threat of death, he retains a 'fighting posture' and does not expect disaster. This level of stress resistance is particularly reinforced during military training, since it is critical to the endurance of continuing adverse stress. If resistance factors at this level are absent or destroyed, an accelerated transition to the final 'chronic' phase can be expected.

Although the 'chronic' behavioural response to severe stress would radically impair one's ability to live in a 'normal' low-stress society, it is often essential for self-preservation in extreme pressure situations. A continuous state of anxiety may develop, often with profound depression of mood and pessimism in outlook. Thought processes, bodily desires and functions become retarded. In this state external stresses produce little distress, the body and mind being already maximally distressed. As in acute stresses, a paradoxical situation may occur in which the victim develops a condition of total denial such as an 'hysterical fugue'. He appears to 'switch off' all awareness, looks bland and untroubled, exhibits no response to pain. His memory or voice may be 'lost', he may lie apparently paralysed. It is as though the mind, being too overstimulated, tripped its relays or blew a fuse and ceased to recognise any bodily or sensory stimuli. In those who cannot 'retire' into either of these two main responses, the mind may 'give up' living. War-time experience is full of cases of individuals who exposed themselves to being shot — a fatal injury was apprehended as a merciful release; a non-fatal wound offered a ticket to a base hospital. Although this was sometimes done deliberately, it was usually subconscious, in that over-stressed men became accident prone. At other times death came by suicide or by just not eating and 'lying down to die' as occurred in the more rigorous prison camps in World War II. 'Giving up' could also take other forms: men became susceptible to illnesses like bronchopneumonia, to psychosomatic diseases such as duodenal ulcers, asthma and bronchitis, to coronary disease, T.B., and even to cancer. It is evident, therefore, that from the point of view of resistance to war-stress and torture-stress, it is the factors which impede the transition from the 'sub-acute' response to the 'chronic' response (i.e. from fight to flight) that are critical. It is precisely in this area that military conditioning seeks to reinforce individuals and that torture seeks to break them down. Before analysing the mechanisms of eroding sub-acute stress-resistance, it is important first to deal with two popular misconceptions.

Medical and psychological aspects of torture 43

During the passage of the wars from The American Civil War through to Vietnam, two erroneous notions were abolished. The first is that by assessment of a man's previous personality one can predict his endurance under stress. People with previous neurotic illness, and social misfits who were unable to cope in normal environments, often did better than those with a clearly 'normal' personality. It was noted at one time that in psychiatric battle casualties about 50 per cent had a 'poor previous personality', and vigorous, recruiting screening procedures were introduced (including a US Navy World War I programme that classified swearing and masturbation as reasons for exclusion). It was not until later that it was noted that psychiatric casualties had on average served longer than the physical casualties and that 50 per cent of highly decorated aircrew also had a 'poor previous personality'.

The second fallacy is that given 'strength of character' one can survive life-threatening stress indefinitely. In World War II in the Mediterranean area, it was noted that men who survived physically unscathed for 100, 200 or even 300 days of continuous front-line fighting became mentally disturbed and without eating or sleeping, continued to fight like automata and had to be forcibly removed from the battlefield for rest and psychiatric treatment. It is significant, furthermore, that the 'Code of Conduct for Members of the Armed Forces of the United States' was altered at the conclusion of the Korean War to take into account the fact that almost all Prisoners of War in the past had divulged information to their interrogators regardless of rigid orders to the contrary. The Secretary of Defense's Advisory Committee which drafted the revised Code concluded: '. . . it is recognised that the POW may be subjected to an extreme of coercion beyond his ability to resist. If in his battle with the interrogator he is driven from his first line of resistance (i.e. 'name, rank, serial number and date of birth, only'), he must be trained for resistance in successive positions.'

The best and most commonplace resistance to pain and stress, whether of a high or low intensity, is the simple denial that it is either a potent pain or stress or even that it is a pain or stress at all. This denial may be either culturally or individually generated. For example, many types of stress, such as severe physical exercises, are regarded as character-building in some educational environments. The removal of a fingernail by a surgeon, although uncomfortable, is patiently borne in the knowledge that it will produce relief of pain and the return to normal health. On a general level, if one believes that the endurance of physical punishment on earth grants one a short stay in Purgatory and more certain heavenly reward after death, pain may be endured gladly. Similarly, if one has faith in a cause such as the defence of freedom or is committed to a revolutionary struggle, pain and death are simply prices that must be paid for victory. Morale may be compounded of feelings of patriotism, comradeship, or justice, of personal feelings of emotional security, or hatred or aggression toward one's antagoniser. It may be supported by little things — by a ray of sunlight, by food and sleep, by news from home, or even, from accounts of solitary confinement, by a bond of love with tiny creatures such as mosquitoes. As long as an individual in a severe and sustained stress situation manages to preserve this compensatory morale, he cannot be said to have entered the chronic response phase. The aim of the torturer/interrogator is, therefore, to erode that morale by destroying whatever props the individual has for his mental integrity.

This means that the victim must believe that he is being tortured before the excessive stress state of torture can be said to begin; he must believe that the stress is malevolent. The pulling off of a fingernail in the course of coercive interrogation, or the insertion of needles into the quick, is a horrendous experience, and the pain is dramatically different from that experienced in the benevolent surgical context. Furthermore, it should be noted that the stress has to be 'correct' culturally to be recognised as a torture. For example, many sophisticated Caucasians believe that Pentothal is a 'truth drug' and that if injected with it one cannot help giving a true and complete response to every question. It is this belief alone which gives the drug its reputation: if one believes a substance to be a drug with a specific effect, there is a 40 per cent chance of that effect occurring even if a totally inert substance is used (the placebo effect). The same sophisticated Caucasian who 'tells all', when given an injection of distilled water (believing it to be a 'truth drug') would probably laugh if a voodoo spell said to have the same result were cast on him. The reverse could reasonably be expected of a Haitian peasant.

In the context of political repression, of course, these essential features of malevolence and appropriateness are inherent in the torture/interrogation situation. Therefore, the first object of the torturer/interrogator is to weaken the compensatory morale and habitual defences of the victim. Commonly, this is achieved initially through systematic debilitation of the detainees. Not surprisingly, methods are relatively universal: semi-starvation, exposure, exploitation of wounds, induced illness, sleep deprivation, lack of proper hygiene, prolonged interrogation under extreme tension, prolonged constraint, forced writing, and fatiguing physical exercises. This debilitation procedure is to introduce the corollary of the principle, 'a healthy mind in a healthy body'. Damaging the anatomical and physiological components of body function progressively impairs the working of the brain and hastens the collapse of will and morale. Starvation deprives the brain of energy to work, malnutrition with Vitamin B deficiency deprives the brain of coenzymes necessary for normal cerebral metabolism. Sleep deprivation is scarcely understood but produces gross disturbance in higher cortical functioning: electroencephalograms clearly indicate that sleep deprivation results in a progressive increase in dreaming frequency, and if sleep is prevented dreams appear to occur in the waking state, resulting in disordered perception and hallucinations.

There are two theories of the functions of this breakdown process — the 'brain-syndrome' theory and the stress theory. Each includes the other as a subsidiary influence. In his systematic study of the induced debility of the interrogation subject, Hinkle * states that the aim of the physical breakdown is to achieve 'an impairment of all those aspects of brain function that are commonly tested when the physician undertakes to assess the 'mental status' of the patient. A patient exhibiting this syndrome can no longer carry on his usual complex activities, assume his daily responsibilities or cope with interpersonal relations. As its symptoms develop

---

* For full references to authorities quoted in this section see Select Bibliography.

he may become restless, talkative and delirious ... information derived from past experience generally becomes less potent as a guide for action, whereas information derived from the immediate experience, pain, thirst, discomfort and threats to life, becomes more potent.' Shallice, while suggesting that Hinkle's concept cannot account completely for the effectiveness of the procedure, acknowledges that the 'brain-syndrome aspects are relevant. The inability to think properly would itself produce stress, it would prevent the prisoner thinking of means to cope with stress and would make him easier to interrogate ... it is an important part of a positive feedback stress-producing process.'

The second major theory of the breakdown process is proposed by Sargant. He offers a comparison with combat exhaustion, as recorded by Swank and Marchland and argues that the breakdown is simply due to the effect of stress. After a period of about 50 days of continuous combat, the soldiers would become 'easily startled and confused', 'irritable' and would over-respond to all stimuli. 'This state of hyper-reactivity was followed insidiously by another group of symptoms referred to as 'emotional exhaustion'. The men became dull and listless, they became mentally and physically retarded, preoccupied and had increasing difficulty remembering details. This was accompanied by indifference and apathy ... In such cases bizarre contradictory behaviour could occur.'

The simplest manifestation of this breakdown process as a result of torture was recorded after the Korean War. In its examination of methods of forceful indoctrination, the Group for the Advancement of Psychiatry points out that during the Korean War a particularly effective means of inducing pain and fatigue was to subject a prisoner to prolonged interrogation while forcing him to remain in a standing position. (Other variants were to make him sit in a sitting position without a chair or stool etc., or to hold up heavy objects — books.) The Group points out the advantages of this form of debilitation torture for the interrogator: the immediate source of pain is not the interrogator but the victim himself; the contest becomes, in a way, one of the individual against himself; acting thus 'against himself' makes the prisoner feel that the interrogator has greater powers (e.g. refusal to comply can mean that the interrogator can resort to overt violence); and the interrogator can say that no one laid a hand on the prisoner, thus giving the interrogator the sense that he is acting legally.

The logical extension of this 'passive' disordering and debilitating torture is the application of sensory deprivation techniques. A vast amount of research has been carried out in the field, and there is a fairly general pattern of findings. Typical of the bibliography of experiments in this field is a programme cited by Lord Gardiner in his minority report submitted with the 'Report of the Committee of Privy Counsellors appointed to consider authorised procedures for the interrogation of persons suspected of terrorism', presented to the British Parliament in March 1972:

> In an experiment in England, fully described in the *Lancet* of 12 September 1959, 20 men and women volunteer members of a hospital staff, aged between 20 and 55, were each placed in a 'silent room' standardised up to a mean sound-pressure level difference of 80 decibels, and the further sensory deprivation consisted of having to wear translucent goggles which cut out patterned vision, and padded fur gauntlets. On the other hand they had four normal meals a day when they were visited by colleagues on the hospital staff and could take off the goggles, and they had 'dunlopillo' mattresses on which they could sleep or rest, or they could walk about. They were promised an amount of paid time off equal to that spent in the room and were asked to stay there as long as they could.
>
> Six remained for 48, 51, 75, 82 and 92 hours, but 14 of the 20 gave up after less than 48 hours (two of them after only 5 hours), the usual causes being unbearable anxiety, tension or attacks of panic. Dreams were invariable in those who slept for any length of time and in a quarter of the 20 included nightmares of which drowning, suffocation, killing people, etc. were features. These were the results, although they were volunteers in their own hospital who knew that there was no reason for any panic and who were not submitted to any wall-standing or deprived of any food or sleep.

Shallice, in his discussion of the application of sensory deprivation research in the Ulster Depth Interrogation techniques, makes a statement critical to an understanding of the real implications of SD in a torture context:

> If we turn to people undergoing SD in a non-experimental situation, where the situation would be phenomenologically very different, the stressful nature of SD becomes even more apparent... In the Ulster situation the internees had a thick black bag over their heads, were subject to a loud masking noise, had to remain in a fatiguing and painful fixed position while dressed in a boiler suit... Sleep was prevented and food was inadequate. Thus cognitive functioning would be impaired. Pain would be present both from beatings and from the use of the 'stoika' position at the wall. Finally anxiety must have been at a high level for the internees even before sensory deprivation began, especially as no one knew... that they were to be arrested and subjected to the depersonalisation and disorientation of the arrest and initial imprisonment process. Thus one would expect the positive feedback process... to operate starting from an initially high level of stress... with cognitive functioning impaired so that rational defences would be impossible.

The testimonies of released internees support Shallice's suggestion. Testified one: 'I heard strange noises, screams and my only desire was to end all this pain and confusion by killing myself. This I tried to do in my thoughts by striking my head on a pipe but without success.'

When an individual's basic stability is threatened in such a manner, he adopts various manoeuvres to relieve the stress. For example, if an unpleasant thing happens to someone he tells a friend about it, and some of its unpleasantness disappears. A group of prisoners may sustain each other by talking (or making jokes) about their experiences, or by talking or singing about other things which distract their minds. This 'letting off steam' is limited, of course, to the stresses that are recognised and the fears which are named. Sedman points out that 'the failure of the prisoner to recognise the sources of the compulsion he experiences in the interrogation situation intensifies their effects, particularly the disabling effects of guilt reactions.' But even the release which comradeship affords is denied the prisoner who is isolated. Deprived of company and kept in suspense as to his fate, the victim begins to experience a lowering of his 'breaking point'. He may become so tense and anxious just waiting that he will develop a 'chronic' stress-response behaviour pattern. Boredom, too, contributes to the spiral of stress which is unrelieved in many instances by any physical exercise. Prevented from taking physical exercise, the victim is deprived of another basic way of dealing with distress and if this reaches severe proportions, he may actually welcome the physical aspects of torture and use it as his 'safety-valve'. As in the testimony of the Ulster internee, 'I tried to strike my head on a pipe', soldiers in World War I, subjected to extreme stress, found enormous relief when wounded. Severely distressed psychiatric patients may injure themselves and become calm, after cutting their wrists, for example, and it is thought that peptic ulcers in highly stressed individuals are a way, albeit subconscious, in which we can transmute unacceptable mental stresses into acceptable physical distress.

It is because of this self-regulating protective potential of the human organism that torturers and interrogators, to be effective at all, cannot rely solely on accumulating stress to mould the behaviour of a detainee or interrogation subject. To do this requires considerable manipulation of the subject's behaviour. It is to that we now turn.

Manipulation and resistance

It is the transition from the sub-acute to the chronic stress response that the torturer seeks to orchestrate, initially by systematically weakening the subject. This forms part of the classic pattern of manipulation described by the post-Korean War research of Biderman. Biderman was instrumental in debunking the myth that the Chinese had used mysterious or magical means to 'brainwash' the Allied Prisoners of War. With Harlow, Farber and West (and others) he classified manipulative techniques according to a scheme known as DDD (Dependency, Debility and Dread). At that time, the behaviour code for POWs expressly forbade any communication with the enemy apart from the 'Name, rank, serial number and date of birth, only' required by the Geneva Convention. Yet, without recourse to excessive physical brutality, the Chinese interrogators had managed to extract confessions which were fabrications at least as preposterous as those elicited by the KGB for the 1930s show trials. By applying elementary principles of conditioning theory, Biderman pointed out that under the physical, social and emotional conditions produced by the introduction of DDD, compliance could be considered a natural consequence of the operation of ordinary principles of human behaviour. The following outline of the DDD schema will show how stress patterns can be and are manipulated.

The function of debility has been discussed above. The victim, by being deprived in the process of debilitation of food, sleep and human contact by his torturer, becomes paradoxically dependent on his torturer for these things. The only person who can provide these reliefs is the torturer, and in the induced abnormal environment where deprivation and stress are the norm and other social contacts are withdrawn, the victim becomes dependent on him as the sole source of support. Occasional unpredictable brief respites, when among other things the torturer becomes a sympathetic listener, make the victim feel obligated towards him.

Just as debilitation leads to dependency, dependency leads to dread. Dread may not be consciously experienced during the application of the debilitation, but during the respites with the fear of returning to this debilitation torture. The induction of dread is a basic aim. To quote Farber et al.: 'Dread is the most expressive term to indicate the chronic fear the Communists attempted to induce. Fear of death, fear of pain, fear of non-repatriation, fear of deformity or permanent disability, through neglect or inadequate medical treatment, fear of Communist violence against loved ones at home, and even fear of one's own ability to satisfy the demands of insatiable interrogators — these and many other nagging despairs constituted the final component of DDD.'

The combination of these three factors, carefully contrived and nurtured, prepares a resistant prisoner for complete compliance. It should be stressed here that complete compliance may mean a whole range of subservient actions by no means restricted to the popular misconception that the aim or result of coercion is disclosure of true subversive information. In fact, the whole process of extracting confessions (whether true or false), or 'softening up' political suspects is simply a ruthless 'teaching' procedure: the radically changed context of the torture situation produces new responses that either compete with or interfere with habitual behaviour. The coercive stresses seriously affect one's customary ways of looking at and dealing with oneself. They operate in part to produce a state of over-arousal by disturbing the feeling of inner and external security and stability (thereby rendering the prisoner susceptible to relatively simple conditioning techniques) and by channelling the normal need to talk to relieve stress so that only certain conversation patterns (e.g. confessions) are allowed and therefore have to be used by the prisoner.

The coercive situation contains features both of selective or instrumental learning (Thornedikean) as well as classical conditioning (Pavlovian). It produces selective reinforcement or certain modes of response. Critical to this entire procedure is the fact that the treatment is constantly varied. There is usually no regular or uniform sequence to the particular coercive techniques. There is no time when a prisoner can be sure that he is through with a particular ordeal. He can be hauled out at any time and re-interrogated — often a mere cover for getting the prisoner into the habit of compliance in talking. In addition, alleviation of the stress, whether due to spontaneous factors or deliberate manipulations, is intermittent, temporary and unpredictable. Hence, relief of hunger, fatigue, isolation or pain, even temporarily, serves as a reward, as do occasional favours (cigarettes), promises ('I'll do what I can for you'), and bonuses for partial compliance ('You can go and sleep now and we'll start again tomorrow'), all of which provide positive motivation for final compliance, hinder adjustment to the suffering, and speed up the onset of the 'chronic stress' response.

The reduction of stress at the time of the occurrence of desired behaviour has a second consequence — the learning of instrumental acts often of a verbal nature. Since verbal behaviour is in a general way already strongly conditioned in all human adults as a means of relieving stress or denying its potency, it is not surprising that prisoners should respond to cues of this basically socialised nature. Some prisoners become victims of the very socialisation process that under ordinary circumstances is regarded as a desirable and, indeed, essential aspect of civilised living. A simple example of this was noted by Burns in POW studies: the stress of refusing to answer questions. In everyday situations, it is taken for granted that questions will be answered if they are 'civil questions' and, as frequently as not, even if they are 'uncivil' ones. Many US POWs found that the ingrained pattern of civility made it difficult for them to decline outright to answer a question. It was not that they could not decline, but merely that the refusal required continuous effort which in the long run they could not sustain.

Furthermore, if it becomes clear that the victim is only sustaining himself by his hatred of his imprisoners, he will suddenly find himself being well-treated or having his aggression discussed in 'psychotherapy' groups until he is made to feel guilty about feeling aggressive. When he is returned to a punishment situation he finds that his aggressive feelings induce reflex guilt, and so he abandons them or turns his aggression either outwardly against his fellow captives or inwardly, becoming depressed or anxious.

These analyses of conditioning techniques used by interrogators make it evident that gross acts of torture (such as electric shock, rape or tearing out fingernails) are situated within a coercive context of which such methods are merely an extension. The accompanying chart, prepared by Biderman, is by no means exhaustive of coercive methods, and it does not include the excessive physical abuse which many forms of torture employ; however, it demonstrates the essential character of stress manipulation and may perhaps, by virtue of its more 'benign' content, reveal the intentions and results of torture with a precision that is almost impossible to achieve when dealing with those massive assaults in which pain and disorientation are compressed.

The victim is trapped in a situation in which the stresses are manipulated so as constantly to frustrate this need to behave in a consistent, learned, personal behaviour pattern and in accordance with an esteemed self-image — both of which are necessary for the protection of basic self-identity.

BIDERMAN'S CHART OF COERCION

General Method	Effects (Purposes)	Variants
1. Isolation	Deprives victim of all social support of his ability to resist Develops an intense concern with self Makes victim dependent upon interrogator	Complete solitary confinement Complete isolation Semi-isolation Group isolation
2. Monopolisation of perception	Fixes attention upon immedate predicament; fosters introspection Eliminates stimuli competing with those controlled by captor Frustrates all actions not consistent with compliance	Physical isolation Darkness or bright light Barren environment Restricted movement Monotonous food
3. Induced debility Exhaustion	Weakens mental and physical ability to resist	Semi-starvation Exposure Exploitation of wounds Induced illness Sleep deprivation Prolonged constraint Prolonged interrogation Forced writing Overexertion
4. Threats	Cultivates anxiety & despair	Threats of death Threats of non-return Threats of endless interrogation & isolation Threats against family Vague threats Mysterious changes of treatment
5. Occasional indulgences	Provides positive motivation for compliance Hinders adjustment to deprivation	Occasional favours Fluctuations of interrogators' attitudes Promises Rewards for partial compliance Tantalising
6. Demonstrating 'omnipotence'	Suggests futility of resistance	Confrontation Pretending co-operation taken for granted Demonstrating complete control over victim's fate
7. Degradation	Makes cost of resistance appear more damaging to self esteem than capitulation Reduces prisoner to 'animal level' concerns	Personal hygiene prevented Filthy infested surroundings Demeaning punishments Insults and taunts Denial of privacy
8. Enforcing trivial demands	Develops habit of compliance	Forced writing Enforcement of minute rules

To shield and to reassure himself that he is in control of the situation and of himself, the victim may finally resort to 'self-defeating' behaviour. A frequent statement of this 'defence' is: 'I decided to give in while I still had my wits about me and could control what they got out of me, rather than waiting until they had broken me completely.' Such behaviour leads one to consider the possibilities for resistance to stressful coercion.

In its study of forceful indoctrination methods, the Group for the Advancement of Psychiatry cited a number of reasons for resistance, among them: moral and duty obligations, altruistic calculations in terms of the interest of the 'movement' or 'cause' and the interest of fellow prisoners; self-interested calculations in terms of fear of 'getting in deeper and deeper'; fear of penalisation by former comrades or other prisoners for collaboration; emotional considerations including the feeling of pride, dignity and self-respect, hatred of the enemy or of the specific individuals inflicting the stress and a sense of outrage or righteous indignation. It should be noted of course that if bodily well-being is maintained it is easier to resist psychological stresses, and the extent to which one is aware of latent anxieties and tensions within oneself will reduce the ability of the interrogator to use unadmitted fears or guilt as a covert force towards compliance.

Despite efforts made, in South Africa for example, to train activists in interrogation/torture resistance, there are obvious limitations. Biderman concludes: 'It would be foolish to disregard the fact that some of the elements of DDD represent a pathological organic state, some consequences of which are probably innately determined. To the extent that this is true, one cannot expect to achieve a great degree of prophylactic success in regard to the effects of DDD, any more than one can reasonably expect at the present state of knowledge to prevent some of the undesirable consequences of lobotomy. Though many of the behavioural consequences of DDD are not innately determined, the conditioning of certain types of responses desired by the enemy many eventually occur, even in the face of superlative resistance.'

Before proceeding to a discussion of the injury which such stress may cause and specific injuries associated with common practices, it is important to point out here the use of

Pharmacological torture

Of all aspects of torture, pharmacological torture is the one which seems most prone to misconceptions. If a drug existed that could make people tell the truth and reveal all their secrets and memories, that could make them change their beliefs and allegiances, no one would embark on the expensive and time-consuming process of psycho-analysis in order to unearth information that they wish revealed, and every drug company, doctor, psychiatrist, and newspaper in the world would be extolling its virtues. To believe that such a drug exists implies not only naïvety but also disrespect for the enormous resilience and complexity of the human brain.

It is really quite difficult to damage the brain permanently by the use of chemicals without hurting the body. People have injected themselves intravenously with almost every known substance from liquid metallic mercury to peanut butter and completely recovered. As mentioned earlier, for a person to suffer mentally he has to be aware that he is suffering, and his brain has to be functioning well to be aware at all.

The primary suffering caused by the threatened use of pharmacological agents is the victim's belief in their effects. A classic example is the short-acting anaesthetic agents, such as thiopentone (Pentothal, Intravel, etc.) and methohexitone (Brietal). Literally millions of people every year receive these by intravenous injection to induce anaesthesia for the relief of suffering. They don't tell the anaesthetist and the surgeon their life history; they go to sleep. Even if by careful injection one managed to induce a drowsy state between waking and sleeping, all the patient (or victim) experiences is a tremendous sense of relaxation. If he has been very tense and apprehensive he may talk freely about the things which have been worrying him, e.g. how he hates his job; he may even shout and scream abuse or may ramble on about a fantasy world which exists only in his imagination. This technique is used in psychiatry for relief of terrible mental stresses and is called 'abreaction'. Its effects resemble drunkenness and may provide an emotional catharsis. It was extensively used in World War II for restoring distressed minds to normality. It is in the victim's belief that he will 'tell all' if such a drug is administered that the threat really lies. Moreover if the abreaction does occur and the victim then falls asleep and ceases to be aware, the torturer can claim that 'all was revealed', and thus trick his victim into revealing the information.

The secondary use of drugs is in the induction of debility. Hallucinogenic drugs, such as LSD, cause great disruption to normal perceptual and conceptual processes. They may be used to confuse, distress, and weaken the victim. Like ECT or sleep deprivation they damage the function of the brain, and memory becomes distorted. What is revealed to the torturer is again a mixture of fantasy, delusional and hallucinatory memories, interspersed with random real ones. The voluntary use of LSD is widespread, and most users recover to their own satisfaction. Even those who are 'permanently' affected by their LSD experiences can be cured or have their condition ameliorated by taking drugs of the type of phenothiazine or butyrophenane.

The phendhiazine (e.g. chlorpromazine = 'Largactil', perphenazine = 'Fentazine') and related drugs ('Moditen', 'Modicate', 'Veractil', 'Stelazine', etc.; the full list is enormous) and the butyrophenones (e.g. haloperidol = 'Serenace') are widely used in medicine and psychiatry and are known rather loosely as 'major tranquillisers'. They are better known for abolishing paranoid psychotic illness and schizophrenic illness; for the relief of emotional stress; for the prevention of nausea and hallucinations of delirium tremens or LSD; as adjuncts to analgesia; or as treatment for prickly heat or skin rashes. They even stop hiccoughs. They are undoubtedly powerful drugs and have side effects which can be very unpleasant. However, many psychiatric patients the world over owe to these drugs their ability to live a normal life. They may take doses of 500-1000 mgm. per day of Largactil for years without side effects. But these do frequently occur. A dry mouth and sedation are the most common sensations reported by people taking it. Stiffness of the muscles or a light tremor similar to mild Parkinson's disease or a motor restlessness may occur, and if noticed can be reversed by stopping use of the drug or giving anti-parkinsonian drugs such as benahezol (artane) or orphenadrine ('Disipal'). Other side effects such as jaundice are incredibly rare.

Much confusion in reading accounts of alleged pharmacological torture arises from difficulties in the determination of what is real and what is illusion. If a man develops paranoid schizophrenia, he may have a *delusion* of persecution. The delusion is culturally determined, and in past centuries men were persecuted by the devil, by the Freemasons or the Church. Now, it is the police, the government, 'spies', the Communists, or even the American astronauts. It is easy to call a man mad who hears voices from the 'President of Mars', but the priest who hears God speak to him is culturally acceptable.

It is all too easy to want to believe a distressed man who claims he is being tortured or persecuted by the police and to regard as further torture what may be an attempt to reduce his distress with phenothiazine, especially if you believe that the police of his country torture people. Normal people believe what they want to believe; it is important that they should want to believe the truth and ways of discovering this are discussed later.

Some drugs are used to induce unpleasant sensations for the production of dread. Apomorphine produces vomiting, and curare or suxamethonium ('Scoline') induces paralysis. If totally paralysed by these agents you stay fully conscious and unable to breathe — a very distressing experience. The lack of oxygen eventually causes loss of consciousness, and artificial respiration may be used until the drug's effect wears off. Recovery from a dose of 'Scoline' may be accompanied by muscle pains. Scoline is routinely used in major surgery when the patient is under anaesthetic. But people who have received Scoline *without anaesthetic* in experiments have all agreed that it is such an unpleasant experience to be able to see, think, feel, hear and yet be unable to move that the drug should not be used.

Heroin and other addicting drugs can be used to induce dependency, for anyone given regular doses of opiates will become physiologically dependent on them and their withdrawal will produce physical and mental distress.

A final word about pharmacological tortures. Because of individual idiosyncrasies, any drug if misused can be harmful.

Two aspirins may cause a fatal gastric haemorrhage, twenty paracetamol irreversible liver damage, and one common antibiotic may irreversibly destroy the bone marrow. If a drug is so used with intention of causing distress, it is then being used as a method of physical torture and the results are analogous.

Injury and long-term effects

Pain is a signal that the body is being damaged or destroyed. To stay alive is undoubtedly one of our basic drives, although death may eventually be counted as a merciful release. But few people can view with equanimity the prospect of living as a damaged body or mind. A 'mind' needs a complete 'body' for complete self-expression. It needs intact genitalia for fulfilment of social ambitions such as marriage, for expression of sexual drives; intact hands for constructive and aggressive instincts; vision, speech and hearing for relating to other bodies/minds. A healthy body is seen as 'good', a disfigured one is 'bad', and therefore the victim sees himself as becoming regarded as a 'bad' person, a 'mind' to be shunned and therefore condemned like the wandering Jew to the continuous torture of eternal loneliness. The immense suffering caused by even minor physical ill-treatment is a reflection of these and other often nameless fears.

The most senseless of all tortures is physical trauma to the brain. If a man's skull is struck, the brain may be shaken up (concussed), bruised (contused) or torn (lacerated). Brain cells die; blood vessels get torn, cerebral haemorrhage and further destruction of brain tissue occurs. Some brain cells, if damaged, recover; but dead cells are never replaced. To damage the organ of a healthy mind can serve no purpose, further no cause. Like picking the wings off a butterfly or the burning of the ancient library of Alexandria, it produces an irreparable loss. Death, coma or a mindless 'vegetable' is a result with no suffering for the victim; but to be left aware that one's mind is damaged or distorted, deficient in its memory, its intellectual skills or its control is a terrible sentence. A profound depression often ensues; one may be subject to convulsions, or outbursts of rage, unable to work, or to adjust to society and unable to co-operate with the authorities even if one wished to.

From reports so far available, it seems that interrogation methods employing sensory deprivation techniques also have traumatic effects. Anxiety, hypochondria and hysteria are the most frequent in clinical situations; phobias, depressions, emotional fatigue and the obsessive-compulsive reactions are rarer. In addition to its subjective results, anxiety can lead to stomach, heart and genito-urinary symptoms as well as to tremors and sleep disturbances. In Ulster Wade reports one man who 'shakes continually and finds it hard to articulate sentences' and who 'could not be alone at any time'. Another is described as 'shuddering spasmodically and (complaining) of violent headaches, insomnia and nightmares when he does go to sleep'. With regard to the long-term effects of sensory deprivation expert medical evidence presented to the Parker Committee stated:

> Sensory isolation is one method of inducing an artificial psychosis or episode of insanity. We know that people who have been through such an experience do not forget it quickly and may experience symptoms of mental distress for months or years. We know that some artificially induced psychoses, for instance those produced by drugs like LSD or mescaline, have in fact proved permanent; and there is no reason to suppose that this may not be a danger with psychoses produced by sensory deprivation. Even if such psychotic symptoms as delusions and hallucinations do not persist, a proportion of persons who have been subjected to these procedures are likely to continue to exhibit anxiety attacks, tremors, insomnia, nightmares and other symptoms of neurosis with which psychiatrists are familiar from their experience of treating ex-prisoners of war and others who have been confined and ill-treated.

The induction of convulsions by passing an electric shock through the brain is, like the use of sensory deprivation, a perverted application of medical practice. Therapy using electrical shock in this way (electro-convulsant therapy) is widely used for alleviating depressive illnesses. Even in medical use when it is given twice a week, it may induce mild confusion and memory impairment for a short period. When repeated many times in a day it causes such cerebral disturbance as to render men demented and incontinent and is analogous to a severe head injury. Paulo Schilling points out the other effects of electricity when applied locally to limbs as a torture:

> The electrical discharge causes a sensation which is difficult to describe: a physical and psychological commotion filled with electric sparks, which together with convulsive shaking and loss of muscular control, gives the victim a sense of loss, of unavoidable attraction for that turbulating electrical trituration. The shock causes a stimulation in the muscle identical to the stimulation of the nerve fibres and the muscle responds with a contraction. The extensor muscles extend and the flexors flex, causing disorderly, uncontrollable movements similar to epileptic convulsions.
>
> The tortured victim shouts with all his might, grasping for a footing, somewhere to stand in the midst of that chaos of convulsions, shaking and sparks. He cannot lose himself or turn his attention away from that desperate sensation. For him in that moment any other form of combined torture — paddling, for example — would be a relief, for it would allow him to divert his attention, touch ground and his own body which feels like it is escaping his grasp. Pain saves him, beating comes to his rescue. He tries to cause himself pain by beating his head repeatedly on the ground. But generally he is tied, hanging in the '*pau de arara*' (parrot's perch), and not even that resource is available to him.

Psychiatric cases encountered after the use of electrical torture in Algeria included instances of localised or generalised cenesthopathies in which 'the patients felt "pins and needles" throughout their bodies; their hands seemed to be torn off, their heads seemed to be bursting and their tongues felt as if they were being swallowed'. Instances of apathy, aboulia and electricity phobia were also evident, the former two in patients who were 'inert' and the latter in patients who feared touching a switch, turning on the radio or using the telephone (Fanon).

The immediate effects of DDD stress have already been discussed in some detail. Studies of the aftermath of such experiences, especially in World War II POW camps, is continuing.

Just as severe damage to our physical system may leave a scar, so may mental stress have long term sequelae. If, during the process of torture, our psychological defences are eroded and the mental systems with which we cope with stress become so overloaded that they are destroyed, we may find on return to our normal environment that we no longer have an adequate system for coping with any life problems. In favourable surroundings we may learn anew, but the new system may be imperfect and based on different values. From their investigation of Korean War POWs, Farber et al. (p. 278) conclude:

> In terms of normative criteria, many ex-prisoners are more than ordinarily anxious, defensive, despondent, suspicious, insecure. Pressed to explain any possibly discreditable acts, they often exhibit a very considerable degree of hesitancy, vagueness, paramnesia and rationalisation. In a word, they behave exactly as one would expect of any individual required to explain and defend his behaviour, many determinants of which he is not aware.

A survey of psychiatric casualties of World War I revealed that almost all were unable to return to normal life after discharge from the Army and were unable to work in their former capacity, if at all. Their minds became preoccupied with grief or bitterness over their misfortunes, or a permanent state of anxiety arose. Contrary to the theological concept that suffering is good for people, extreme suffering is usually harmful. This does not alter what is clearly apparent, that the many people who have been through severe mental stress appear to make full mental recoveries. It is probable that we do sublimate our mental stresses to produce physical illness, and severely stressed people are shown to have more disease and earlier deaths than controls. In World War II the mortality of American Army prisoners of war in Japan was 30 per cent compared to 1 per cent in Germany, reflecting the former's greater hardships. In the two years after release the two groups were compared and the Japanese groups were found to be twice as likely to die of cancer or heart disease, four times as likely to die from an accident and nine times as likely to die of pulmonary tuberculosis.

In laboratory work on stress, using goats, a neurotic response of undue anxiety was induced. If, on the first symptoms of anxiety appearing, the stress was stopped the goats recovered. If the stress was continued for too long then a state of permanent anxiety and neurotic behaviour developed despite the eventual termination of the stress. These latter goats remained neurotic, poor mixers, were poor mothers whose kids had a higher mortality and who developed identical neurotic traits which they in turn passed on to their progeny.

Distressing dreams and memories can occur many years after the severe stress, being re-awakened by another severe stress, and similarly a pattern of behaviour (such as a state of abject terror) acquired during torture may suddenly reappear. Much can be done by the use of suitable environments, sedations, anti-depressants, even electroconvulsive therapy, abreaction and good social rehabilitation and psychiatric support to restore disturbed torture victims to normal. The earlier treatment is initiated the better.

It is within the context of breakdown through manipulated stress that physical abuse is employed. The function of beatings, burnings, gaggings, finger irons and needles is clearly exhausting, demoralising and disorienting. In his study of the results of tortures of this order, Fanon reported cases of agitated nervous depressions, patients who were sad and depressed, who shunned contact and were liable to show signs of very violent agitation without obvious cause. Perhaps the most serious problems were encountered in patients who, after torture, exhibited a phobia against all forms of physical contact with other people. Nurses who came near the patient and tried to touch him, to take his hand, for example, were at once pushed stiffly away. It was not possible to carry out artificial feeding or even to administer medicine (Fanon p. 227). It is perhaps cases such as this that best illustrate Jean Amery's statement: 'Torture is the most terrible event remaining in man's memory.'

* * *

The April 1974 coup in Portugal should have significant consequences for research on the subject of torture. It is possible that the study of the past uses of torture in Portugal will help us better to understand phenomena such as the psychology of the torturer and the long-term psychological and medical effects of torture on the victim. A unique opportunity exists to study these phenomena, and fortunately, an experienced Portuguese psychiatrist is leading a team of researchers who are in the planning stages of a five-year programme of medical and psychological testing and personal interviews with the victims of torture under the previous regime. Their findings may well supersede earlier scientific data on the subject in that their planned research will deal directly with aspects of torture rather than with related topics such as the effects of traumatic stress on the prisoners of war during the Second World War and the Korean War.

Torturers: psychological aspects

It may be that some torturers are, and always have been, grossly abnormal personalities. If this is so it would seem that they possess to an excess that capability for aggression that is present and latent in us all. Aggression can arise *de novo* or by a defence mechanism against feelings of guilt or frustration. It is a rare mother who has not felt a sudden upswelling of anger, a desire to hit her most loved child when for example it cries uncontrollably and she is unable to comfort it. If people in authority urged her to express her emotions thus, 'baby-bashing' would be more common. People may feel guilty about imprisoning their fellow men, it gives them an unpleasant feeling, and they may punish their prisoner because he is responsible for this. When their prisoner shows distress their guilt is exacerbated and so is their aggression and they may destroy their victim. When the victim is dehumanised, for example by being made to wallow in his own excrement, he becomes somehow a being that can be perceived as deserving punishment, or that produces the unpleasant emotion of disgust and makes aggression justified. For normal people the conflicts of emotion involved in torturing produce so much distress that they cannot continue long in so doing. Regretably, normal people may be brainwashed and if our education systems, newspapers, and politics teach us from earliest days that members of one race, or religion, or political belief are not to be regarded as humans like ourselves, then it will be normal if we treat them inhumanly.

The professional torturer is likely to be a man who achieves a relief of mental stress by aggressive acts, who acts out his own conflicts and fantasies by destroying others. He is at the other end of the spectrum to the successful interrogator. The latter, whatever his ideology, must be able to be humane and empathic, able to understand his subject's difficulties, to be shrewd and intelligent. To get reliable information takes time, patience and individual attention. Solitary confinement in a dark cell may be done for the same purpose as isolation from one's own people in comfortable surroundings. The latter, though likely to be more effective in achieving co-operation, is more expensive and time-consuming, produces less dramatic effects and needs greater expertise.

An analogy can be drawn between the relationship of a torturer to his victim and that of a master to his slave — both torturer and slave driver are caught up in a deliberate effort to break the will of other human beings.

In his autobiography Frederick Douglass, a black slave in the pre-Civil War American South, recorded his struggle against a Negro-breaker. The Negro-breaker's task was to tame unruly slaves who refused to submit to their role as forced labourers. In other words, like a torturer, it was his aim to break the slave's will. Douglass writes:

> I was whipped, either with sticks or cowskins every week. Aching bones and a sore back were my constant companions... His plan was never to approach in an open and direct manner... He would creep and crawl in ditches and gullies, hide behind stumps and bushes and practise so much of the cunning of the serpent that Bill Smith and I, between ourselves, never called him by any other name than 'the snake'.

'Who is the non-human here?' asks Angela Davis in her *Lectures on Liberation*. 'I would go so far as to say that he is even more profoundly affected than the slave... by a tendency towards unconscious self-annihilation.'

This tendency may also account in part for the refusal or inability of the torturer to recognise himself in the agony of his victim. If there is any threat that the victim might, for an instant, touch the torturer's humanity, a black bag is thrown over his head or he is strapped to the other end of a machine. Usually, however, social or military conditioning brings about the required dehumanising. Talking of the field tortures he witnessed in Vietnam an American veteran put it this way: 'It wasn't like they were humans. We were conditioned to believe this was for the good of the nation, the good of our country and anything we did was okay. And when you shot someone you didn't think you were shooting at a human. They were a Gook or a Commie and it was okay' (Vietnam Veterans Against The War).

Another veteran reported (ibid.):

> My first reaction (to the killing of a 12 year old boy) was, I guess, you would call normal. It would be horror, pain, and when I realised that I caught myself immediately and said 'No, you can't do that', because you develop a shell while you are in the military. They brainwash you. They take all the humanness out of you and you develop this crust which enables you to survive... And if you let that protective shell down, even for a second – it's the difference between you flipping out or managing to make it through. I caught myself letting the shell down and I tightened up right away.

For a period of time, of course, a man can cut himself off from the atrocities he commits or condones. But recent research reveals the longer-term difficulty of living a life which denies the recognition of the humanity of his victims. Soldiers, secret police and torturers build up elaborate defences for themselves, usually based on group spirit, rivalry and rituals.

In Brazil, it has been alleged that there now exists a

sub-culture of torture, with its own values, its apprenticeship, its initiation rites. It has even acquired its own language. The list of atrocities has been codified to sound like a cartoon show: the parrot's swing, the dragon chair. In the Operacao Bandeirantes of San Paulo, an interrogation centre once described as 'an advanced school of torture', the entire ritual of torture is known as the 'spiritual seance'.

This whole process of mystification suggests that most torturers must build up defences in order to carry on their work. In the recent wave of torture in Greece, the torturers at the Bouboulina Street Asphalia headquarters went so far as to call themselves 'doctors'. The atmosphere surrounding the torture operation seems to rely on this kind of perverted irony, an *esprit de corps* which, like forced bravado in wartime, is necessary to sustain the belief that somewhere a higher authority will take responsibility for crimes committed in the name of the state.

This kind of postponed accountability or elaborate personal defence cannot always be indefinitely guaranteed. Franz Fanon, in his capacity as a physician in Algeria during the Liberation War, encountered many cases of torturers who were unable to escape their own guilt. In *Les damnés de la terre* he cites many instances, among them A-----, a French policeman assigned to an anti-FLN brigade.

> A-----'s trouble was that at night he heard screams which prevented him from sleeping. In fact, he told us that for the last few weeks before going to bed he shut the shutters and stopped up all the windows (it was summer) to the complete despair of his wife who was stifled by the heat. Moreover, he stuffed his ears with cottonwool in order to make the screams less piercing. He sometimes even in the middle of the night turned on the wireless or put on some music in order not to hear his nocturnal uproar.

This case is only a bizarre illustration of the fact that a torturer is himself subject to considerable pressure and frustration. The torturer is seldom of high rank; he is forced, often in situations of extreme urgency, to extract information from unwilling suspects in order to satisfy the demands of superior officers. This double pressure was examined by Dr Stanley Milgram.

Milgram recruited volunteers who believed they were to take part in an experimental study of memory and learning. Each volunteer was asked to administer electric shocks to a learner-victim whenever the learner-victim gave an incorrect answer to a question. Ostensibly, this was to demonstrate the role of punitive treatment as an aid to learning.

In fact it was a carefully arranged 'cover' to find out just how far the volunteers would go in punishing their victims. The learner-victim made pre-arranged responses according to an increasing scale of electrical voltage, labelled for the benefit of the volunteers from 'slight shock' to 'danger: severe shock'. The experiment was described by R.D. Laing:

> When the punitive shock reached the 300 volt level, the learner-victim kicked on the wall of the room in which he was bound to the electric chair. At this point the teacher-volunteers turned to the experimenter for guidance. The teacher-volunteer was advised to continue after a 5-10 second pause. After the 315 volt shock, the pounding was heard again. Silence followed. At this point in the experiment the teacher-volunteers began to react in various ways. But they were verbally encouraged, and even ordered in a firm manner, to proceed right up to the maximum level of voltage.
>
> Dr Milgram states that contrary to all expectation 26 of the 40 subjects completed the series, finally administering 520 volts to the now silent 'victim'. Only 5 refused to carry on after the victim's first protest when 300 volts were apparently administered. Many continued, even though they experienced considerable emotional disturbance, as clearly shown by their spoken comments, profuse sweating, tremor, stuttering and bizarre nervous laughter and smiling. Three subjects had uncontrollable seizures. The teacher-volunteers who continued the shock frequently voiced their concern for the learner-victim but the majority overcame their humane reactions and continued as ordered right up to the maximum punishment.
>
> One observer related: 'I observed a mature and initially poised businessman enter the laboratory smiling and confident. Within 20 minutes he was reduced to a

twitching, stuttering wreck, who was rapidly approaching a point of nervous collapse. He constantly pulled on his earlobe and twisted his hands. At one point he pushed his fist into his forehead and muttered: 'Oh God, lets stop it.' And yet he continued to respond to every word of the experimenter and obeyed to the end.'

The difficulty of investigation

While investigation of long-term effects of torture on the victim and of the character of the torturer have been conducted with growing sophistication in the past thirty years, the essence of torture research remains careful documentation of the victim's experiences. Detailed first-person accounts, skilful interviews, a thorough medical and pyschiatric examination, information on the victim's previous life style, personality and health, and periodic follow-ups would together constitute the necessary evidence that can be used not only to prove that torture or brutality has taken place but also to find ways to make its techniques ineffective. Circumstances have hardly combined, however, to make this kind of investigation possible, and the interested scholar may supplement his findings with research into other forms of stress, such as warfare, which may in part at least be applicable to torture.

But research into the effects of torture is sadly open to perversion, and the psychiatric studies to find cures for abnormal mental states must be scrutinised to ensure that they are not abused but are used to alleviate the distress of those exposed to torture. In recent years psychotherapy, aversion therapy and brain surgery have been used in prisons to try to change the mental attitudes of certain prisoners. It is vital that these procedures should be supervised by completely impartial physicians and psychiatrists. In medicine, a doctor who wishes to perform a kidney transplant is not the doctor who decides when the potential donor cannot be resuscitated. If a prisoner's aggressive outbursts can be traced to a temporal lobe tumour, it may be reasonable to offer him brain surgery to remove the tumour. But cerebral surgery to make a man less troublesome to the authorities is reprehensible. All reports of treatments to prisoners should be published and carefully assessed so that we neither prevent prisoners from having medical help nor allow them to be subject to experiment or inhumane treatment. By the same token, no research into torture or such subjects as sensory deprivation should be undertaken without consideration of the motives of the sponsoring organisation or individual, so that at least some estimation can be made of the eventual use to which the results of the work will be put.

Even the experiments themselves may pose serious practical and ethical problems. Subtle techniques of psychological torture are known to have long-term effects; must the researcher inflict the possibility of permanent neurosis on his subjects in order to conduct a useful experiment? Surely no one in his right mind would volunteer to participate in such a study, but unless a subject is in his right mind he cannot be said to be a volunteer. Moreover, research and publication of techniques and their aftermath may serve to spread expertise and advance the technology of torture when the opposite was the intention of those who designed the research. Perhaps the study of non-brutal methods of interrogation would provide a balance and an alternative to the dehumanising methods so widely employed today.

Yet even if the revelation that less violent forms of treatment may be the most efficient means of interrogation were advanced in all the Ministries of the Interior in all the countries in the world, this scientific reality would pale before the political reality of a torture state. Obtaining information is only one purpose of torture; in most states it is one of relatively little significance. The deterrence power of fear of pain and of a long agony of dying would not be equalled by a potential dissenter/victim's belief that while he might be induced to reveal some information he certainly would not be tortured. The prevention of torture then lies not in medical research but in political and legal remedies.

2 *Legal Remedies*

This section outlines the remedies available to torture victims. It briefly examines the role of relevant governmental and non-governmental organisations at the world and regional levels. Three case studies — the occupied territories of the Middle East, Greece, and Northern Ireland — illustrating international efforts in the first case, regional efforts in the second case and domestic remedies in the third, demonstrate the possibilities and limits of such remedies.

The question of remedies involves two fundamental but competing principles of the international system — one is the right of the sovereign state to be free from outside interference in its internal affairs; the other is the right of the individual to his basic human rights and the international protection of those rights. Paradoxically, no two international norms are more violated that these two, non-intervention and human rights. The problem is that when states do intervene, they generally do not do so to protect the human rights of others, and thus rather than having only one principle sacrificed for the other, both are sacrificed.

The key role in the international system continues to be played by the state, and remedies for torture victims depend ultimately on the state. For the victim the immediate problem is what can be done so that his torture stops. It is at this level of urgency, this cry for help, that the family, friends and concerned organisations must confront their own relative helplessness. The state that tortures is normally not one that respects the rule of law, and such local measures as *habeas corpus* will rarely be available. Within this kind of arbitrary system, personal intervention by the powerful often offers the only hope. Internationally there exists no mechanism for dealing with torture, with the exception of a few European states in the European Convention system, but even that procedure offers no immediate redress. Thus each case, each cry for help, triggers an *ad hoc* operation shaped by the particular circumstances. In fact the use of the legal term 'remedies' is perhaps misleading as it implies a developed system like that of domestic law in which remedies are available. For the torture victim, at the immediate level of what can be a matter of life or death, there are no such legal remedies.

The means currently employed to stop torture are designed to put pressure on the state and the torturer so that they will not use torture methods. Means employed directly at the state level include diplomatic intervention by other states, hopefully more powerful ones, and the intervention of important institutions of personalities, e.g. the Catholic Church or Nobel Prize winners. Publicity through the media is another important, though less direct, means. Non-governmental organisations like Amnesty International are often important channels for appeals, pressure and publicity. Pressure from other organisations such as international businesses can be effective defence of human rights (the removal of the education tax on Jews emigrating from the USSR is a case in point). All of these pressures are exerted on the assumption that the state will decide it has less to gain from continuing to torture the victim than from ceasing. The state remains the key element, not only in the sense that it is the offending party, but also in that at the international level most efforts are designed to persuade states to exert their influence on the offending state. We are still in a world ruled by power politics; the effective power of those individuals and organisations who defend human rights is as yet no match for the state. Even though most nations now worry about the international reaction when they ill-treat their citizens, the right of the individual to be free from torture remains a right without an international remedy.

International governmental organisations

The United Nations has neither effective means nor institutions for dealing with the problem of torture. The most that can be said is that it does provide a number of forums throughout its various organs and agencies in which the problem of torture can be raised. The appropriate division of the United Nations family for this issue is the Commission of Human Rights, part of the Economic and Social Council. Despite its promising title the Commission has neither the will nor the power to defend the Universal Declaration of Human Rights, and especially its article prohibiting torture:

> No one shall be subjected to torture or to cruel, inhuman or degrading treatment or punishment.

The Commission itself is made up of members representing states; consequently, it is a political forum which expresses the political interests of member states. Because states share an interest in upholding the doctrine of non-interference, no effective mechanism for examining human rights violations can be set up. This is not at all surprising as so very few states live up to the high ideals of the Declaration. Some smaller powers which do in fact respect the Declaration in their own countries have shown a willingness to adopt more effective measures, but these efforts are blocked by the others, especially by the Great Powers. The wolves are left to guard the sheep and the result is predictable. What makes it more depressing is that the wolves all feel obliged to insist in public that they are sheep.

There are two instances, however, of the political situation having permitted some international activity, namely in the occupied territories of the Middle East and in Southern Africa. Hearings, investigations and public reports under the aegis of the Commission have dealt directly with the question of torture in South Africa and the Portuguese colonies. The Middle East investigations are dealt with below.

Sub-commissions of the Commission which are made up not of official representatives of states but of individual experts in the field of human rights have done more independent work. They show a tendency to defend human rights rather than the policies of their governments.

Even if the Commission did show a willingness to take up the problem of torture in a number of member states, their effective power would be very limited, as the case of Southern Africa has demonstrated.

Since 1970 there has been a new development which for the first time permits, at least in theory, a private individual or non-governmental organisation to complain to the Secretary-General about the violation of human rights and to have these complaints investigated by an impartial international body. This new procedure, laid down in ECOSOC Resolution 1503 and filled out in its detail by the Sub-Commission on Prevention of Discrimination and Protection of Minorities, is hedged with a thicket of conditions and obstacles and depends finally on the consent of the state accused to permit the investigation; however, it is the first slight opening within the UN of the possibility of international action on behalf of an individual whose human rights have been violated.

There are three stages of the new procedure. The 'communication' or complaint moves first through a Working Party of the Sub-Commission, and then the Sub-Commission, and then through the full Commission, which can either take it up for thorough study or appoint an *ad hoc* committee to investigate the complaint 'in constant cooperation with the state' concerned. The operative criteria for promotion from instance to instance is whether the complaint 'appears to reveal a consistent pattern of gross and reliably attested violations of human rights and fundamental freedoms'. While this is a strict standard, there is of course no shortage of cases which could meet this standard.

State torture as an administrative practice fits perfectly into a 'consistent pattern of gross violations' and the three cases that have been declared admissible by the Working Group — Greece, Iran and Portugal — include torture as one of the violations. It remains to be seen what will happen under this new procedure, but after the meeting of the full Commission in the spring of 1973 in Geneva, it is clear that many state their wish to close even this modest opening. (See *The Review of the International Commission of Jurists*, December 1072, p. 5, 'Disappointing Start to New UN Procedure on Human Rights'.)

The First United Nations Congress on the Prevention of Crime and the Treatment of Offenders adopted, on 30 August 1955, the Standard Minimum Rules for the Treatment of Prisoners. These rules were endorsed with minor alterations by the United Nations Economic and Social Council on 31 July 1957. They also formed the basis of Standard Minimum Rules adopted by the Council of Europe's Committee of Ministers on 19 January 1973.

Article 31 of both the UN's rules and those of the Council of Europe provides:

> Corporal punishment, punishment by placing in a dark cell, and all cruel, inhuman or degrading punishment shall be completely prohibited as punishment for disciplinary offences.

Both sets of rules provide a code for the humane treatment of prisoners.

Regional organisations

The European Convention on Human Rights was signed on 4 November 1950, and came into force on 3 September 1953. The Convention was conceived in the post-war period when the memory of recent tragedy was fresh and the spirit of European unity strong. The Council of Europe and the Convention on Human Rights were viewed as institutions expressing a common heritage of democracy and human rights which would serve as steps toward European Unity.

The Convention is the one ratified document in the field of human rights that attempts to make legal obligations to the principles expressed in the Universal Declaration of Human Rights. The Convention sets out the basic civil and political rights, institutes machinery for providing remedies for the violation of these rights, and seeks in a realistic fashion to balance the rights of the individual with the right of the state to defend itself. It is the only existing international agreement for the protection of human rights equipped with sanctions, and it is the only agreement that thus far has given the individual standing before an international tribunal.

The organs of the 'Convention System' which are charged with making the system work are the Commission of Human Rights, the Court of Human Rights, and the Committee of Ministers. In the framework of the Council of Europe, the Court and the Commission can be thought of as the judicial side, while the Consultative Assembly, made up of parliamentarians of member states, can be thought of as the parliamentary side. Actual power is very limited, and the Commission and the Consultative Assembly only have the power to recommend to the Committee of Ministers. It is the Committee, made up of the Foreign Ministers of the member states, which has the power to make decisions and levy sanctions.

The Commission is considered by many commentators to be the greatest accomplishment to date of the Council of Europe, and it is the organ that has confronted directly the problem of torture. Once a petition is accepted, the Commission is given two functions: the first 'a friendly settlement of the matter on the basis of respect for Human Rights in this Convention'. This 'European conscience' has been likened to a *juge d'instruction* who carries out a preliminary investigation; yet the Commission, which can proceed in a very flexible manner, is essentially a judicial organ. It is also the 'workhouse' of the Convention system, as it has received thousands of applications and heard inter-state cases.

Torture has been raised directly in inter-state cases on three occasions: the Cyprus Case between the United Kingdom and Greece; the Greek Case between the Scandinavian countries, Holland and Greece; and the Northern Irish Case between the Irish Republic and the United Kingdom. In April 1973, the Commission declared admissible the individual petitions from Northern Ireland against their own government, the United Kingdom, claiming that they had been victims of ill-treatment as prohibited under Article 3 of the Convention.

Western Europe is probably the area of the world where the rule of law is most respected; consequently, a system of this kind has a chance to work. The Greek Case (which is discussed below in more detail) showed that the Convention system can protect human rights in member states only when the states themselves have the will to protect them at the level of municipal law, and when the rule of law is an operational reality. The Convention System is really designed to handle the occasional aberration, the exceptional denial of justice that will occur even in the most conscientious of states.

In 1959, an Inter-American Commission on Human Rights was set up by a resolution of the Organization of American

States. This autonomous seven member entity of the OAS was confirmed by treaty in 1967. It was seen by the member states as an advisory and study group on human rights which would 'promote' rather than 'enforce' human rights. The Commission has developed a more vigorous concept of its own role and within its very slender mandate has used its possibilities of making on-the-spot investigations and reports in the most effective way. While the member states did not intend to confer on them the right to receive individual petitions, the Commission has resolved that it could 'take cognisance' of such communications submitted to it. It has published periodic reports on human rights violations particularly on those states which have refused to cooperate or admit the Commission. An American Convention on Human Rights drafted in 1970 sets up a system comparable to that of the European Convention system with its Commission and Court, but this convention awaits ratification, and it is doubtful that it will receive the ratifications necessary to bring it into force, particularly as the larger states of the hemisphere do not at present intend to ratify it.

> No one shall be subjected to torture or to cruel, inhuman or degrading punishment or treatment. All persons deprived of their liberty shall be treated with respect for the inherent dignity of the human person.
> Article 5.2 American Convention on Human Rights

Non-governmental organisations

In the international community it is the non-governmental organisations that have been the most vigorous in defence of human rights and in condemnation of the practice of torture. The United Nations has granted, as provided for in the Charter, Consultative Status to 251 'NGOs' in a first category which gives them this status throughout the United Nations organisation, and there are a further 280 organisations in a second category, which are recognised by particular agencies of the UN. This number covers a varied range of organisations; most represent the interests of a particular constituency like trade unions, professional groups, student organisations, religious groups or veterans, while others are organised on the basis of a certain principle like peace or the abolition of slavery. Fifty-three of these organisations are listed on the Special Committee of NGOs on Human Rights and some of these have shown a special concern for the problem of torture.

Despite the energetic efforts and deep concern of many NGOs they have only limited possibilities to combat torture. Their activities can be summarised in the following categories:

(1) Gathering information about torture and disseminating it to interested parties, including the news media;
(2) Sending investigators to the countries concerned;
(3) Sending observers to trials where the issue of torture is likely to be raised by the accused;
(4) Lobbying with those who can influence governments that employ torture, such as other governments or institutions;
(5) Developing and proposing long-term actions which would strengthen human rights protection and support existing mechanisms such as the European Human Rights Commission. It is evident that NGO's must rely on public opinion and governments to achieve their goals.

CASE STUDY A: THE UN AND THE OCCUPIED TERRITORIES OF THE MIDDLE EAST

In the aftermath of the six-day war in June 1967, the UN, concerned with human rights in the area of the conflict, took several initiatives to investigate human rights question (see generally, Rodley, N., 'The United Nations and Human Rights in the Middle East', *Social Research*, No. 38, p. 217, 1971).

Within a week of the war, the Security Council passed resolution 237 of 14 June 1967, which called upon the government of Israel to ensure the safety, welfare and security of the inhabitants of the area where military operations have taken place and to facilitate the return of those inhabitants who have fled the areas since the outbreak of hostilities. It recommended to the governments concerned the scrupulous respect of the humanitarian principles governing the treatment of prisoners of war (Third Geneva Convention) and the protection of civilian persons in time of war (Fourth Geneva Convention) contained in the Geneva Conventions of 12 August 1949. The Secretary-General was to follow the effective implementation of this resolution. In pursuance of his mandate, the Secretary-General sent a Special Representative (Mr Nils-Göran Gussing) to the Middle East. After one mission to the area, his activities were eventually halted when the government of Israel insisted that he would have to investigate the conditions of Jews in the area of conflict if he were to be allowed to investigate that of Arabs. Conflicting interpretations of the resolution led to an impasse. When, a year later, the Security Council by resolution 259 (1968) explicitly restricted the mandate to the occupied territories, Israel continued to refuse cooperation.

Because of this stalemate, the General Assembly, in 1969, set up a Special Committee to Investigate Israeli Practices Affecting the Human Rights of the Population of the Occupied Territories (Special Committee of Three). The membership of the Special Committee of Three consists entirely of countries that have no diplomatic relations with Israel. For that reason, among others, the Israeli government has refused to co-operate with it and has restricted itself to discrediting the Special Committee and its findings, none of which, as a result of Israel's non-cooperation, have been based on investigations *in loco*.

The Committee, in its first report, ventilated a variety of accusations of torture and expressed its acceptance of the credibility of some of those making the allegations. Subsequent reports have played down the torture question, confining themselves to following developments regarding those allegations that were mentioned in the first report.

Since there was some delay over the establishment of the Special Committee of Three because of a constitutional wrangle over the procedures by which members were appointed, the Commission on Human Rights addressed itself to the problem. Re-affirming 'the inalienable right of all the inhabitants who have left since the outbreak of hostilities to return', the Commission by Resolution 6 (xxv) set up a Special Working Group of Experts (Special Working Group) to investigate allegations concerning Israel's violations of the Fourth Geneva Convention. This was the only time that the Commission has launched an investigation, outside Southern Africa, under its authority to make thorough studies of situations that reveal a consistent pattern of gross violations of human rights. Composed of the same persons who had investigated Southern Africa, and covering much the same evidence as the Special Committee of Three, the Special Working Group concluded that it seems that means of coercion are always applied to extract information and confessions contrary to the relevant provisions of the Geneva Convention. It did not consider that it had been in a position to verify allegations of torture juridically.

By confining human rights investigations to Israeli-occupied territories and Southern Africa, while refusing to act on recommendations to investigate other countries, e.g. Greece and Haiti, the United Nations has not elicited confidence in its impartial support for the international protection of human rights.

CASE STUDY B: REGIONAL AND INTERNATIONAL RESPONSE TO THE USE OF TORTURE IN GREECE 1967-1973

The recent example of the use of torture by the military regime in Greece provides an excellent case study of the limits and possibilities in any international effort to combat torture. While the Greece of the Colonels is not the worst example of state torture in the contemporary world, it is an archetypal military regime which depends on torture to govern, and, most important, for our own purposes, it is historically the case where the international efforts to prevent torture were pushed the furthest.

The violation of human rights in Greece has received considerable attention internationally, clearly a disproportionate amount in terms of all the attention focussed on these problems globally, but still insufficient for those who suffer. Special, if not unique, circumstances explain why international efforts were pushed the furthest in Greece and why the torture issue became for a time the major issue in Greece's foreign affairs. A major circumstance was the fact that Greece is considered a Western and European country and is tied politically and economically to the West. Western public opinion was particularly sensitive to what was happening in Greece; Greece had been a parliamentary democracy. Even though the Colonels tried to place the coup in the context of the Cold War, public opinion, because of the general *détente* and the open repression of non-communists in Greece, was more willing to look at the reality rather than the propaganda. The regime prosecuted and alienated the most articulate Greeks who then became effective lobbyists since they knew how to use Western institutions. Moreover previous Greek governments had signed a number of international agreements, many of them with human rights commitments, most notably the European Human Rights Convention, which meant that many international organisations had the legal right to concern themselves with human rights violations in Greece. Finally Greece enjoys a peculiar sentimental position in the West for it is seen as the 'cradle of democracy', the land where 'the Western adventure began' and as such the practice of torture was considered all the more shocking when it occurred in that country.

To analyse the problem of torture in Greece in terms of articles of international agreements violated might be an interesting theoretical exercise but it would miss the point. The issue can only be understood in terms of a total political reality; these agreements themselves only have meaning in terms of reality.

After the German occupation of World War II a civil war broke out in Greece which became part of the developing Cold War between the United States and Russia. With a weakened British Empire no longer able to help the *ancien régime* in Greece, the United States stepped in and Greece became an American client state in the emerging bloc system. The relationship between Greece and the United States was the determining fact in Greece's post-war history in general and was to be the major determinant on a specific issue like that of torture under the Colonels' regime.

On 21 April 1967, a group of military officers carried out

a successful coup. Instead of the elections that had been scheduled for May, there were mass arrests, purges, martial law, censorship — all the familiar features of a military dictatorship. Torture began from the first day and became an integral part of the state mechanism of repressing opposition.

(Note: There is a considerable bibliography on the subject of torture in Greece under the Colonels. The most authoritative is the Report of the European Commission of Human Rights in *The Greek Case*, volume 2, part 2. See also Becket, J., *Barbarism in Greece*, New York, 1970, which lists the names of 438 victims and 126 torturers. Personal accounts of victims include: *Dans les prisons des colonels*, Paris, 1971; Fleming, A., *A Piece of Truth*, London 1973. There have been three books in English which are considered to be favourable to the Colonels' regime and which, while not totally denying torture, deny that it is a state policy: Young, K., *The Greek Passion*, London, 1969; Holden, D., *Greece Without Columns: the Making of the Modern Greeks*, London, 1972; Stockton, B., *Phoenix with a Bayonet*, Georgetown Publications, 1971.)

Policies and attitudes

In terms of power and influence the US government plays the predominant role in Greece. The self-declared interests of the US in Greece are strategic — it needs bases and facilities for its armed forces in a congenial environment of political stability. The Greek military regime has more than met these requirements, providing new bases and facilities in the high stability of a dictatorship. Consequently the regime has enjoyed the effective support of the US government throughout this period. For the US government the issue of torture has been a totally peripheral one and has only had significance in the measure that it could be politically expressed with enough force to interfere with broader American policy. American policy on the torture question as expressed in official statements and official testimony has been to deny it where possible and minimise it, where denial was not possible. This policy flowed naturally from general support for the military regime.

In the post-war division of Europe the Soviet bloc was the enemy of the Greek state. The bloc aided the losing side in the Civil War and absorbed many thousands of refugees after the defeat. The Greek Communist Party (KKE) continued to function in exile and left-wing forces regrouped in Greece in the EDA party whose basic decisions were taken in Moscow. Relations began to improve in the 1960s as part of the general détente, but it was with the advent of the Colonels that the Soviet bloc made a special effort to improve relations with Greece. Russian policy has shown a marked preference for this regime and economic, political, and cultural relations have expanded.

While the media in the Soviet bloc have been critical of the Greek regime, particularly at its outset, the most astonishing aspect was that the line among party members in Eastern Europe is that the Colonels 'have done many things'. Most shocking has been the action of the Bulgarians in returning escaped Greeks who asked for political asylum. (For the foreign policy of various Eastern European countries see *Greece under Military Rule*, London 1972 pp. 222-5. See also *Christian Science Monitor*, 'Athens warms to advances by Moscow', 4 January 1973.) At a conference held in Geneva of National Committees for Democracy in Greece on 29-30 June 1968, the Soviet delegate urged the following boycotts be pressed for by each national committee in their country; boycott of foreign investments, Greek ships, tourism, artistic activity, sports. Since that time the USSR has enlarged relations in all these spheres including the economic sphere through the construction of electric power stations and the development of peat industry. (See *Procès-Verbal de la Conférence des Comités Nationaux pour la Grèce Democratique Genève, Maison des Congrès, 20-30 juin 1969* (mimeo).)

Just as the US has its own nominalism so does the Soviet Union. The Soviet Union states it supports socialism, proletarian revolution and international working-class solidarity while opposing capitalism, fascism and imperialism. As the Colonels are a right-wing military dictatorship who nominally denounce communism and have imprisoned thousands of communists and tortured hundreds of others, Russian friendliness creates a certain gap. An attempt is made to bridge it by stating that while the Party disapproves, the state is obliged to seek friendly relations with other states in the interests of 'peaceful coexistence'. Furthermore they argue that it is better to have good inter-state relations in order to be able to intervene effectively on behalf of those imprisoned in Greece. This policy has led to disintegration of the Greek Left, just as American policy has led to considerable disillusion in liberal quarters in Greece.

The Greek issue has been an important political issue in Western Europe because Greece is part of that region. The Greek question has been raised continually on the state level and has been a concern of major political parties, cutting across party lines, though more consistently taken up by social democratic parties than conservative parties. The governments of the three most important states in Europe, Germany, England and France, have all tried to maintain good commercial relations with the colonels, while Germany and England have made political statements criticising the lack of parliamentary democracy and human rights. In regional organisations such as the Council of Europe and the Common Market those two states have taken positions against the Greek military regime; though in the wider Atlantic context, principally NATO, they have not.

The Scandinavian countries, Norway, Sweden, and Denmark, have been the only ones willing to make sacrifices for the sake of principle. They have acted at the state level on violations by Greece of its international obligations. They have brought the issue to the Council of Europe.

The policy of the military regime in Greece was first to survive, then to survive handsomely. Greece is ruled by a military junta with a dictator occupying the principal posts of power in the traditional cabinet form. (Col. George Papadopoulos occupies the posts of President, Prime Minister, Regent, Defence Minister, Minister of Foreign Affairs and was at one time also Minister of Education.) The government bureaucracy maintained its structure with military officers put in sensitive posts. A new development was the rise in size and power of the apparatus of repression, the military police and other army units playing a role along with the police in matters of security. These forces were in direct liaison with the junta. They used and use torture. The official position of the Greek state has been and remains that there has been no torture. This has been denied and denied again at every international level. The traditional state mechanism, including the Foreign Office, the Ministry of Justice, the Press Office, have all been used to combat these accusations. Censorship has prevented it from becoming a domestic issue.

The question of torture has not been a concern of the United Nations at the level of the Security Council and the General Assembly, but the question of torture in Greece has been raised in the Human Rights Commission of the United Nations where it has made little headway and in the International Labour Organisation, one of the Specialised Agencies of the UN, whose Commission of Inquiry found that the Greek regime had violated two ILO Conventions.

At the regional level of Europe it has been a different story, since the torture issue has been of great importance and has resulted in measures such as the exclusion of Greece from the Council of Europe. This was made possible by an existing machinery to investigate human rights violations, by states which were willing to use it, and by the fact that the major supporter of the regime, the US, could not, as a non-member, legally veto these efforts. Greece's status in the EEC has been frozen partly as a result of its violation of basic human rights.

It was at this level that organisations took a very active role and a strong position on the issue of torture in Greece, though their lack of power set limits to their effectiveness.

There were first of all organisations directly concerned with human rights. Their methods included sending representatives to Greece to investigate, sending observers to trials, gathering information and publishing reports with the hope that states would take measures. These organisations include Amnesty International, the International Commission of Jurists, La Ligue de Droit de l'Homme, the Associations of Democratic Jurists, and others.

The International Committee of the Red Cross played an important role in the investigation of prison conditions and the question of torture. It was able to visit political prisoners, and it submitted reports to the regime on its findings. As a result of the Greek Case before the European Commission of Human Rights the Greek regime signed an unprecedented accord with the ICRC granting their delegates the right to examine police stations and other places of detention at any time. This accord officially lasted for a year though it became quickly apparent that it had little effect, particularly on the military, once its political *raison d'être* — to stay in the Council of Europe — ceased to exist.

The issue of torture was also taken up by nongovernmental organisations representing particular groups such as workers, students, journalists, religions, e.g. World Council of Churches, International Press Institute, World University Service, the ICFTU, etc.

Western political parties took an interest in the Greek question and one of their concerns was torture. It was generally the parties in opposition that took strong stands of condemnation. Once in power their positions were often softened, but the Greek case became part of many political platforms, was an issue in electoral policies, and was a frequent subject of parliamentary debate where accusations of torture were an important component of the argument used by opponents of the Greek regime. The attitude of the Labour Party in Britain is a good example. While George Brown said in November 1967 that excluding Greece from NATO 'would weaken and destroy the alliance', the Party Congress adopted at the same time a resolution favourable to Greece's exclusion. (The Greek question was also an issue of sharp difference between the candidates in the 1972 American Presidential elections.)

A number of groups were set up in various Western countries to help the political prisoners. These were essentially pressure groups and charitable organisations which sought to alleviate the conditions in which prisoners were held and in which their families lived. They were distinct from resistance groups of Greeks. These concerned organisations became a source of information for people abroad who were interested in the Greek situation as well as remaining a source of aid for the prisoners.

The press, television, and radio played a key role in the

question of torture in Greece. Without the dissemination of the information that there was torture there would have been no issue. Without the continual treatment of this issue by the media it would not have become a political problem. The removal of Greece from the Council of Europe in December of 1970 can be almost directly related to the breaking of the news of the findings of the Human Rights Commission in the press before the meetings. This created an atmosphere where it would have been very difficult for certain states to keep the military junta, now condemned as torturers, in the organisation. While the media in Europe had the most impact, the media in the United States also placed the government on the defensive on this particular issue.

History of the issue

... the Delegation can objectively state that torture is deliberately and officially used and was convinced that the use of torture is a widespread practice against Greek citizens suspected of active opposition to the Government... Report of Amnesty International Delegation to Greece, 17 January 1968

'International Communism' launched on the morrow of the Revolution of 21 April 1967 an unprecedented vile attack about alleged torturing of political prisoners ... These communist charges were comprised in a report of 'Amnesty International', *The Truth Regarding the Deported Communists and the Alleged Tortures* (pamphlet published by the Press and Information Department of the Ministry to the Prime Minister, spring 1969; full text in Becket, *Barbarism in Greece*, pp. 192-9).

The first period: April 1967-November 1968: charge and counter charge

The first period is characterised by the struggle of the one side to make the problem of torture known and the effort by the other side to deny and suppress the issue. At the same time there was the struggle to convince public opinion by each side; the issue was becoming more important in the press and was becoming the concern of non-governmental organisations and finally of states and international organisations.

The carrying out of the coup involved the arrest and deportation of thousands of persons. A few were killed during this period, many were beaten and ill-treated, and some were systematically tortured, generally to find out where certain people were hiding. Many people were taken into custody by the security forces and beaten as a measure of intimidation. Once the basic situation was in hand and the new regime consolidated its power, the use of state torture began in a systematic and regular way. A number of state organisations, both civilian police and military forces, practised torture. Reports of torture began to filter out of Greece almost immediately. It was not until November of 1967 however that an authoritative report appeared in a 'serious' Western newspaper. This article appeared in the *Guardian*, and was based on conversations with people accused of supporting the resistance organisation called the Patriotic Front by such acts as publishing leaflets and hiding Mikis Theodorakis. Many of these defendants had been tortured but none dared declare it openly in the courtroom. The article did not mention any names and took particular care that no one could be identified, for the risk of being tortured again was a very real one.

The large number of political prisoners and reports about ill-treatment prompted Amnesty International to send two lawyers to Greece at the end of December 1967. During their inquiries about prisoners they continually heard stories of torture. Despite the extreme difficulties in making contact with any victims, they managed to interview sixteen persons who claimed they had been tortured, and they gathered the names of thirty-two others who were still in prison, but who, according to second-hand evidence, appeared to have been the victims of torture. When they left Greece at the end of January they published a report on their findings which listed the methods of torture, the places of torture, and certain torturers, but it mentioned no victims by name as they feared reprisals and would not permit the use of their names. This report received considerable attention in the press, and the issue was seriously posed though the government of Greece did not yet react, and the report suffered from the fact that it gave no names. One of the lawyers then returned to Greece two months later where he was allowed to visit certain prisoners in prison. Nine of the 12 prisoners he saw said they had been tortured by falanga or electric shock. Amnesty International's Second Report then, with the consent of the victims, gave names.

The issue could no longer be ignored by the Greek regime or their supporters. The publicity about torture was beginning to compromise their interests. International newspapers like *The Times* of London, *Le Monde*, and the *New York Times* had carried stories on the subject. The Greek regime, following the second Amnesty Report, took the offensive on this issue. Inside the country they tightened up security and intimidated victims in order to prevent reports of torture from getting out. For public opinion abroad, the regime attacked the reports as slander and part of the 'communist conspiracy', attacking Amnesty's representatives personally. When it realised that this tactic was no longer sufficient it sought 'independent' sources to back up its denials. They invited journalists and parliamentarians to come to Greece with all expenses paid, and they hired public relations firms abroad to help the regime's 'image'.

By the end of April, 1968, they presented evidence which they held disproved 'the slander':

(1) the visit of a British inter-party group of MPs, one of whom made the statement that he didn't believe there had been tortures in the deportation camps;
(2) a report of the Delegate of the ICRC on his visit to Bouboulinas Street where the majority of tortures reported were alleged to have taken place;
(3) a statement by Francis Noel-Baker in the British parliament.

The reports of torture had not come from the island detention camps but rather from police stations and military camps, and so the statement by the British MP was not relevant.

Mr Francis Noel-Baker also did not deny the existence of torture, but attacked the Amnesty delegate for 'his strong political views' and said that reports of torture had been 'inflated to a superlative degree'. The Report of the Red Cross was treated by the Greek government as its strongest argument even though the Report gave the position of the victims, who stated they had been tortured, and the position of the police, who claimed there was no torture. Despite the fact that out of 131 prisoners, 46 complained of torture or ill-treatment, the Greek government used selected excerpts from the confidential Red Cross report to announce publicly that the Red Cross had found no evidence of torture. The Red Cross complained about publishing it in this way and the whole report was released.

As a result of inquiries about torture from American citizens, the US government, through the State Department, had to take a position on the issue. The official texts included here are excerpts of letters from the State Department to members of the Congress who made inquiries at the request of their constituents. The answers of the Greek Government to charges of torture were exceedingly crudely phrased and created an unfavourable impression on public opinion abroad. The State Department answers are drafted for a more sophisticated audience and the language of the letters is the guarded language of the lawyer seeking to protect his client. While the language and style are different, the purpose is the same: to convince public opinion of something they themselves know is not true.

The first inquiries produced what was to be the basic position taken by the State Department from April 1967 to July 1968:

> Our tentative conclusion is that there have unfortunately been instances of mistreatment of prisoners in individual cases. Our impression is that these instances occurred particularly with the rounding up, the detention and trial of members of the Patriotic Front, which is regarded by Greek officials and public opinion generally as a Communist-dominated group. During that period, which had its highpoint in the summer and fall of 1967, a series of home-made bombs were exploded in public places in Athens resulting in the death of an innocent bystander, and the police seem to have resorted in a number of cases to excessive means in order to uncover the responsible persons. Since the dispersal of the Patriotic Front, reports of mistreatment of prisoners have declined.

The uninformed reader, while he might note the extreme caution of the highly qualified language, would get the impression that in Greece there were, as in other countries, individual cases of 'mistreatment' by the police, but here it involved violent Communist bombers who killed innocent bystanders. Anyone familiar with the actual facts would get a different impression. Members of the Patriotic Front, a left wing organisation including persons from varying political persuasions, had been arrested and rounded up during August, September and October. The last Patriotic Front trial ended on 22 November 1967. On 30 November 1967 a bomb exploded on the roof of the Ministry of Justice and a passer-by, Katerina Milona, was killed by a section of falling pipe. This was the only fatal bombing incident in 1967 and 1968 and it occurred *after* the Patriotic Front had been arrested, tortured, tried and imprisoned. No one was ever tried for this incident. Most important, reports of what the State Department could only bring itself to refer to as 'mistreatment' of prisoners had not declined since November but had greatly increased.

In the middle of February some prisoners were taken from jail and brought to the laid-up warship *Elli* at the Scaramang Naval Base for interrogation. The government alleged a plot against the navy by 115 intellectuals and navy enlisted men. Here they were tortured by beatings, electroshock, and water torture. Those in Athens who worried about these matters knew of what was going on and tried to alert public opinion abroad. It was known soon after that one prisoner, Naval Petty Officer Constantinos Paleologos, had died under torture, and the details regarding the others became known when some of the victims were returned to prison at the beginning of March. One of these victims, Gerassimos Notaras, described his tortures to the Amnesty delegate and confirmed the reports that the *Elli* had been used for torture. This was published by Amnesty on 6 April 1968. The next day the report was denied by the Greek secretary of the Press. On 9 April, in a letter from the State Department signed by the Under-Secretary of State whose regional responsibility included Greece, the following was written to a US Senator:

As you requested, we asked the Embassy in Athens to look into this matter. It has not been able to develop any information to substantiate the allegation. As of this moment, it does not appear to us that the charges that the *Elli* is being used as a place of torture are valid inasmuch as the *Elli* is located close to the shore, a sizeable crew is maintained on the ship, many naval crews are stationed nearby and, in these circumstances, the comings and goings of guards and prisoners would be difficult to conceal. No reports of such movements have come to the Embassy's attention.

While those who cared about these matters abroad knew the name of the man killed under torture, and while Amnesty had already printed the testimony of one of the victims, the State Department, commanding the resources of an Embassy staff of more than 200 diplomats, a CIA mission of more than 600, including foreign nationals, and a military presence in Greece of thousands, could not 'develop any information to substantiate the allegation', and believed the charges that the *Elli* was being used as a place of torture were not valid.

The next development in their standard letters came on the State Department's initiative. In the beginning of May, new letters were sent to interested members of Congress with a few 'additional sidelights ... regarding charges of mistreatment of Greek political prisoners [which] ... have come to our attention'. These 'sidelights' turned out to be the Red Cross report, and the visit of the British inter-party delegation — in sum, just the evidence produced by the Greek Government, not any of the abundant available evidence confirming torture.

Torture reports increased, coming from Athens, Salonika, Crete, and outside Athens at the Dionysos military camp. Many groups were victims: Democratic Defence; Rigas Ferraios, a student group; right-wing army officers. Yet the State Department continued to include in its letters the same paragraph about 'our tentative conclusion' and the decline in the reports of mistreatment.

On 3 July, Gerassimos Notaras stood before a military court and denounced his torturers saying that his confession was false and had been extracted after long periods of torture, the last sessions on board the *Elli*. The court did not contest his statement and the prosecution confirmed that prisoners had been held on the *Elli*, only torture was considered judicially irrelevant. But Notaras had set a precedent, for it was the first time a victim of torture publicly denounced his torturers. This was later to become a commonplace of every political trial, but at the time it was a blow to the regime that they could no longer keep the victims quiet. A week after this on 10 July the State Department sent the following letter to an interested Senator, which did not bring up this new 'sidelight':

> Our Embassy in Athens has replied to our recent inquiry about renewed stories of torturers in Greece. *It has no new information* of significance and points out that claims of torture continue to be spotlighted by the international press and particularly by those papers which actively oppose the present Greek Government as a policy line. To the best of our knowledge here and that of our Embassy, many of these charges are false or gross distortions by political enemies of the regime... The treatment of prisoners generally by the Greek Government is a topic which the State Department and our Embassy in Athens have pursued diligently. The Greek Government has been made very much aware of the adverse image which such charges create of it. We believe that they have made an effort, particularly since January 1968, to curb any excesses by investigators. We will continue to do all that we can to establish the truth of these charges and to take advantage of every opportunity to press for *continued* fair treatment of prisoners. (*Our italics*)

By the summer of 1968 the torture issue had been brought out into the open. In Europe the struggle for public opinion on the issue of whether or not the regime had deliberately been using torture could be considered a draw at this point. The regime turned out strong denials accompanied by authoritative sounding sources like the Red Cross and British Parliamentarians. On the side of the victims, the press was carrying more signed accounts of torture, the continual trials before courts martial were now being highlighted by declarations by the accused that they had been tortured, and concerned non-governmental organisations were publishing reports, sending observers, and collecting and disseminating information. For European public opinion clearly all was not right in the kingdom of the Hellenes, but there still was a tendency to believe or disbelieve allegations of systematic torture according to one's ideological predispositions. The debate was now to move into a new arena — the European Commission of Human Rights, and it was to cross the Atlantic and become an issue in the American press.

The second period: November 1968 — the European Commission of Human Rights

> The Commission has found it established beyond doubt that torture or ill-treatment contrary to Article 3 has been inflicted in a number of cases and given the 'repetition of acts' and the 'official tolerance', the use of torture in Greece constitutes an 'administrative practice'. (Report of the European Human Rights Commission in the Greek Case, made after a two-year investigation in Greece and Europe in which 88 witnesses were heard, hundreds of documents submitted, 20,000 pages of testimony taken, and a report of 1,200 pages released, listing 213 victims of torture.)

> I rather suspect if they (the Greek authorities) go rough, it was more in the early stages, during the arrest period when they picked these fellows up; there may well — I am sure there have been cases where the police were unnecessarily severe in the early days. But as far as the general proposition, torture policy of the Greek government, there is no evidence to support that. (Testimony by the Ambassador of the United States to Greece, the Honourable Henry Tasca, before the House Armed Services Committee in Greece in January 1972).

This period was highlighted by the proceedings before the European Human Rights Commission which, in the form of an advisory hearing before an impartial tribunal, examined evidence on the violations of the European Human Rights Convention by the Greek regime, especially the violation of Article 3 forbidding torture. Placing this issue before the Commission had two important results: it heightened the interest of public opinion, and it had the effect of suspending the issue at official levels. Within the Council of Europe difficult decisions were postponed in anticipation of the decision of the Commission. The meeting of the Committee of Ministers of the Council of Europe voted on 5 May 1969 to postpone any decision on Greece until its next session in December when the Commission's Report would be ready. States fended off inquiries with the explanation the subject of torture was now *sub judice* and the Commission's decision had to be awaited. This building up of the significance of the Commission's decision gave political importance to what was essentially a judicial finding.

While Europe concentrated on the hearings held in Strasbourg, this period in Greece was characterised by a stream of trials before military courts where the defendants regularly denounced the tortures they had undergone. The barrier of fear had been broken, partly because there was hope that telling the truth might not be a futile gesture but would help the Commission. The other significant development was that the torture question became an important issue in the American press. The Greek regime could only escalate their denials.

The governments of Norway, Sweden, Denmark, and the Netherlands had already filed applications to the European Commission of Human Rights in September of 1967, charging the Greek regime with violating eight articles of the Convention. For a year the case before the Commission was to involve oral arguments and written briefs dealing with basic procedural and legal questions. The original Scandinavian application had not included Article 3, the one prohibiting torture, but after the Amnesty Report and other evidence the Scandinavian application was amended to include Article 3. (This involved the most important procedural decision by the Commission in the first year, as they allowed the amendment, thus rejecting the Greek argument that local remedies had not been exhausted. They held that these remedies could not be considered 'effective' or 'sufficient'. The dismissal the day before of Greece's thirty top judges aided in this decision.) A Sub-Commission was formed of seven European jurists and they prepared to hear the evidence of witnesses. One of the basic issues they were to determine was 'whether or not political prisoners had been tortured or subjected to inhuman or degrading treatment by police officers of the respondent Government and, if so, whether this amounted to an "administrative practice" '.

The decision to admit Article 3 changed the nature of the case. Not only was it of greater interest to the general public as the issue of torture roused European public opinion, but it changed the pleading strategies of the two parties. Article 15 of the Convention specifically excludes Article 3 from those articles which a state can legally suspend in times of emergency. In other words, the Convention holds that no situation permits a state to use torture to defend itself. The case then turned on these two articles, though if the Scandinavians could prove torture, the Greek regime would have no legal defence and would clearly be in violation of the Convention.

Both parties and the witnesses journeyed to Strasbourg for hearings which were to begin on 25 November 1968. Only one torture victim had escaped from Greece and was willing to testify before the Commission and the Scandinavians thus had limited direct evidence. This lack was remedied in a highly dramatic fashion, when two witnesses, brought by the military regime to testify they had not been tortured, escaped their armed guards and came to the hotel where the Scandinavians were based asking for sanctuary. They then testified before the Commission that they had been tortured. This story returned to the front pages when a month later one of the *transfuges* turned up in the Greek Embassy in Stockholm, retracted his story, refused to come to Strasbourg again, and returned to Greece.

The Sub-Commission then prepared to go to Greece to hear witnesses there and examine certain places. It is this feature of the Convention that gives it the first step toward a machinery for the international protection of human rights, the power to investigate in member states. After considerable delays and the imposition of conditions by the Greek Government, the Sub-Commission arrived in March 1969. This was a historic occasion for those interested in human rights, for there in Greece a body of foreign jurists heard evidence and confronted alleged torturers with their victims. An exchange which appears in the Report between the President of the Commission and a policeman when a victim was to be brought in, well expresses the opposed concepts of absolute national sovereignty versus the international protection of human rights.

> *Mr Fotinos*: Isn't it necessary to have an approval for this? Isn't it necessary to have the approval of the Government?
> *Mr President*: The Sub-Commission, Sir, does not need such approval from the Government, because the Government is a party to a Convention which enjoins it to observe the rules. *When the torture victim entered the room and identified the policeman as his torturer, Fotinos rose and tried to run from the room.* (Report, vol. 2, part 1, p. 180)

The Greek government ceased to co-operate and refused access to witnesses on the Sub-Commission's list, so the jurists left Greece under protest. By this time more torture victims had escaped from Greece, and they were heard in Strasbourg in June and July. The evidence was now overwhelming, and the Greek side boycotted certain meetings to try to delay the proceedings and the publication of the Report.

Attention was focussed anew on the issue when at the end of May the mass-circulation American magazine *Look* had as its lead article 'Greece: Government by Torture'. The Greek Embassy in Washington rejected 'the slanderous and totally foundless (sic) allegations'. Prime Minister Papadopoulos announced that he would execute personally and publicly in Constitution Square anyone proved to have administered torture. He further challenged the author of the article and the person who supplied the information to come to Greece to make an 'objective investigation'. The challenge was taken up, but the Greek government then changed its mind. Papadopoulos contented himself with telling an American Congressman that there had been no torture, and if there had been he would on his military word of honour commit suicide.

Concern was building up in Washington, particularly in the Congress, though there seemed to be some hesitation within the newly installed Nixon administration about policy toward the Colonels. The Secretary of State, Mr Rogers, in answer to a leading question from one of the best-informed and most concerned Senators, went further than any American official has gone before or since:

> *Senator Pell*: I realise that the country is going back toward normal. But this is a regime built on the basis of torture and the denial of civil liberties. Can you not take a hard line in future aid negotiations, and ask for assurance that torture not be a normal way of governing.
>
> *Mr Rogers*: Yes, Senator, we share your concern, not only for the torture phase but the other civil liberties. We are at present doing what we can through diplomatic circles to effect that, and we also will be conscious of the factors that you mention in subsequent negotiations. (*Christian Science Monitor*, 13 May 1969, article by Saville R. Davis)

This statement received little attention, perhaps as it was not intended as a definitive statement on the question of torture and the expression 'torture phase' is open to different interpretations. The issue however was to pick up momentum in the press in the United States.

During the summer of 1969 the Sub-Commission was drafting its Report. There was considerable behind-the-scenes negotiation. Efforts were made, as required by the Convention, for the two parties to come to a 'friendly settlement'. The Greek government as a result of these negotiations signed an accord with the International Committee of the Red Cross giving them free access to all detention places in Greece, including police stations. The stumbling-block in negotiations appears to have been over a time-table for elections and the restoration of democracy. The Scandinavians demanded a fixed date for elections, but the Greeks were unwilling. The Report was submitted to the full Commission and adopted on 5 November 1969. It was sent to the Foreign Ministers of member states on 18 November 1969. The Report found that torture was an administrative practice of the Greek government. A confrontation was building up for the Council of Ministers meeting of the Council of Europe in Paris on 11 December, a confrontation between those countries who wished to expel Greece and those who wished to keep it in and thus retain influence over it.

The US government, while not a member of the Council of Europe, had played an active diplomatic role from the beginning. Diplomatic pressure had first been put on the states bringing the action to abandon it. When the US was not successful in this endeavour, it had its ambassadors in Europe put pressure on the member states of the Council not to expel Greece, urging that this would lead to difficulty within NATO. The US government was in an awkward position: on the one hand all the European States believed only the US could change the situation in Greece, and at the same time the US was defending the regime and arguing that it should remain in the Council of Europe, an organisation based on democratic principles.

The coming clash was sharpened by the leaking of the Report to the London *Sunday Times* and other newspapers. This created a climate of public opinion which the Ministers could not ignore. The Council of Europe had never received so much attention. The Greek delegation arrived prepared to defend their position and stay in. Despite an eloquent speech by Foreign Minister Pipinelis, the votes were clearly against him, and under orders from Athens he walked out before the vote, and Greece denounced the European Convention of Human Rights. Tanks moved in Greece, flags were ordered flown, but the victory against those who used torture was only a moral victory.

In terms of the European Convention system and in terms of the history of the international protection of human rights, the Greek Case pushed the available international remedies the furthest yet, but these alone were clearly insufficient to stop the practice.

Where power counted, in the US government, the Report was nearly ignored. The attitude can be seen in the following exchange before a Congressional Committee:

Congressman Fraser: Isn't it true that the present Greek government was about to be expelled — thrown out of the Council of Europe?
Mr Davies (Deputy Assistant Secretary of State for Near Eastern and South Asian Affairs): They left the Council of Europe as a result of their feeling that it was improper for the Council to inject itself into Greek domestic affairs.
Mr Fraser: The inquiry being conducted was into the question of political torture, torture of political prisoners. As I recall, the Greeks were signatory to the treaty that created the right of the Europeans to look into that

question. Am I wrong in that?
Mr Davies: I don't have the basis for an answer, Sir. (p. 77, Joint Hearings: Committee on Foreign Affairs, House of Representatives, 92nd Congress, 'Political and Strategic Implications of Homeposting on Greece', March 7 & 8, April 12, 13, 18, 1972).

'I have been brutally tortured and kept under unspeakable conditions.'
Stathis Panagoulis at his trial in Athens, January 1973

'What did you expect, the Athens Hilton?'
Lt. Col. Karamaios, Chief Judge of the Military Tribunal

January 1970 — torture as usual
The major remedy had now been exhausted; yet in the torture chambers of the Greek military and security police it was business as usual. After three years it was clear that the Greek regime believed that it still needed to use torture in order to stay in power. As long as there were arrests for security reasons there was torture. It had been proved that torture was an administrative practice, but simply proving it was hardly sufficient to stop it. It was now obvious that only a change in the regime would stop the practice; it was not the temporary expedient of some early transitional period, but an integral part of a system that depended on dictatorial means to govern.

A change in the regime looked even more unlikely when the United States resumed full military aid to Greece in September 1970, and arranged for thousands of American servicemen and their families to live in Greece under the new base agreements. American policy statements now emphasised 'the firm commitment of the United States to a policy of non-interference in the internal affairs of other countries', and denied or minimised the practice of torture in Greece.

A new international remedy was opened in August 1971, when the Sub-Commission on the Prevention of Discrimination and the Protection of Minorities of the United Nations Economic and Social Council adopted new procedures under which individuals and non-governmental organisations could complain of violations of human rights to the UN Human Rights Commission. A completely documented communication on Greece was filed on 19 May and 20 June 1972, on behalf of the individuals who were either victims or witnesses of torture. Given the considerable delay inherent in the procedure and the lamentable record of the Commission of Human Rights in the defence of human rights, this 'remedy' offered no hope except as a first step in a long-term effort to create some meaningful system of international protection of human rights and fundamental freedoms.

With the issue of torture in Greece now effectively removed from the active concern of international organisations, the matter was dealt with directly only by the press and non-governmental organisations. Amnesty International, the International Commission of Jurists, the League for the Rights of Man, the International Association of Democratic Lawyers and other organisations continued to send observers to trials and gave as much attention as possible to the declarations of defendants about their tortures and to the fate of arrested persons who were held incommunicado. The foreign press continued to report accounts of torture, but the practice was now so institutionalised that it was not 'news' unless the victim was 'news', and it was difficult to sustain editorial indignation or reader concern, especially in the face of a steady flow of descriptions of barbarity from all corners of the world. The relative impotence of international organisations and international opinion even became integrated into the torture process. Victims were mocked during their suffering with such comments as, 'The Human Rights Commission can't help you now ... The Red Cross can do nothing for you ... Tell them all, it will do no good, you are helpless.' The torturers from the start had said that the United States supported them and that was what counted. Their appreciation of the international system and the effectiveness of the international protection for human rights was certainly more accurate than the hopes of the intellectuals and professors they were torturing.

This essay has dealt exclusively with foreign public opinion and foreign actors, and only with Greeks who represent the state or are victims of torture. But Greek experience is also instructive on public opinion inside Greece. Greek public opinion on the torture question does not in a sense exist because of press censorship and the absence of political parties and of institutions independent of the regime; the only public expression on this subject takes place only in the form of denunciations by the victims at their trials. And yet for the system 'public opinion' about torture is important. This kind of regime has a seemingly paradoxical interest, it wants all its citizens to know that torture is the penalty for dissent so that they will be deterred, and yet it must publicly deny the use of torture to conform to its nominal values, eg. 'Greece of Christian Greeks', 'a civilised nation'. Strangely enough this seeming paradox functions well at the practical level. Released prisoners have been shocked at the refusal of even life-long friends to believe their stories of torture.

There is first of all the general phenomenon of 'the willing suspension of disbelief' on the part of people to accept that their own countrymen would commit such practices; the Germans in the last war, the French in Algeria, the Americans in Vietnam are contemporary Western examples. In a police state, public reaction is much more complicated than defensive chauvinism. If the citizen was to believe, his own value system would require him to act; it is then much more convenient and safer on this level not to believe or to put it all at a distance, and thus avoid the moral dilemma. Another defense mechanism to avoid the issue is to label a report 'exaggerated' and thus dismiss it entirely, though this response really says the attention given is exaggerated, not the quantity of victims or the quality of torture. Those who do believe either are effectively deterred by fear of torture or by their own impotence against the state, or they do decide to act. The Greek experience has shown, and this is probably the case elsewhere, that only a handful of people will act *because* torture and other barbarities are practised by the regime. With large state security forces, with modern means, these 'dissidents' can be isolated, arrested, and themselves ground up in the torture machinery. The vast majority of the population 'mind their own business', while the few who act are isolated by the state. The state is not handicapped by the apparent paradox which immobilises the majority of potential opponents for whom the price is too high, and limits active opposition to a manageable number.

Torture continued as an administrative practice with the military police taking the lead. New trials produced new denunciations of torture; one of the most publicised was that of Wing Commander Minis who was held by the military police for 111 days. His torturers not only told him that the Prime Minister was following the course of the interrogation as Minis was an important prisoner, but they wanted him to tell everyone of his torture so all who entered military police quarters would tremble.

Most recently, six young lawyers who had defended students were arrested at the end of February 1973 and held by the military police without any charges being brought against them. A smuggled message read: 'Please do whatever you can, the suffering is unbearable'. In an unprecedented action, distinguished lawyers were sent from England, the US and Canada representing human rights organisations, with the sole mission of helping these lawyers. Despite their polite inquiries, the visitors were rudely rebuffed by the government. Again in June 1973 Amnesty received reliable information that at least nine of the naval officers arrested in connection with the attempted mutiny were being tortured.

During this period the State Department made another statement on the torture issue:

> To the question of 'torture' being practised by the Greek government, the best information available to the Department of State suggests that there may be instances of maltreatment of prisoners. However, we are not in possession of conclusive evidence that the mistreatment of prisoners is the result of systematic, much less official, policy. We deplore the mistreatment of prisoners wherever it occurs and have made our concern that all detainees receive fair and humane treatment very clear to the Government of Greece. (Letter from George Churchill, State Department).

It is difficult to see the change in the American position since 1968: 'torture' is put in quotation marks; the language despite six years of evidence, is still cautious — it 'suggests' that there 'may' have been instances of maltreatment of prisoners. The one change seems to be in the tense of the verb: from the past 'might have been', it is now the present. It would appear that Greece is not a case of 'government by torture' but 'government by instances of maltreatment'.

Conclusions

A number of generalisations can be made from the Greek experience:

1. Torture can become an integral part of a system of government. Since it is an integral part of the system, the only apparent way to stop it, as opposed to marginally restricting its use, is to change the system of government. This is a political problem totally outside the power or the design of any international mechanism for the protection of human rights.

2. A bureaucracy will defend the torturers if the decision-makers determine that the practice serves a policy interest. In the Greek case this was true both to the Greek bureaucracy and the American foreign relations bureaucracy.

3. Organisations and individuals opposing torture in a given situation depend on at least the following conditions in order to have any effect: a) the general acceptance of the principle that torture is a repugnant and illegal practice; b) correct information about torture; c) the possibility of disseminating that information; d) the existence of public opinion; e) the acceptance by states that they should justify their actions and enter into rational dialogue.

4. Only states have real power in the international system. Action against torture must ultimately be taken at the state level, particularly the superstate level, if it is to be effective. There must be a responsive link between public opinion and state power if popular feeling against the use of torture is to be expressed as state action. This existed in the Greek case with Scandinavian public opinion, but although these states were willing to pursue

the issue on a limited scale internationally, they are states with only marginal power.

The first two generalisations imply a *Realpolitik* vision of international affairs. The *Realpolitik* theory offers a persuasive explanation for the behaviour of states. And yet, in the Greek case, it is an incomplete view. If it were the whole explanation, states would simply say that they did torture and in effect be asking how many divisions the opponents of torture could muster. On the contrary, states always deny that they use torture. While states will not only announce bombing and murder, but glorify those that bomb and kill, the state never announces torture or glorifies the torturer. Moreover most states somehow feel the need to justify those actions they cannot conceal, and this inevitably leads them into national dialogue. Nevertheless, the case before the Council of Europe was unique, insofar as torturers were confronted by their victims. It may be argued that the case had a prophylactic influence, and that it strengthened respect for the Convention on Human Rights in Europe. It is in this area that those opposing torture can operate. In the Greek case both the Greek regime and the American State Department felt compelled to make statements on this subject. Each declaration prompted a reply and new declarations. The truth does have value when both sides accept the rules of the game, that is of rational debate. The major strength of those in the international system who have no real power is to present facts and to force states to deal publicly with these facts and to justify them within their declared value system.

It is difficult to estimate how effective the considerable international effort to halt torture in Greece was in terms of *limiting* the practice, but it is reasonable to believe that torture became less severe, for certain limited periods, as a result of foreign pressure.

* * *

Since this section was written, fundamental changes have taken place in Greece. In August 1973 nearly all political prisoners were released in an amnesty, but in November 1973 student demonstrations resulted in many arrests and in the replacement of the Papadopoulos regime by one similar in kind, although different in personnel. Martial law, which had been declared by Papadopoulos before his downfall, was maintained, and in the following months hundreds of people were imprisoned or deported. From the moment of the first arrests allegations of torture began to reach the outside world. Attempts by delegates from international organisations, and in at least one case by a doctor, to see prisoners were not successful, but detailed accounts of the condition of tortured prisoners came from relatives and released prisoners.

In July 1974 the military regime was replaced by a civilian government, and all political prisoners were released in an amnesty. Reports of the physical condition of many of the released prisoners as well as their own accounts of their treatment confirmed beyond reasonable doubt that the commitment of the military regime to the use of torture had been absolute throughout their rule. David Tonge reported in the *Guardian* (London), 28 July 1974: 'The physical scars on many of the Greek prisoners released since Thursday's general amnesty prove that their maltreatment in the past few months has been far more extensive than had been feared earlier.' Amnesty International has requested the new government to investigate the torture allegations of the past and to rehabilitate and compensate the victims.

CASE STUDY C: THE UK GOVERNMENT AND NORTHERN IRELAND

In the Greek situation, both domestic and international efforts to stop torture were ultimately frustrated by the authoritarian government. Although initially the Greek government was evidently sensitive to the adverse publicity created by accusations of torture, once the finding that torture was in fact occurring had been accepted by the Council of Europe, not only was there no voluntary compliance or cooperation on the part of the Greek government, but Greece simply denounced the Convention and withdrew from further participation in the investigation.

In the British situation, however, domestic and international publicity given to allegations of brutality and torture in Northern Ireland preceded investigations of these allegations made not only by such organisations as Amnesty International but by the government of the United Kingdom itself. The conflicting results of some of these investigations as well as their differing terms of reference and the degrees of co-operation obtained from the various parties seem to point to the conclusion that an administrative practice of torture may exist despite contrary domestic legislation and perhaps without the knowledge of the highest domestic political authorities.

Frequent and extended brutal interrogations that occur inside an Army or police compound with the participation of military, police and medical personnel must be practised with the knowledge of at least some officers. The difficulty lies in detecting at what stage in the chain of command toleration or encouragement stops and deception begins. Given the natural tendency of security forces to 'protect their own', it becomes very difficult for civilian political leaders to investigate allegations of torture and brutality without the cooperation of the soldiers or policemen involved. Still less can one expect an internal inquiry of a torture allegation to be an honest and thorough one where the acts complained of are in fact widely practised and accepted at certain levels of the forces.

It is thus understandable that those who hold political power are likely to dismiss as 'propaganda' allegations of torture or intimidation, since the information they receive from below is likely to be coated with many layers of 'covering up' by the time it reaches the top. As long as the government has faith in the integrity of the security forces at all levels, it is unlikely to take very seriously the accusations against them, and will treat as only isolated cases those incidents which they are forced to accept as well-founded.

In trying to break the pattern of torture as thus outlined, the goal is not necessarily to change an established government policy which encourages such activity, but rather to make the executive realise what is occurring and then to rely on the established domestic procedures for law-enforcement to take over. Thus the task should be politically easier than that involved in pressuring all levels of the regime itself into conforming to international standards of human rights.

Internment without trial was reintroduced in Northern Ireland on the 9 August 1971, under the Civil Authorities (Special Powers) Act (Northern Ireland) 1922. Three hundred and forty-two arrests were made on that day, and large numbers of arrests continued for several days. (Until 10 November, there had been 980 arrests.) By the end of the week the first reports of brutality on the part of the British Army found their way into Irish newspapers (the British press did not deal with the allegations until mid-October). On 31 August 1971, the Home Secretary appointed a three-man Committee of Inquiry, chaired by Sir Edmund Compton,

> to investigate allegations by those arrested on 9 August under the Civil Authorities (Special Powers) Act (Northern Ireland) 1922 of physical brutality while in the custody of the security forces prior to either their subsequent release, the preferring of a criminal charge or their being lodged in a place specified in a detention order.

The Compton Committee visited Northern Ireland from 1 September until 26 October; the report was published on 16 November 1971.

The inquiry was hampered from the start by procedures which effectively if not intentionally prevented the complainants from testifying before the Committee. These procedures were adopted 'to protect the lives of those who had conducted the arrests and interrogations' (Introduction, para 13). The hearings took place *in camera*, and no opportunity was given to the complainants to confront the members of the security forces against whom complaints were made. Both complainants and members of the security forces were allowed to be accompanied by a legal representative, but the lawyer was not permitted to cross-examine witnesses or to have access as of right to transcripts of evidence. While such procedures may have protected members of the security forces from IRA retaliation, the complainants believed not only that the constitution of the Committee could not ensure an unbiased hearing but moreover that its procedures did not adequately protect them from RUC or Army retaliation, and therefore they did not cooperate with the Committee. Of the forty complainants whose cases were covered in the Report, only one appeared in person before the Committee and one presented a written statement. Thus virtually all the evidence of complaints was hearsay.

Perhaps as a result, the Committee was able to make definite findings in very few cases. It did conclude that certain techniques complained of (e.g. hooding, loud noise, deprivation of sleep) had in fact been employed and did constitute ill-treatment. Twenty complaints were considered individually: a measure of ill-treatment was reported in two cases; a finding of no ill-treatment was made with reference to all or part of the allegations in four cases; in eighteen cases no finding was made on all or part of the complaint, although in three of these the allegations were thought probably not to be true. In five incidents about which a number of complaints were received, the Committee made no finding in one and no finding with reference to allegations of assault in another, found that there was no deliberate ill-treatment in one, and concluded that slight ill-treatment had occurred in three incidents. The Committee also criticised the planning and administration of medical coverage of the events of 9 August.

Yet although the broad substance of all the allegations was either confirmed or left undenied, the Compton Committee vitiated any restraining effect it might have had on interrogation procedures by appearing to justify the use of the techniques and by relying on semantics. In para. 52, the Committee stated:

> These methods have been used in support of the interrogation of a small number of persons arrested in Northern Ireland who were believed to possess information of a kind which it was operationally necessary to obtain as rapidly as possible in the interest of saving lives, while at the same time providing the detainees with the necessary security for their own persons and identities.

The complaints received by the Committee were couched in terms of physical brutality and torture; the conclusions were in terms of 'physical ill-treatment' (para. 105),

> Where we have concluded that physical ill-treatment took place, we are not making a finding of brutality on the part

of those who handled these complainants. We consider that brutality is an inhuman or savage form of cruelty, and that cruelty implies a disposition to inflict suffering, coupled with indifference to, or pleasure in, the victim's pain. We do not think that happened here.

According to this definition, the regretful use of electroshock to obtain information would be neither cruel nor brutal. The Committee made the state of mind of the interrogator the linchpin of its definition, and its conclusions thus turn on the element most easily disguised — and even forgotten — by the soldier or policeman in the dispassionate atmosphere of an official enquiry, and it uses to its great advantage its ability to diminish the gravity of the charges made against government agents merely by changing to 'ill-treatment' the definition of the actions described by victims as brutality or torture.

On 16 November, the establishment of a Committee of Privy Counsellors to consider interrogation techniques was announced in the House of Commons, and its final constitution was made public on 30 November. The three members. Lord Parker of Waddington (Chairman) Mr J.A. Boyd-Carpenter and Lord Gardiner, held their meetings in private, considering both written and oral evidence on behalf of both individuals and organisations. Their brief was to consider 'whether, and if so in what respects, the procedures currently authorised for the interrogation of persons suspected of terrorism and for their custody while subject to interrogation require amendment'. A majority report and Lord Gardiner's minority report were published on 2 March 1972.

The majority report, in addressing the question of whether or not the interrogation techniques currently employed were consistent not only with the established guidelines for security operations but also with the moral standards of a civilised and humane society, concluded that the answer depends on the intensity with which the techniques are applied and on the provision of effective safeguards against excessive use. Moreover the context in which these techniques are used is an integral part of the argument in their favour: active urban guerrilla warfare in which innocent lives are at risk and the safety of the security forces, their facilities, and their detainees is threatened. A 'measure of self-defence' is justifiable and the degree of urgency points to the use of those techniques which the Compton Committee described as physical ill-treatment.

Lord Gardiner, however, refuted the conclusions of the majority on legal, moral and practical terms. He contended that the procedures used, even if anyone had purported to authorise them, are certainly illegal by domestic law and probably illegal by international law. There is nothing in the special legislation applicable to Northern Ireland that extends the ordinary police powers of interrogation. He questioned the effects and usefulness of the sensory deprivation techniques complained of and challenged the conclusion of the majority that the information thus obtained would not have been revealed had other techniques been employed. Lord Gardiner was unwilling to accept the possibility that Parliament should make these procedures legal, in violation of international human rights standards, and he concluded:

> The blame for this sorry story, if blame there be, must lie with those who, many years ago, decided that in emergency conditions in Colonial-type situations we should abandon our legal, well-tried and highly successful wartime interrogation methods and replace them by procedures which were secret, illegal, not morally justifiable and alien to the traditions of what I believe still to be the greatest democracy in the world.

Lord Gardiner's views, rather than those of the majority, were accepted by the British government, which announced that the techniques of interrogation in depth such as hooding and exposure to constant loud noise would not be used in future as an aid to interrogation.

About two weeks before the Compton Committee's report was published and the Parker Committee was announced, Amnesty International formed an International Commission of Enquiry to examine the allegations of ill-treatment of prisoners and internees detained under the Special Powers Act, as well as the conditions of imprisonment and internment. It dealt primarily with those cases arising after 9

Legal remedies 111

August, 1971, in which, with one exception, interrogation in depth did not figure. The Commission, consisting of a Norwegian lawyer, a Swedish journalist and a Dutch doctor, met in Belfast in December, 1971; the latest date of a complaint heard by the Commission related to men arrested on 18 November. Its report was published in March 1972.

In contrast to the official government enquiries, the Amnesty International Commission heard evidence given by and on behalf of detainees and internees and ex-detainees and ex-internees. Evidence was not heard from the government however, as members of the security forces were not permitted to testify before an independent international enquiry on what was considered to be an internal matter. The United Kingdom authorities also refused to grant facilities to the Commission and did not accept an invitation to send an observer to sit with the Commission. As there was no cooperation from the authorities, the Commission decided to concentrate its work on investigating allegations of ill-treatment and to deal with cases outside the terms of reference of the Compton Committee. Evidence consisted of written affidavits and medical statements, oral evidence from the six complainants not still detained or interned and from physicians who had examined nineteen of the complainants. On the basis of this evidence, the Commission concluded that persons arrested under the Special Powers Act had been subject to brutal treatment by the security forces during arrest and transport and that there were cases where suffering had been inflicted on those arrested to obtain confessions or information from them. These incidents were considered to be in violation of Article 3 of the European Convention and of Article 5 of the Universal Declaration of Human Rights. Four cases heard by the Commission had also been investigated by the Compton Committee, and in three of them the Commission concluded that the ill-treatment constituted brutality, disagreeing with the findings of the Compton Committee.

On 24 March, the Home Secretary stated that he had seen the Amnesty International report, and that the cases were being investigated by the police with Army cooperation. This investigation was subsequently suspended because all of the cases dealt with by Amnesty International were by then the subject of civil proceedings which had not yet been resolved. In fact, recourse to the civil courts seemed to be virtually the only palpable remedy available to torture victims in Northern Ireland.

A civil action brought in the Lurgan county court against the Chief Constable of the RUC and the Ministry of Defence in February 1972 resulted in an award of £300 for wrongful arrest and assault. Damages were awarded two months later to nine internees and seven former internees who had alleged assault causing physical and mental suffering and degradation after their arrest in August 1971. Two army privates were each fined £25 in May after pleading guilty to assaulting and causing actual bodily harm to the plaintiff, who had been arrested in January. In October, a jury in Armagh found two marines guilty of assault and fined them both £25. Other investigations promised or actually initiated have been seriously hampered by the fact that the authorities persist in having the enquiries conducted by the security forces against whom the accusations are made.

But although victims of the alleged mistreatment have been reluctant to cooperate with domestic enquiries, they have not felt similarly constrained in the case brought by Ireland against the United Kingdom which is now before the European Commission of Human Rights. In October 1972, certain parts of Ireland's application were admitted for further investigation, namely those made in connection with Articles 1, 3, 5, 6 and 15 of the Convention. In April 1973, the Commission admitted for further investigation complaints brought by seven individuals against the United Kingdom government of ill-treatment by security forces in Northern Ireland. The Commission did not accept Great Britain's contention that these cases could not be heard unless and until all domestic remedies had been exhausted, apparently holding that an individual has the right to bring an application to the international level, where he alleges that he himself is a victim of an administrative pattern of violations of the Convention. Both his own treatment and the existence of the pattern itself may be put into issue, thus providing the individual with perhaps the only meaningful way of challenging widely-practised torture.

The right of the individual to bring a case of this nature

before the European Commission in Strasbourg also means that the government might be more likely to take the allegations it has been receiving more seriously. An objective investigation from Strasbourg will provide the government with a strong incentive to re-assess its own investigative procedures. In a situation of this type it is impractical to believe that prosecutions, on an individual basis, of those responsible for ill-treating prisoners can themselves have a great effect on the cessation of such practices. Strong pressure from above should be capable of forcing the lower levels of the command structure into line.

It is felt by many in Northern Ireland that this high-level pressure to stop torture and brutality is absent and that the report of the Compton Committee and the reasoning behind the majority report of the Parker Committee provide evidence to support this belief and to support the conviction that a domestic remedy is not available against widespread violation of the right not to be tortured.

3 World Survey of Torture

The nature of the evidence

One of the ironies inherent in any study such as this is that the availability of information is likely to be limited in precisely those countries where abuses of human rights in general and of the freedom from torture in particular are most likely to occur. Moreover, in a number of states where allegations of torture have been found to be substantiated, the official co-operation received during Amnesty International's investigations was precisely the factor that enabled the organisation to draw the serious conclusions it did. At the same time it is undeniable that there are a number of countries which are believed to practise torture on a large scale as an administrative policy but from which no satisfactory corroborative information can be obtained. Yet Amnesty International must draw attention to torture when it does obtain valid and substantial information, even if by doing so it may give an unbalanced view of the practice of torture in the world as a whole. Thus the statement that one country practises torture bears no relation to the presence or absence of accusations made against other countries. To criticise one government is not to praise another about which Amnesty International has no information.

In most of the brief summaries that follow, some comment has been made about the quality and quantity of information available on torture as well as on political detention in each country. It hardly needs to be said that several biases affect the availability of information. In most of the world only the famous or the wealthy are likely to be able to focus international attention on their plight once they are imprisoned and ill-treated. Only the educated — and specifically the European educated — are likely to know that an organisation such as Amnesty International exists and wishes to alleviate their situation. Most important, since the prohibition of torture itself springs from a European conception of human rights, victims from other cultures may not have a realistic view of the amount of public indignation their plight could arouse. The incarceration of government ministers, of poets and musicians, of internationally respected professors or physicians will be noticed by others than their families. Approaches will be made on their behalf to the press, to international organisations, to Amnesty International. If the responsible government is at all sensitive to foreign opinion, it is possible that the torture of that particular victim will stop. But what of the student, the taxi driver, the worker or the farmer? Even if their existence should be known to the outside world, perhaps the regime that tortures them is immune to foreign economic or political pressure and can see no gain in stopping a practice which contributes to its maintenance of power.

Given that Amnesty International's information may represent only a small part of the practice of torture, it is none the less confronted with the task of evaluating the evidence it does receive. The first judgment to be made in reaching a conclusion about the reliability of an allegation involves an examination of the source.

The most confidently accepted evidence is that which has been studied in a tribunal that provides impartial judges and an adversary procedure. In the Greek case before the European Human Rights Commission, lawyers on both sides argued their cases, testimony was heard by torture victims and government witnesses, and accused torturers were confronted with their victims. After many months the Commission concluded that torture had been inflicted as an administrative practice in Greece. It should be added that the confrontation between the torturers and their victims, in an international court, was an event unique in the history of the world.

Allegations of torture by British troops in Northern Ireland led to the establishment of the Compton Commission which concluded that the techniques complained of had indeed been used and officially condoned, but that they constituted 'physical ill-treatment' rather than 'physical brutality'. However, only one of the 144 witnesses from whom oral evidence was taken was a complainant, and thus the investigative procedure, although quasi-judicial, cannot quite be compared with the European Commission's treatment of the Greek case. In contrast to the government-appointed committees, Amnesty International's investigation of the torture allegations received the co-operation of the complainants but not the authorities.

Unlike the evidence, accepted by the European Commission, which can be taken as proof of the torture allegations, other kinds of evidence do not of themselves constitute proof. Although these may, like sworn, witnessed affidavits, written and signed by the torture victim, have a high degree of credibility, they are not accepted at face value without corroborative and supportive evidence about the experiences and allegations of the writer and the circumstances in the country of which he writes. Statements of a less official nature are very frequently received; cramped notes on scraps of paper or fabric smuggled out of the prison and the country. These too are evaluated in the context of the prevailing situation. Personal interviews are of great value, for credibility and motivation can be assessed and understood. It is not surprising that a communist would want to discredit a right-wing dictatorship, or, say, a priest a communist state by accusing it of torture; but even in spite of his motives his allegations may be absolutely true. Statements from witnesses of torture and from physicians who have examined torture victims are invaluable corroborative evidence but are not of themselves absolute proof of torture allegations.

Amnesty International also receives allegations of torture that are made on behalf of victims by organisations and news media. Again, the bias of the source is significant. A group of political refugees; an international organisation of churchmen or lawyers; a radical newspaper: they all have their reasons for giving publicity to one set of facts. In regard to official statements, Edmund Burke's 'geographical morality' comes into play: a politician may condemn an invidious practice in another country and condone it in his own.

It should be added that an important element in determining Amnesty's reaction to any evidence is the government's readiness to investigate allegations, and to punish any offenders.

Finally, it should be said that in the countries where torture is used the collection of evidence on the practice becomes difficult, if not impossible. The atmosphere of terror and intimidation created in that way prevents enquiry, from inside or outside the country concerned.

Thus, in the following pages, the reader must bear in mind the limitations of the evidence available. Amnesty International is confident of the information in each country mentioned, but it would be the first to point out that because of inadequate information the extent of the practice of torture in one country may be underestimated and its existence in another may not even be mentioned.

AFRICA

During their struggle for freedom, the nationalist movements of various African states were exposed to the use of torture on their militants, and on persons suspected of being their sympathisers. This torture was inflicted by the military and political personnel of the colonial powers, as it was, for example, used by the French in Algeria, and as it is now used by the Portuguese in their colonies of Angola, Mozambique, and Guinea-Bissau. Where the remnants of colonial rule persist in the form of white minority regimes, the practice of torture has been detected by international enquiries and condemned as a flagrant violation of the rights of the African majority. Notwithstanding the aspirations towards justice and the protection of the human person from torture or humiliating treatment which are incorporated into the constitutions of most African states, the use of torture seems undeniably to be employed by many of these countries, for a variety of motives and in a number of different ways.

Torture has occurred in connection with the large-scale ethnic conflicts which have marked the past decade in Africa. In Nigeria, in Sudan, and in Burundi, atrocities committed by troops against civilians, and often by civilians against other civilians of differing ethnic backgrounds, have been reported in the international press (here it should be noted that massacres of this kind are not exclusive to 'Black' Africa — as the Sharpeville massacre of 1960 in South Africa and the events in Mozambique in 1971-2 indicate). In some states torture appears an adjunct to political trials, as a means of extracting 'confessions' and incriminating statements from the accused or from witnesses. Here South Africa figures prominently, as do such states as Morocco, Tunisia, Cameroun, and, in Tanzania, Zanzibar. There are instances of torture being used not as a means of interrogation, but as a punishment for political prisoners, or as an instrument to suppress dissent on the part of political or religious minorities. In this role, torture has been used against political prisoners in Togo, against Jehovah's Witnesses in Malawi, and against students in Ethiopia, to name but a few examples. In extreme circumstances, such as those prevailing in Uganda at this moment, torture appears to be a sadistic accompaniment to the murder of the politically suspect. Another disturbing development, both in white- and black-ruled states, is the increasing use of torture not only in political cases, but also against common law offenders. Reports that electroshock has been used in South Africa and Senegal against persons suspected of criminal offences are echoed by happenings in the Central African Republic and Ghana, where incontrovertible eye-witness reports have confirmed that torture (sometimes up to the point of death) had been used against suspected or convicted thieves and other criminals. Amnesty does not wish to suggest that the states cited in the following pages are the only ones which have employed torture over the last decade — evidence that torture exists has come also from other countries, among them Mali, Senegal, Lesotho, Guinea, Zaire, Gabon, and Mauritania. But we give here a selection of the accounts which have reached us over the past decade, and which we have been able, within reasonable limits, to substantiate. The readiness of governments in Africa to resort to torture, and the proliferation of such sophisticated methods as electroshock, is an indication that there are at the moment few states in Africa, whether 'independent' or ruled by ethnic minorities or colonial powers, where torture has not been used over the past decade against internal political dissidents or suppressed racial or religious groups and few, if any, which are willing to investigate such practices. (The Portuguese colonies in Africa are dealt with in the European section of the Report under Portugal.)

Burundi

The chronic conflict between the Tutsi tribe, who form the

ruling minority in Burundi, and the majority Hutu people, who comprise 85 per cent of the population, has given rise since 1964 to numerous allegations of the use of torture. In some instances these have been connected with the vicious inter-tribal fighting which took place periodically throughout the last decade, most notably in 1965, 1972, and the spring of 1973. In the last instance there were reports of Tutsi soldiers and members of the 'Jeunesse Revolutionnaire' (the youth wing of the ruling Uprona Party) killing and torturing Hutu, including women and children. Torture is also reported to have been used before a political trial in late 1969, when a number of prominent Hutu personalities, both military and civil, were arrested and charged with plotting to overthrow the regime of the Tutsi President, Colonel Michel Micombero. One of the accused, Cyprian Henehene, a former Minister of Health, died in detention while awaiting trial. Burundi students in Europe claimed that he died as a result of physical tortures, including elecroshock, flogging, and exposure of the eyes to powerful lights. The Burundi government claimed that he had died of a heart attack. In the light of recurring reports of the torture and massacre of Hutu by Tutsi, and the government's failure to investigate these allegations, it would a appear that torture, as an instrument of ethnic suppression, has been widely used in Burundi since its independence.

Cameroun

Since 1966 the ruling party in Cameroun, the Union Nationale Camerounaise (UNC), has struggled to consolidate its hold on power in the face of guerrilla activity on the part of the banned opposition party, the Union des Populations de Cameroun (UPC). Administrative internment camps have been established in Mantoum, Tcollire, Lomie, Yoko, and Tignere. In spite of government action, the UPC has continued clandestine and often violent opposition to the UNC since before independence, drawing most of its support from ethnic groups in the southern part of the country. Allegations of torture of UPC members and supporters have appeared in the international press. This was especially the case at the end of 1970, when Ernest Ouandié, the UPC leader, the Roman Catholic Bishop Hdongmo of Nkongsamba, and over 100 alleged UPC supporters were brought to trial. Ouandié claimed that he had been subjected to torture in order to extract statements from him, the bishop was said to have been induced to sign statements by being shown the 'torture room' at the headquarters of the secret police, and it was reported that women had been tortured to 'confess' that they had slept with the bishop; they retracted their statements in court. The agents accused of carrying out these tortures were members of the Service de Documentation (SEDOC), Cameroun's political police. Renewed allegations of physical torture were published in the French press in the spring of 1972, coupled with descriptions of ill-treatment and poor prison conditions. These were denied by Cameroun officials, but similar allegations were once again made in the press in September of the same year. This time the torturers were said to be soldiers from northern Cameroun, and the methods involved included suspension by the arms, electro-shock, and beating. The Cameroun government had not investigated these allegations of torture nor prohibited its practice.

Ethiopia

Emperor Haile Selassie, Africa's elder statesman, continues to rule Ethiopia as he has done continuously since 1941, when he returned from exile after the liberation of his country from Italian occupation. His government faces unrest from a number of directions — the insurgent Eritrean Liberation Front continues a guerrilla struggle for the secession of the northern province of Eritrea from the rest of Ethiopia, student unrest has been rife, and there has been sporadic discontent amongst ethnic groups who resent the domination of Ethiopian political life by the Amhara people. The Eritrean struggle has led to large-scale detentions of civilians and reports of atrocities by Ethiopian troops against non-combatants in the area of armed struggle. The student unrest and ethnic discontent have led to charges of torture being made against the Ethiopian authorities. The first such reports to reach Amnesty from private sources date from 1967, when several leaders of the Mecha and Tulema Association, an ethnic organisation of the Galla tribe, were arrested and tried on charges of plotting to overthrow the government. It was alleged that some of the accused in this trial were extensively tortured by the Ethiopian police over a period of six months in order to extract from them confessions to be used in court. The tortures alleged included beatings, deprivation of sleep and food, and suspension from a rod. Subsequent to this torture several witnesses retracted in court what they claimed to be statements extorted under duress. Following the sentencing of the accused, ill-treatment reportedly continued during their confinement to prison in Addis Ababa. The General Secretary of the Association, Haile Mariam Gemada, died in prison in 1969. His colleagues in the Association claim that he died as a result of torture, and was paralysed and bedridden for two years before his death. The Ethiopian authorities state that he died of 'natural causes'. More recent allegations of torture by the Ethiopian police were reported by a reliable source soon after the arrest in February 1972 of a large number of students following disturbances at Haile Selassie I University in the capital. First-hand reports were given of students who claimed to have been beaten by the police, and unverified descriptions of torture by electroshock and by the release of CS gas into windowless cells were reported. The government has not apparently investigated these allegations of torture, which are in direct contradiction to Article 57 of the Ethiopian constitution, which provides that 'No one shall be subjected to cruel and inhuman punishment'.

Ghana

Ghana was one of the earliest African states to achieve independence following the period of colonial rule, celebrating its freedom from British administration in 1957. In 1966 its first president, Kwame Nkrumah, was overthrown by a military coup which installed in power civilian rule three years later. The Progress Party regime then introduced lasted a scant twenty-seven months before it was in its turn overthrown by the military led by Colonel I.K. Acheampong in January 1972. A military National Redemption Council now rules Ghana by decree.

At the very beginning of Nkrumah's presidency, a number of political parties were banned, and in 1964 Ghana became a one-party state. A Preventive Detention Act promulgated only a year after independence allowed detention without trial for five years and was used against opponents of the Nkrumah regime. Early in Amnesty International's existence, evidence of torture came out of a number of detention centres where large numbers of political detainees were held without charge or trial. Exiled political groups claimed that Mr Obetsebi-Lamptey died as a result of tortures in 1962. A letter from a group of prisoners to Mr Wilson, then the Prime Minister of Great Britain, was transmitted to exiled United Party members in 1965; it alleged that several of their number had been tortured over a period of five to six months in the 'special block' of Nsawam Prison, and that one of them, Dr J.B. Danquah, had died after having been detained there for about a year. During the summer of 1972, Amnesty International again began to receive allegations that torture was being used in Ghana.

In July Amnesty received reports from private sources that several persons arrested in the middle of that month in connection with an alleged plot to overthrow the National Redemption Council had been beaten during interrogation. One such person, Ambrose da Rocha, died in mysterious circumstances shortly after his arrest. When nine persons were brought to trial on charges of subversion in September 1972, a number of the accused complained in court of having been stripped, insulted, and beaten by army personnel during the course of interrogation in order to make them sign false statements. One defendant accused a member of the National Redemption Council of participating in the beatings and showed the court scars he claimed were the results of torture. These cases were widely reported in the Ghanaian press. Amnesty International requested a government enquiry into these allegations, but received no reply.

During 1972 Amnesty International also received reports from sources in Ghana that army personnel were enforcing military 'drill' (exercises, carrying of heavy stones, etc.) on civil servants who arrived late at their offices and on other civilians. This brutalisation allegedly extended to some of those civilians held under the Preventive Custody Decree (over 1,300 were detained immediately after the coup of 13 January 1972). One detainee who died in hospital at Sunyani is alleged to have been 'shaved' with a broken bottle and forced to carry heavy stones. Torture has also been used as a deterrent to crime in the case of petty criminals and, again, it is the Ghanaian army which has been responsible for its infliction. In December 1972 a reliable eye-witness account reached Amnesty describing how a suspected thief had been beaten, whipped, and burned with cigarettes by three soldiers under the command of a corporal. The informant said that eight men had been thus 'drilled' that day, and that in another town a man had died and five had been hospitalised as a result of similar torture. He was told that others had died in the village where he witnessed the 'drilling'. Amnesty International knows of no attempt by the Ghanian government to investigate such allegations or prohibit this practice.

Malawi

Under the rule of its Life President, Dr Hastings Banda, Malawi has been the source of numerous reports of ill-treatment and torture of political detainees and religious dissidents. In the main, the motive behind the use of torture in Malawi seems to be the intimidation of political prisoners and the terrorising of religious dissenters rather than the more usual motive of extracting information. In most instances, the agency involved in inflicting the tortures seems to have been the Malawi Young Pioneers, the youth wing of the Malawi Congress Party (MCP). In 1965 Amnesty received eye-witness accounts of severe beatings administered to political detainees in Dzeleka, the largest detention centre in Malawi, which is now thought to hold over one thousand persons detained under the Public Security Act of 1965. Between 1965 and 1968, Amnesty records show that at least seven detainees died as a result of this treatment, for which the Young Pioneers were largely responsible.

The Young Pioneers have also been active in harassing the Jehovah's Witnesses, who have angered the MCP by their refusal to purchase party cards, this being against their religious convictions. According to first-hand accounts and reports in the international press, the Young Pioneers took a leading role in the persecution of the Jehovah's Witnesses in 1967 and again in 1972. The role of the Young Pioneers in this respect is explained in part by amendments to the Young Pioneer Act which were introduced in 1965. These amendments provide that no policeman can arrest a Young Pioneer without consulting the local Young Pioneer District Commander, nor can a policeman release a person who has been 'lawfully arrested' by a Young Pioneer without a similar consultation. Well-substantiated reports indicate that both in 1967 and in 1972 the Young Pioneers and their supporters inflicted torture on the Jehovah's Witnesses in the form of rape, beatings, shaving with broken bottles, and burning. In the autumn of 1972 these persecutions caused a number of deaths and the migration of some 21,000 Jehovah's Witnesses to Zambia, where several hundred died in an inadequate refugee camp. The harrassing of the sect appears to have the support of the MCP and government officials, who therefore must be regarded as giving at least tacit assent to the tortures and atrocities inflicted on the sect's members.

Morocco

The past decade of Morocco's history has been marked by a steady deterioration in the relationship between the monarchy of King Hassan II and the major opposition political parties, the Istiqlal, and, especially, the socialist Union Nationale des Forces Populaires (UNFP). This deterioration has been characterised by persistent demands for constitutional, social and economic reforms on the part of the UNFP, and an alternating policy of apparent conciliation and repression on the part of the King. The decade is punctuated by a series of mass arrests and trials of UNFP members and other left-wing elements, frequently on charges of plotting armed subversion against the state. From the accumulated evidence, which takes the form of personal affidavits, statements before courts of law, medical certificates, and allegations by opposition groups, there is little doubt that the use of torture has reached the level of established administrative practice in Morocco. Most reports of torture share certain characteristics: the techniques used were primarily physical and they were in the main employed to extract information about suspected anti-government activities and to force detainees to sign false confessions for use in political trials. The agencies responsible for inflicting this torture appear to have been elements of the Moroccan police, particularly the Service Urbain de la Police Judiciaire and the Corps Mobile d'Intervention; the torture has often taken place in police commissariats, particularly in Rabat.

One of the earliest torture allegations was made by Mehdi Aloui, a UNFP leader, who claimed that in 1963 he was arrested and tortured for information about Mehdi Ben Barka, the UNFP leader. During November 1963, 104 members of the UNFP were accused of planning the assassination of the king. Amnesty's observer at this trial, a French lawyer, reported that allegations of torture were made. From the outset of the trial defence counsel claimed that the defendants had been tortured by the police, and a number of the defendants showed the court scars caused by this torture. Claims were made during the trial that witnesses had been forced to testify from fear that they would die under torture if they did not co-operate. Another mass trial of UNFP members took place in 1971, and was attended by three Amnesty observers. One observer commented in his report: 'After careful examination of all available means of information one has to state that most of the accused had been tortured or maltreated in the preliminary proceedings [i.e., while they were in police custody] ... Methods of torture were unanimously given as forcible bending of the body, brutal blows, plunging of the head into dirty water, and burning with cigarettes.' Medical certificates relating to traces of torture on some of the accused were produced. One defendant died in suspicious circumstances while in police custody, and another suffered a fractured skull. In 1972 Amnesty received detailed statements made by two young leftists, Abraham Serfaty and Abdellatif Laabi, describing tortures (similar in some instances to those mentioned in connection with the 1971 UNFP trial) which they had undergone while detained in late January and early February at the Commissariat Régional of Rabat.

In July 1972 information was received from private sources of a group of fourteen torture victims, mostly teachers and students, who had been arrested in February and March and tortured over a period of two weeks in Dar El Mokri near Rabat. A second group of eleven, arrested at the same time, was taken to the Casablanca station of the Corps Mobile d'Intervention and tortured during a two-week period. At the end of the year, Amnesty received a hand-written letter and a typed signed statement from the sister of Abraham Serfaty, Evelyne, who stated that her brother had been tortured in January 1972, and decribed in detail her own experiences while she was detained from 26 September to 4 October 1972 in the Commissariat of Rabat and was tortured by the police for information about her brother. Two medical certificates describing her resulting injuries accompanied the letter. In spite of the numerous allegations of torture that have been made and supported by documentary evidence — of which examples have been shown above — the Moroccan authorities appear to have taken no steps to investigate or prohibit the practice of torture.

Rhodesia

Amnesty International has received a number of torture allegations from Rhodesia. More recently, the United Nations Commission on Human Rights Ad Hoc Group of Experts have published allegations of torture in Rhodesia as part of a report on questions relating to human rights in Southern Africa.

The political, legal and social conditions which made torture possible in the period immediately preceding the Unilateral Declaration of Independence (UDI) by Mr Ian Smith's government in November 1965, have not changed for the better. Although actual reports of torture have decreased since UDI, the present crisis in Rhodesia, with security forces attempting to stamp out guerilla activity in various parts of the country, has given rise to renewed allegations that harsh and brutal methods have been used to extract information from civilians concerning the whereabouts of guerillas.

The first in a series of widespread torture allegations relating to Rhodesia occurred around August and September of 1963. This was at a time when the political situation was deteriorating as nationalist movements opposed to white minority rule were gaining strength. Physicians' reports of a number of cases of persons who had been arrested confirmed the victims' descriptions of torture they had suffered at the hands of both African and European police.

In 1964 there was an increase in the number of allegations of improper police conduct. Maltreatment was being used to force detainees to make statements. On 6 August, the Minister of Law and Order stated that 33 cases had been cited by the press in the first six months of the year. He contended, however, that in subsequent investigations the accusations against the police had been rejected. Yet three policemen were convicted of assault against their prisoners in 1964. Early the following year Alexander Mashawira was found dead in Salisbury's central police station after having been detained for five days for interrogation by the sabotage section. He had evidently been tortured in a deserted building nine miles from Salisbury. In February and March of the same year eight Africans were acquitted because the court refused to accept their confessions in view of the circumstances in which the confessions were probably obtained. Although this court decision and the occasional prosecution of policemen were indications that the government of Southern Rhodesia was sensitive to the accusations of torture, the general official slowness to investigate such charges, coupled with reports that complainants have been re-detained and tortured to withdraw their allegations, indicate that torture was not simply the excessive act of a few sadistic policemen, but was already by 1965 a practice that received tacit official approval.

Two cases reported since UDI exemplify the close cooperation between the police of Rhodesia and South Africa. On 2 January 1968, a South African Asian teacher, Desmond Francis, was arrested in Rhodesia at Victoria Falls. His affidavit states that he was transferred to the Bulawayo Central Police Station. After several days' detention, he was tortured over a period of a week, in the Public Works Department Workshops, by a member of the Rhodesian Security Police, Peter Watermeyer, who questioned him about the African National Congress. Francis was deported to South Africa on 18 January where he was again tortured and was in solitary confinement for over a year (see section on South Africa). Benjamin Ramtose was tried in Pretoria in

1970, for offences under the Terrorism Act. He claimed that he had been kidnapped from Botswana by Rhodesian troops. After four days of detention and torture, two South African police arrived and participated in the torture. He was later taken to Pretoria.

The most recent specific allegation of torture which has come to Amnesty's notice was that of Nimrod Alick Khumalo, who died on 30 July 1971, just after being released from Gray's Prison in Bulawayo. The circumstances of his death are not clear, but there were strong allegations from persons who had seen him in detention that he had been tortured. The authorities claimed that he had died of meningitis.

South Africa

Police brutality has long been a feature of South Africa, where discriminatory policies and laws give rise to continual unrest within the underprivileged communities. However, allegations of torture have been more widely documented since the introduction of strict and far-reaching security laws by the Nationalist government after it came into power in 1948. These laws were passed mainly to deal with African political opposition. They introduced preventive detention, increased the police's powers over political suspects to a point where the security police can hold virtually anyone for as long as they felt necessary, until he had 'satisfactorily replied to all questions ... or (until) no useful purpose will be served by his further detention ...' (Section 6 of the Terrorism Act, 1967).

For the last decade Amnesty International has received a great deal of evidence that torture is an administrative practice in South Africa. Affidavits, eye-witness accounts and newspaper reports show that torture and maltreatment have been used as part of the interrogation process. In 1964, concerned at the evidence in South African courts that prisoners were frequently tortured to obtain confessions or to elicit information from them implicating others, the United Nations Special Committee on Apartheid called for an international enquiry to investigate the ill-treatment of prisoners in South Africa.

After a great deal of research the UN collected sufficient evidence to affirm that torture was used systematically in South Africa. In 1968 the General Assembly passed a resolution condemning 'any and every practice of torture, inhuman and degrading treatment of detainees in South African prisons and in South African custody during interrogation and detention . . .'

Ironically, allegations of torture began to increase around this period. A year earlier the South African government had passed the Terrorism Act, Section 6 of which provided for detention for an indefinite period, without access to a lawyer or the detainee's family. The South African Security Service is well respected all over the world as one of the most efficient intelligence systems with vast financial resources at its disposal; it is noted for its quick action on any sign of anti-apartheid activity within the country and has a reputation for anticipating the actions of political activists and dissidents. Thus for instance when Desmond Francis, a young South African teacher of Asian origin who was living in Zambia, crossed the Zambian border into Rhodesia one afternoon in January 1968 to book an air passage to South Africa for his mother, he was detained by the Rhodesian police who subsequently handed him over to the South African security police. Francis later signed an affidavit giving an account of the treatment which he received at the hands of the security police while in detention for more than 400 days. Francis was deported to South Africa on 18 January 1968. He was driven to Beit bridge on the South African/Rhodesian border by a young security policeman of Afrikaner extraction, who apparently had been his torturer during the few days that he spent in the custody of the Rhodesian police.

At Messina, a little town in the Province of the Transvaal he was handed over to a Major Swanepoel (now Brigadier Swanepoel), who accompanied him to the security police headquarters in Compol Buildings, Pretoria. Francis said he was subjected to various forms of torture and physical assaults during the next four months while a statement was being extracted from him. All through this period he suffered a great deal of pain, and bled internally. Finally, he was made to sign a statement while his head was covered with a canvas bag. He was then told that he would give evidence at a trial of persons 'who were unknown to him'. A year after his arrest, he was driven to Pietermaritzburg to appear as a witness at the trials. However, instead of giving evidence he told the judge that he had been tortured. The judge replied that his experiences at the hands of the police during his 427 days of detention were not the concern of the court.

A great deal of documented torture relates to political cases; black people for obvious reasons pose a greater political threat to the Nationalist policies, and therefore are more likely to be arrested for the more serious political offences. Also, traditional attitudes among the South African police play an important part in their treatment of those in custody. For this reason most of the allegations of torture have come from the so-called 'non-white' prisoners. However, as white political dissidents increased, torture was used on this section of the community to get confessions. A Report of the UN Special Committee on Apartheid, 1973 — on the torture and maltreatment of political prisoners in South Africa — states: 'The growing impunity of the Special Branch is reflected in the fact that while only Africans and other non-whites were subjected to physical assaults in 1963, white men have also been assaulted since July 1964 . . .' However, except for two known cases, there has generally been restraint as far as white women were concerned, but both 'non-white' men and women have been subjected to brutality.

A lesser known facet of police brutality in South Africa is the torture of common law offenders. It is generally supposed that the detention clauses under the Security Laws are only used for political cases, but in fact suspected criminal offenders have been held and interrogated under the 180 days detention clause of the Criminal Procedure Act. Many trials of 'non-white' criminals involving murder and robbery are usually accompanied by allegations of torture. The allegations are used as a major issue in contesting the admissibility of 'confessions' made to the police, or even to magistrates after interrogation. In November 1971, damages of R5,000 were awarded against the South African police following an action by Mr Temba Mkize, who was taken into police custody, evidently in connection with criminal charges. Temba Mkize alleged that he had been tortured by two policemen during February 1971, who gave him electric shocks from a hand generator while he was suspended from a broomstick hanging between two pieces of furniture.

The techniques mentioned by a UN report of 1973 on the maltreatment and torture of prisoners in South Africa, as well as in information that has come directly to Amnesty International, encompass both physical and psychological techniques, including long periods of solitary confinement as well as more subtle methods aimed more at the mind than the body. But clearly physical brutality is still the most important feature of South African torture procedures. Allegations have been made that there is an appliance for administering electric shock torture in almost every police station in South Africa, but the uniformity of the methods even in small local police stations, and the fact that some interrogators seem to travel from one centre to another, led the UN investigators to suggest that the police must receive some training in the use of torture:

> The conclusion is inescapable that cruelty against opponents of *apartheid* is the application of a deliberate and centrally directed policy, and that torture by the Security police is condoned, if not actually encouraged, by the Government. Allegations of similar tortures have been made from so many centres and have involved so many local officers — in addition to certain interrogators who travel from Pretoria to other areas — that there is reason to believe that Security Branch officers have been trained in these methods. (*Maltreatment and Torture of Prisoners in South Africa*, Report of the Special Committee on Apartheid, New York, 1973, pp. 10, 25).

The names of a number of security police officers crop up again and again in connection with allegations of torture. The name of one man in particular appears repeatedly in the accusations of a decade: Theunis Jacobus Swanepoel. Swanepoel rose from the position of Lieutenant in 1962 to that of Brigadier in 1969, and was simultaneously appointed Chief Interrogator of the Security Branch of the police.

At least 20 deaths in political detention between the years

1962 and 1971 are believed to have resulted from torture and maltreatment by the police. Inquests were held into many of them, but in none of them were the police held to bear any responsibility. The government has resisted suggestions that it should hold impartial inquiries into allegations of torture, and death in detention. The case of Ahmed Timol, a school teacher who fell to his death from the tenth floor of a window of the security police headquarters in Jan Vorster Square, Johannesburg, in October 1971, is a case in point. There were public calls for the government to appoint a full judicial inquiry. The Prime Minister, Mr Jan Vorster, said he saw no reason for this since there would be an inquest. Some newspapers questioned police assertions that Timol had committed suicide. They pointed out that a similar death had occurred seven years earlier — when Suliman Salojee, a 32-year-old attorney's clerk, had fallen from a window while being interrogated by the police. The police had given assurances that they would take immediate steps to ensure that a similar incident would not occur. The press insisted that the room from which Ahmed Timol had fallen had heavily barred windows, and the whole section had been claimed to be escape-proof.

Lawyers, doctors and churchmen have spoken out against police brutality, and have publicised cases with which they have been familiar. There is also clearly an independent opinion within the judiciary, shown by the courageous stand taken by some members in the face of government disapproval. However, generally speaking, the South African judiciary gives the impression of being establishment minded and inclined to favour the views of the police rather than the rights of the individual. The government itself has shown little interest in controlling the use of physical brutality in its police stations and prisons, nor has it thought it necessary to change the legislative conditions that make torture possible. Individual senior members of the government have made statements which seem to indicate that the government refuse to believe that torture and maltreatment exist as part of police interrogation methods. The South African authorities have tacitly admitted some torture cases where these were proved in court; the attitude however has been that these were isolated cases of a few unethical individuals.

Recently there has been a noticeable move on the part of the government and its institutions to reply in detail to all the allegations of torture and maltreatment; but the fact is that police repression is built into the South African system, and the detention clauses merely add to the extensive powers that the police already have over a great section of the population.

Namibia

Namibia, a United Nations Trust Territory, has been ruled by South Africa since the end of First World War. Namibia's police are therefore integrated with those of South Africa and essentially allegations of torture of Namibian prisoners have been made against the South African police.

The first group of documented allegations relates to the years between 1962 and 1969 when many suspected guerrillas and collaborators were arrested by the police who were trying to root out nationalist elements. Many of these were detained under the security laws and 37 were subsequently tried under the Terrorism Act in Pretoria in 1967. The first of these allegations was made in court when one of the accused, Joseph Halao Shityuwete, applied to the judge to produce a detained man, Gabriel Mbindi, to give evidence about assault allegations. The judge directed that steps should be taken to protect Mr Mbindi from assaults by the police and the hearing of Shityuwete was fixed for 20 February 1968. But then it was announced that, after 8½ months in custody, Mr Mbindi had been released and taken back to Namibia. The police had paid him R3,000 as an out of court settlement. Mbindi's case was thus never heard in court.

In an appeal to the United Nations on behalf of 10 Namibian detainees, three years later, a South African lawyer living in exile, Joel Carlson, revealed that he had obtained affidavits from 27 of the 37 accused in the 1968 trial about alleged torture inflicted on them by the security police during interrogation. One man did not live through the trial and was alleged to have died of injuries inflicted while he was being interrogated.

A trickle of information on torture continued to reach Amnesty in the late 1960s but suddenly in 1972 reports indicated that large scale police repression was taking place in

Ovamboland in the northern portion of Namibia. A few months earlier, about 3,000 migrant workers had taken part in a nationwide strike and were repatriated home to Ovamboland by the administration. A state of emergency was declared in the area and hundreds of people were arrested. Amnesty learnt from a number of sources that the detainees had been maltreated by the police and subjected to various forms of torture including physical assaults, electric shock and solitary confinement. One of these was an Anglican priest, Olavi Nailenge, who was allegedly tortured to elicit information from him about the activities of the Anglican and Lutheran churches.

Reports of recent torture received from Namibia have generally been second-hand because of the fear of reprisals if complaints were registered by the victims themselves or even by their families. Frequently cases are described in great detail, but names are not given. Amnesty International received eight such detailed and specific accounts during 1973. All of these reports mention physical tortures, including electric shocks, and appalling conditions of detention. Both black and white policemen were alleged to have participated in the beatings. All the torture in these cases took place in Ovamboland, some at a camp in the Ukwanyama area near Chikango. It was an adjunct to interrogation about alleged terrorist activities and sabotage, as well as about church and mission activities, and was part of the effort to force victims to confess crimes. Churchmen within Namibia who were concerned about torture allegations protested to the officials of the administration, but the allegations were denied.

In April 1973, a delegation of leading churchmen for the Lutheran mission in Namibia had a private meeting with South African Prime Minister John Vorster, at which they expressed to him their belief that torture was widely used by the authorities in Namibia. They called for a commission of inquiry and handed to Mr Vorster a list containing the names of thirty-seven black Namibians who claimed that they had been tortured and who would be willing to substantiate their allegations before such a commission — if the Prime Minister would personally guarantee their safety. Five months later, a communication from the Prime Minister's office assured the churchmen that, upon investigation, the allegations had been found to be groundless. However, by April 1974, when they made public their previous contact with Mr Vorster, the church leaders were convinced that a number of persons on the list had still not been questioned about their torture claims. Moreover, they believed that many more Namibians had been subjected to torture since their meeting with the Prime Minister one year before. They were joined in repeating their demand for a judicial inquiry by the Anglican Bishop of Damaraland, who claimed that the authorities were employing electric shocks, beatings and statue torture (enforced standing) against detainees. A former political prisoner who alleged that he himself had been tortured also joined the public appeal.

In fact, over the last two years it has become increasingly clear that the South African authorities who administer Namibia are prepared to use every means, including torture, to intimidate into submission those who would resist the full implementation of South Africa's *apartheid* policies in Namibia. Particularly vulnerable, therefore, have been members of the South West Africa People's Organization (SWAPO) and the Democratic Development Co-Operative Party (DEMKOP), two organisations which have been unflinching in their opposition to the continuance of South African rule in Namibia. At the Katutura township outside Windhoek, the Namibian capital, meetings called by SWAPO have been forcibly broken up by the police, and many party members have been arrested during large-scale police raids. According to information received by Amnesty International, after one such raid in February 1974, at least two SWAPO leaders were tortured with electric shocks and beatings. At about the same time, a number of other SWAPO officials were detained who have been held incommunicado ever since. To date, only two have been charged and brought to trial, and at their first appearance in court they were said to be suffering from mental disorientation as a result of their long period in solitary confinement.

It is not only in the urban areas that SWAPO and DEMKOP have strong support. They also have a considerable following in Ovamboland, where they are regarded as a threat by the leaders of the pro-Government Ovamboland Territorial Authority. The Tribal Authority, which owes its very existence to the *apartheid* policy of the South African government, has therefore co-operated with the South African authorities in the persecution of members of SWAPO and DEMKOP. In particular, it has become common practice for political dissidents against whom the South African police have been unable to bring charges to be handed over to the Tribal Authority for summary public flogging. Tribal policemen have carried out the flogging against some three to four hundred persons, including women, using the firm central rib of the makalani palm branch, which can cause severe pain and bleeding as well as injury to the spine and kidneys.

The South African govenment claims that it cannot intervene in 'tribal customs' to stop the floggings, although in fact it controls, directly or indirectly, all important matters of political and economic life in Namibia. Both Bishop Leonard Auala, himself a Namibian by birth, and a 90-year-old churchman with an impressive memory have given sworn testimony in court that flogging is not tribal in origin, but was introduced as a systematic punishment about thirty years ago by a white commissioner named Hahn, who was known as 'Sjambok' (or, the whip). Their testimony has been corroborated by that of an anthropologist who has had extensive experience of Namibian tribal laws and customs.

In an attempt to prevent further floggings, Bishop Richard Wood of the Diocese of Damaraland, Bishop Leonard Auala of the Evangelical Lutheran Ovambo-Kavango Church, and Thomas Komati, who is a member of SWAPO as well as a victim of the floggings, brought a series of court actions during late 1973 and early 1974 before judges in Namibia. A temporary interdict was obtained but has since been lifted, and at the time of this writing the floggings continue while the Chief Justice deliberates. In July 1974, as part of an effort to stop the floggings, Amnesty International published extracts of affidavits from victims. Meanwhile, Thomas Komati has undergone a period of detention in solitary confinement and many supporters of SWAPO have fled across the Namibian border into Angola, hoping to find safety.

In August 1974, Amnesty International submitted to the United Nations a communication under Resolutions 1235

(XLII) and 1503 (XLVIII) of the UN Economic and Social Council concerning 'A Consistent Pattern of Gross and Reliably Attested Violations of Human Rights Perpetrated by the Government of South Africa upon Inhabitants of Namibia'. This communication incorporated affidavits from victims of the floggings and from a surgeon who examined two of the victims, together with photographs of the wounds inflicted and of the instrument used.

Tanzania

In regard to Tanzania, a clear distinction must be made between the Tanganyika mainland and the island of Zanzibar, with which it was constitutionally united in 1964 to form the United Republic of Tanzania. Although Zanzibar is formally a part of the republic, it appears that the central government has little desire or ability to interfere in the internal affairs of the island. This is a reflection on the mainland government itself, since it is on Zanzibar and its sister islands that the administrative practice of torture has been undoubtedly present since the overthrow of the elected Zanzibar Nationalist Party government in January 1964. Information about this abuse of human rights has reached Amnesty at regular intervals over the past decade from a variety of sources — the news media, exiled political groups, and the accounts of individuals who had themselves been tortured. The victims have been those who are presumed to be opposed to the rule of the Afro-Shirazi Party (ASP), which came to power by a violent revolution in 1964, and for many the tortures have accompanied interrogation about alleged anti-government activities and groups. The torturers are the Zanzibari police and Secret Police, and some allegations have stated that they are trained by police from the German Democratic Republic. Methods with both primarily physical and mental effect have been used, and the requirements for equipment and technical expertise go far beyond mere beating. The two ASP regimes against which allegations of torture have been made (that of Sheikh Abeid Karume up to his assassination in April 1972, and the present regime of Abond Jumbe) have not demonstrated any concern about these widespread reports, and to Amnesty's knowledge no attempt has been made to investigate the charges or to stop the use of torture against political prisoners.

The first allegations of torture in Zanzibar date from the period shortly after the coup of January 1964, in which the ASP overthrew the month-old ZNP government. In a pogrom following the coup thousands of people, mostly members of the island's Arab and Persian ethnic minorities, were killed, and many hundreds arrested. A typical example of an atrocity of this period was the killing of Sheikh Muhammed Salim; who was reportedly shot after having been tortured and was buried in a grave which he himself had been compelled to dig. Letters that were smuggled out of Zanzibar over the next few years by detainees repeatedly alleged inhuman treatment and torture, although few names were cited for fear of retribution. The letters stated that many people had been tortured to death, including three former ministers of the ZNP government. In 1972 Amnesty received a first-person statement from a Zanzibari who had been arrested in 1964. He was sentenced to ten years' hard labour but released in 1967 and then re-arrested twenty months later and taken to the Security Jail in Zanzibar, where much of the torture is alleged to have taken place. Although kept there in appalling conditions for months, he was himself tortured for only one day. Reports continued to reach Amnesty, although most lacked specific details in order that the writer should escape detection. Most letters claimed that 'hundreds' of detainees had been tortured; all spoke of the inhuman conditions in which they were detained. A letter of April 1971 claimed that tortures had left Amani Thani on the point of death, Hassan Sheikh blind and Ali Khalifa mentally unbalanced, and that others had been tortured to death. Reports of torture have not abated since Karume's assassination in April 1972. Both psychological and extreme physical tortures on persons arrested on the island in the wake of the assassination were allegedly used.

There is no evidence that torture is used as an administrative practice on mainland Tanzania, although the international press reported allegations of police brutality against arrested aliens in 1969 and 1970. In both instances official investigations were conducted. Likewise, in 1972 the mainland authorities are reliably reported to have halted torture being inflicted in mainland prisons by officers sent over from Zanzibar, on persons detained following the Karume assassination.

Togo

Since the overthrow of the government of President Grunitzky in January 1967, Togo has lived under military rule headed by General Eyadéma, who has sought to establish a consensus of support through such measures as the founding of a unique party, the Rassemblement du Peuple Togolais (RPT) but has also not hesitated to use torture against opponents of his regime. This was particularly the case during 1970 and 1971, following the reported discovery in August 1970 of a 'plot' to overthrow Eyadéma. Evidence regarding the existence of this alleged plot was so scanty that diplomatic sources in the Togolese capital, Lomé, doubted the truth of government statements regarding it, and the evidence against four of the defendants was found by the magistrates to be insufficient to bring a case against them. None the less, prison sentences were passed, and a number of individuals arrested at the time of the reported discovery of the plot remained in detention without trial. Following the arrests and the trial, Amnesty received reports of the use of inhuman treatment and torture on detainees held at the military camp at Tokoin in Lomé and at the prisons at Sokode and Bassari. These accounts emanated from sources in Togo and Paris, some of whom were very close to the detained persons. Evidently the victims were tortured not as a part of an interrogation procedure, but often merely for the diversion of their torturers, who appear mainly to have been Togolese army personnel, and as a punishment to the detainees and a warning to other dissidents. The methods used were primarily physical, involving beatings with steel-wire whips and electroshock, and there were also reports of soldiers forcing detainees to beat each other. At least three of the detainees are known to have died as a result of their treatment while at the camp at Tokoin. The official cause of death was given as 'collapsed circulation', but even had no other evidence been available, the Togolese Ministry of

Information's photographs of these prisoners was indication enough of the treatment they had received and the undoubted part that torture had played in their deaths. The bodies of the detainees were never returned to their families. General Eyadéma ordered an inquiry into these deaths in 1971, but its findings were never published.

Tunisia

A one-party state under the firm control of its President, Habib Bourguiba, Tunisia seems to have employed torture frequently at least since 1968, mainly in the context of the trial for alleged political offences of students and intellectuals who have expressed opposition to Bourguiba and the Destour Socialist Party (PSD). Allegations of torture have been made by defence lawyers and by the accused during trials, and Amnesty has received accounts of torture from a number of observers who interviewed detainees after their release. First-hand accounts of torture have also been published in the international press. The torture seems in most instances to have been carried out by the Tunisian police, and in one instance a victim was able to recognise his torturers as members of the Direction de la Sureté de l'Etat (DSE), the political police. The motive behind the use of torture seems to have been almost exclusively the extraction of statements or 'confessions' from persons facing political charges, in order to facilitate their condemnation by a court of law. As one political detainee put it to an Amnesty observer: 'I suppose the aim of all this [i.e., the torture] was not to make me give them any real information or confess any special crime. The idea seemed to be just to have somebody tell them something that showed that a political crime had been committed — no matter which — by one or several persons opposed to the regime. The policemen were quite simply in a position where they had to report something — true or not — to their superiors . . .' From consistent and well-documented reports of torture reaching Amnesty in 1968, 1969, 1972 and 1973, it would appear that torture in political cases in Tunisia has reached the status of an administrative practice.

During a trial in September 1968, when more than 100

students, teachers, civil servants, and workers were charged with plotting against the state, allegations of torture were repeatedly made, both by defendants and their lawyers. Evidence to the Amnesty observer from persons who communicated directly with the prisoners included accounts of various physical tortures, including beating of the soles of the feet and suffocation. These accounts were confirmed the following year by a Frenchman who had been among those arrested but who was subsequently released. Further allegations of torture arose in 1972, during the trial of 41 university professors and students on political charges. Once again, the trial was attended by an Amnesty observer, who was able to collect first-hand accounts of torture which reportedly took place during the early spring of 1972 while the detainees were being held at police stations. Separate interviews with two former detainees elicited very similar accounts. Both had been hooded and transported to a villa outside of Tunis where they were tortured by six or seven men in civilian clothes. Other detainees were reportedly tortured — one woman prisoner was raped several times by policemen during nine days of detention early in 1972, and one man had burn marks from cigarettes on his hands and shoulders. Allegations of torture were made again in March 1973 when a Belgian student and a number of Tunisians were tried for political crimes. This trial was also attended by an Amnesty observer. In spite of the fact that the reported use of torture is in clear violation of the articles of the Tunisian constitution which guarantee basic human rights, Amnesty has no knowledge of any government investigation into these reports or prohibition of the use of torture. When interviewed by an Amnesty representative in September 1972 Mr Mohamed Bellalouna, the Minister of Justice, did not deny that the Tunisian police might exercise torture. He stated that torture was used in other countries, and that the police were not answerable to his Ministry.

Uganda

Since achieving independence in 1962, Uganda has survived a number of political crises, which have increased in frequency during recent years. In 1966 Prime Minister Milton Obote ousted the President, Kabaka Mutesa of Buganda, and broke the power of his tribe, the most politically powerful ethnic group in the country. After five years of increasingly oppressive rule, Obote was himself dislodged from the Presidency by an army coup in January 1971 which was led by General (now President) Idi Amin. Although the overthrow of Obote originally was a popular move in the country, and especially in Buganda, President Amin's failure to satisfy Bugandan ambitions, his chaotic and impulsive political leadership, his increasing resort to methods of terror in repressing opposition to his regime and consolidating his power, and his inability to control an ill-disciplined army riven by tribal dissensions have made Uganda the African state where human rights are most consistently and seriously violated.

Reports of the use of torture as an administrative practice in Uganda have reached Amnesty International since 1967, when the constitution then in force guaranteed that no one 'shall be subjected to torture or to inhuman degrading punishment or other like treatment'. The evidence has ranged from eye-witness descriptions and testimony in court to hearsay accounts published in newspapers. Whereas the motive for using torture has in some instances clearly been to obtain a confession from the victim, since Amin's coup torture has been more widely used as an adjunct to tribal massacres and as a prelude to the physical elimination of the regime's opponents.

Under the Obote regime, the Ugandan police, especially the Criminal Investigation Department, were alleged to be responsible for torture. Following the Amin takeover, a policewoman, Sgt Robina Nakibule, testified that 'it was common practice for CID officers to torture suspects in order to obtain confessions' during the previous regime. Individual allegations of torture by the police, using beatings and electroshock, were reported in 1968, and again following the release of Obote's political detainees in January 1971. During Obote's increasingly harsh rule, unconfirmed reports alleged that political detainees held in Luzira Prison suffered solitary confinement in 'punishment cells' for very long periods, and not only exceedingly poor conditions but also apparently deliberate ill-treatment that evidently increased at the end of 1966.

The reports of torture and brutality that have emerged from Uganda since Amin seized power are different in both their nature and scale from the maltreatment that was commonplace under Obote. Massacres and mutilations were added to the evidence of torture. The agencies responsible appear to have been units of the Uganda army and the State Research Department (the ordinary police). Soon after the Amin coup there were reports of inter-tribal fighting within the army, accompanied by atrocities and torture inflicted on soldiers and civilians from Obote's home area. Photographs appeared in the international press of the bodies of Africans who had been mutilated before death. There were eye-witness reports that officers loyal to Obote had been flogged to death in the grounds of the Ministry of Defence in Kampala. In August 1971 the United States government claimed to have strong circumstantial evidence that two Americans who disappeared in Uganda the previous month had been tortured before being murdered by Ugandan soldiers. A judicial enquiry into this incident later put the blame for the deaths of the Americans on members of a Ugandan army battalion. Ugandan exile groups continued to make allegations of the massacre of President Obote's tribesmen, which were substantiated by eye-witnesses who escaped to Tanzania. British journalists detained briefly in Makindye military prison in the autumn of 1972 saw floggings and beatings with rifle-butts and learned from other prisoners that African prisoners had been forced by Ugandan soldiers to smash each other's skulls with hammers. Guards at Makindye were often drunk and were 'given to selecting prisoners for rather brutal fun and games.' Large numbers of civilians, some of them prominent members of the judiciary, the civil service, and the professions, have 'disappeared' since Amin took power in Uganda; it is believed on good evidence that most if not all of these individuals were killed after having been arrested by soldiers or by members of the State Research Department. In some cases, such as that of the former Minister of the Interior, Basil Bataringaya, there are allegations that brutal torture preceded death.

The Ugandan government has not replied to requests from Amnesty for an enquiry into the alleged tribal massacres. It has instead tended to deny the reports of bloodshed, and blame the 'disappearance' of civilians on the activities of pro-Obote guerillas. In February 1973 a number of individuals were executed for these alleged activities, after summary *in camera* trials. Although President Amin has occasionally issued warnings to the army not to molest civilians, serious steps to stop the killings and halt the use of torture have not been taken, and clear evidence indicates that in one case where a judicial enquiry into a 'disappearance' was held (the case of the two Americans mentioned above), the proceedings were seriously hampered by the interference of the government and the non-cooperation of the army. In these circumstances it is quite clear that the present widespread brutal use of torture in Uganda has at least the tacit sanction of the Amin regime.

Zambia

During 1971 and 1972 Zambia went through a period of political crisis which began with the formation of a new political party, the United Progressive Party (UPP) in the spring and early summer of 1971. The UPP threatened to capitalise on the discontent felt throughout Zambia (and especially among the politically-important Bemba tribe) at the policies of President Kenneth Kaunda's ruling United National Independence Party (UNIP) and at the economic difficulties caused by the drastic decline in world copper prices during the previous year. President Kaunda acted quickly to disarm this threat, especially after one of his cabinet ministers, Simon Kapwepwe, resigned in August 1971 to lead the UPP. On 20 September police detained over one hundred UPP officials in a wave of arrests lasting several days. In February 1972 the UPP was officially banned, and a further 123 of its supporters detained, including Kapwepwe. Most of the UPP supporters remained in detention until after the official introduction of a one-party state in Zambia at the end of 1972, with UNIP as the unique party. It is in the context of this struggle to introduce a one-party system that the use of torture by Zambian authorities has been alleged. Evidence of torture has been obtained from victims and their relatives, from reports in the international press, and from cases proven before the Zambian law-courts. Torturing appears to have taken place while the victims were under detention, and the Zambian police, Special Branch or CID, are uniformly alleged to be the agents inflicting the torture, usually during interrogation, and apparently usually at a police station. The techniques alleged were almost entirely physical.

Although in at least one case the torture seemed to be punitive in nature, all the allegations from UPP members said that it was used to obtain information about the UPP and its activities. In June 1972 Amnesty received reports that Simon Kapwepwe and another UPP leader, Justin Chimba, had been beaten while in detention. At approximately the same time an eye-witness, who had himself been in detention in Zambia earlier in the year, reported having seen Chimba and J.M. Chapoloko with swollen faces resulting from beatings. In November of the same year five UPP members, including Chimba and Chapoloko, all of whom were still in detention, claimed damages against the government for assault and battery and false imprisonment in a case which was brought before the Zambian High Court. In December the court ruled that the five had been maltreated by Special Branch officers and subjected to tortures including stripping, beatings, and, in one instance, electroshock. The five men were awarded £20,000 damages. The Attorney General was said to have notified the court that he was not defending the action. Amnesty is unaware that any action was taken by the Zambian government to identify and discipline the responsible policemen. There have also been allegations of beatings administered by Zambian police to dissident members of Rhodesian guerilla organisations, over forty of whom are now under detention without trial in Zambia.

ASIA

This report describes the situation in seven countries, but few parts of Asia are free from the political and economic tensions which generate torture. The countries described below have been selected not because they present unique problems but rather because the quality of information at Amnesty's disposal enables some assessment to be attempted. The omission of China, Thailand, Burma and parts of South

East Asia does not imply the absence of any torture in any of these countries.

Unlike Europe and Latin America, no Asian human rights convention exists and a supra-national consensus has not yet been reached on the prohibition of torture, although it is generally proscribed at a national level. This should not suggest that brutality is less repugnant to Asian cultural patterns than to European traditions; but in societies where the problems of malnutrition, disease and illiteracy have not yet been solved, torture and the denial of human rights may stand out with less clarity than in more economically developed areas; in most Asian countries, these problems are further compounded by population pressures, and in some by deep ideological division. Apart from the United Nations Human Rights Declaration, the only international text which attempts to curb torture is the draft Covenant on Civil and Political Rights; only one Asian UN member has taken even the initial step of signing — the Philippines. No international organisation — Amnesty or the United Nations — has made any investigation into the use of torture in any part of Asia, although Vietnam has been the subject of several independent enquiries, while the International Commission of Jurists has prepared related enquiries on Tibet and Bangladesh. At a national level, Sri Lanka (Ceylon) is the one country where an independent judicial enquiry has taken place, and reported publicly.

This report must therefore rely on the comparatively slender body of evidence and allegations submitted to Amnesty in recent years, but it must be remembered that these do not necessarily reflect the gravity of the situations which they describe. Where there is a high level of legal awareness, as in the Indian subcontinent, violations of human rights will be precisely documented and publicised. But in areas where the rule of law has been systematically subordinated to the political and military requirements of the state, the very prevalence of torture may make impossible the collection of direct testimony. In Indonesia, to take only one example, this situation is aggravated by a low popular level of legal awareness which means that many victims are deterred from describing their treatment not only through fear, but also through ignorance of the fact that they have basic rights which are being violated. Conversely, in the case of Vietnam, the availability of evidence is determined not only by the gravity of the situation but also by the international character of the conflict.

In reading the report, certain political and legal factors should be borne in mind. India, Sri Lanka, Pakistan and Bangladesh are working democracies in which the judiciary, while it may at times be bypassed, is politically independent. Although a strong legal profession does not prevent torture, it can act as a check on the police and army; for each million of the Indian population, there are 183 lawyers, in Indonesia 17 (compared with 1,575 in USA). The Philippines, despite its strong judicial traditions, is now in a state of martial law, while in Indonesia the army has dominated the country's political life for the last eight years. In both these countries, as in South Korea and South Vietnam, left-wing politics are proscribed, and although all remain democracies in theory, in practice political freedom exists only for the voters to the right of the spectrum. In North Korea and North Vietnam, the same situation exists, but in reverse order.

In reporting these situations, we have tried to draw a clear distinction between deliberate torture and collective atrocities as they occur in conflict situations. Thus the report does not deal with the Bangladesh war, or with the killings in Indonesia in 1965 and 1966 or with the Malaysian racial disturbances of 1969. But in some places the line has been hard to hold: in Sri Lanka, after the JVP rising in April 1971, actual fighting and interrogation of suspects were often part of the same military operation. In Vietnam, where torture is certainly used to extract information, it is also applied indiscriminately within prisons to instill terror into potential dissidents. In such circumstances, it is difficult to maintain a logical distinction between collective atrocity on a battlefield and collective brutality inside a prison.

A final word must be said about one important omission — the People's Republic of China. This omission reflects both the difficulty of establishing accurate information about human rights in China and also the fact that Amnesty International has only recently begun to do research in the area.

The only part of China that Amnesty has been concerned

with in detail hitherto has been the island of Formosa (Taiwan). Amnesty has received several allegations of torture from Taiwan, specifically, the torture of political suspects held for interrogation at the Garrison Command in the capital, Taipei, where under the martial law that has been in force for over two decades, defendants may be held incommunicado for months at a time, pending trial by a military court.

Allegations have also been received as recently as late 1972 of the torture and ill-treatment of prisoners held for political reasons in prisons in the Lhasa district of the Chinese Autonomous Region of Tibet. These reports have come from Tibetan refugees in northern India and Nepal, but they remain uncorroborated.

Finally, reference must be made to the many allegations of torture and maltreatment of various sorts of political dissenters that emerged from China during the 1965-9 Great Proletarian Cultural Revolution — allegations made variously by the Chinese themselves, by Tibetans and foreigners resident in China or detained by the Chinese during that period. To take just one example of the latter, the British engineer George Watt, arrested for spying in the early stages of the Cultural Revolution while working on contract in the far-western Autonomous Region of Sinkiang, has described since his release not only the serious maltreatment that he alleges he received during interrogation and detention in Peking, but also the beatings, violent street trials and summary executions of Red Guard victims that he claims to have witnessed before his arrest. Several such accounts have corresponded with the many other first- and second-hand reports that filtered out at the time.

The violence that characterised certain Red Guard factions, as well as certain stages of the Cultural Revolution, and that has been freely conceded in retrospect by Prime Minister Chou-En-lai, seems now to have died away completely. However, we do not yet know how the 'normalisation' of China since 1969-70 has affected the treatment of political dissent.

Singapore is another, if smaller, omission from the report. Throughout the 1960s and early 1970s the Singapore government used political detention as an instrument for containing dissent. This seems to have been accompanied by occasional brutality rather than by systematic torture. We have complaints that solitary confinement has been used and that this resulted in lasting injury to some detainees; one lawyer's statement states that Mr Chwa Seh Kea was subjected to systematic ill-treatment during his interrogation in April 1970.

India

The Indian State of West Bengal has an extremely high population density, while its capital, Calcutta, is by far the largest city in the Indian subcontinent, with a population of more than seven million. During the late 1960s bitter poverty and massive unemployment made West Bengal suitable ground for the development of a Marxist-Leninist movement known as Naxalism (named after a peasant uprising in the village of Naxalbari). The greatest number of allegations of torture from India have come from this area.

The Naxalites' selective assassinations of landlords, policemen and other 'agents of the state machinery', which began in the West Bengal countryside in 1967 and shifted to Calcutta in 1970, were met by an increasingly rigorous police programme of counter-insurgency. Thousands of suspected Naxalites were rounded up, and many of them have been held without trial ever since. They are detained under several preventive detention laws, of which the most widely used (the 1971 Maintenance of Internal Security Act) was declared unconstitutional by the Indian Supreme Court in April 1973.

On 15 May 1973, *Le Monde* reported that a recent convention of socialist parties in New Delhi underlined in documents presented there 'the bad treatment inflicted on revolutionaries when they are arrested — tortures, burnings with cigarettes — or during their detention — absence of medical treatment, beatings etc. Several dozen prisoners — and in winter 1972 the head of the Naxalites, Charu Mazundar — have died during their incarceration or in the course of "struggles" inside the prisons.'

Amnesty International has received allegations from the Legal Aid Committee in Calcutta, the West Bengal Association of Democratic Lawyers and other left-wing groups that police brutality towards those suspected of Naxalism has been widespread, especially during the tense times of 1970-1, when killings by the Naxalites were increasing.

In September 1970 the West Bengal Association of Democratic Lawyers set up an unofficial enquiry into allegations of police brutality. Their report lists a long series of complaints made against the police by individuals claiming they had been tortured, usually by being beaten immediately after arrest. The New Delhi government is not known to have responded to these allegations.

The pattern that emerges is that although incidents of police and prison warden brutality continue to occur, the worst period was in 1970-1, when the threat from the Naxalites was judged to be greatest. While police brutality seems to have stemmed from a desire to extract information about Naxalism, beatings and other abuses of prisoners inside the prisons themselves may have reflected the grossly overcrowded and inadequate conditions of the big Calcutta detention centres such as Alipore and the Presidency Jail.

Amnesty International has also received allegations of torture and ill-treatment of civilian detainees from two other parts of India, Nagaland in the far north-east and Kashmir in the north-west.

Since an armed insurrection against Indian rule began in Nagaland in 1956, the area has been marked by bitter fighting, and more recently by sporadic acts of terrorism. (The secession of Bangladesh in 1971 was a major blow to the Naga rebels.) While it was still operative in 1970 the self-styled Federal Government of Nagaland, established by Naga dissidents in opposition to the government in New Delhi, alleged on at least three separate occasions that the Indian Army had perpetrated numerous 'atrocious deeds' against Naga citizens. These included rapings, beatings and other tortures of men and women suspected of helping the rebels.

In the predominantly Moslem State of Kashmir, where the Plebiscite Front has persistently campaigned for self-determination, supporters of the Front have often been held under preventive detention legislation and subjected to various forms of oppression, though the situation has improved since 1972. In May 1972, a former prisoner of conscience was interviewed; he had been detained in 1966, apparently because of his leading role in the Plebiscite Front. The man alleged that he had been subject to prolonged torture during interrogation; in particular, he said he had been forcibly kept awake for fifteen days and nights, as a result of which his eyesight has been permanently impaired.

Korea

Since the announcement, in July 1972, that North and South Korea were to begin talks on eventual reunification of Korea, the South Korean Central Intelligence Agency has continued to apply itself vigorously to the task of suppressing alleged Communist sympathisers and infiltrators. The South Korean CIA is responsible for 'special investigations' into the cases of alleged Communist suspects, as well as for eliciting 'confessions' from them.

On 4 January 1973 the *Guardian* cited the case of Park No-su, a research student at Cambridge University, who had returned to Seoul and been sentenced to death and executed for alleged espionage activities for North Korea. According to the report, Park had explained in notes left behind after his execution the reasons he 'confessed'. Scribbled in the margin of a transcript of the court proceedings is the list of tortures he had undergone: injections, water torture (forcible swallowing), being kept awake for two weeks, beating by groups of investigators, torture of the reproductive organs.

Amnesty International has not been in a position to confirm this allegation. In another well-publicised political trial, however, there can be little doubt that torture was used to extract a 'confession' and may even have driven the defendant to attempt suicide. This was the case of Soh Sung, a Korean student who had visited North Korea twice, once before settling in South Korea from Japan. Several months after his second visit, he was arrested, interrogated for two weeks by the CIA, and made an oral 'confession', largely on the basis of which he was charged and found guilty of spying for the North. During his interrogation, he apparently tried to commit suicide by throwing himself into an open fire, as a result of which he sustained grave and disfiguring burns. Soh told an Amnesty legal observer at his Appeal Court trial that during his interrogation he had been beaten and had suffered 'physical and mental pain'. The observer's report was sent to the appropriate South Korean authorities, but no comment was forthcoming.

In July 1974 William J. Butler, the representative of the International Commission of Jurists to the UN, visited South Korea on behalf of Amnesty International. His report adds to the accumulating evidence that the torture of political Prisoners by the Korean CIA is both commonplace and intense. Mr Butler spoke with six lawyers who were defending 32 students on trial before military courts. The lawyers told him that in order to obtain confessions from the students, the authorities subjected each of them to such tortures as electrical shocks to the genitals, beatings, sleeplessness, and the forcing of cold water through the nostrils. The national poet Kim Chi Ha also testified that he had been tortured, and Chang Chun Ha, a leading publisher and former member of the Korean Assembly, claims that he was burned with a flame on several parts of his body as he was hanging upside down. These victims are usually accused of being spies for North Korea even though their only offence often is that they have criticised the authoritarianism of President Park. Most of these tortured critics are clearly not communists, for example the outspoken critic of President Park, Bishop Chi Hak Sun of Wonju, who was allegedly tortured and was sentenced in August 1974 to 15 years in prison.

Amnesty has not received individual allegations of torture in North Korea, a thoroughly inaccessible country which *Le Monde* has described as the 'most closed society in the world'. The difficulty in obtaining information about the use of torture in North Korea (which must face many of the same political problems, except in reverse, as the South) does not, of course, rule out its existence.

Indonesia

Reports of torture relate to the period since October 1965, when a left-wing coup attempt was defeated by the army. In the months which followed, the army assumed an increasingly dominant role in the government and administration of the country, and the Communist Party (PKI), with its claimed following of 15,000,000, was outlawed. Formal directions for the elimination of the Communist movement were issued in a March 1966 decree which stated that 'swift, precise and firm steps' should be taken against the PKI nationally and locally. But even before this, the machinery was in motion for an indiscriminate purge of the political left, in which at least 300,000 suspected Communists were killed and similar numbers arrested. This purge continued through the 1960s, though its initial violence was abated, and frequent arrests are still reported of those said to have been 'involved' in the Communist movement before 1965, or to have later tried to bring about its revival. Where torture has been used, its purpose has been to extract admissions of past political activity, which often means no more than affiliation with one of the many legal pro-communist organisations before 1965, and to identify a prisoner's political colleagues, thus assisting the Indonesian Army in its overt task of 'cleansing' the country of Communism.

Amnesty has not been able to investigate the incidence of torture, and has comparatively few first-hand accounts in its file. But the *prima facie* case is extremely strong for believing that torture is practised as a matter of routine both by the police in ordinary criminal investigations and by the army in political cases. In the case of criminal prisoners, this was officially admitted as recently as May 1973 when Dr Hudioro, Grand Commissioner of Police, was reported in a military newspaper as saying that police officers were 'still unable to conduct investigations without force'. His comment referred to the acquittal on appeal of a civil servant previously convicted of arson, on the grounds that his confession had been made only after torture, which had involved electric shocks to the genitals, and crushing his toes beneath the legs of a table. In June, 1972, the National Police Chief, Mohammed Hassan, told the Parlimentary Commission on Law that policemen guilty of torture would be treated severely, but no general enquiry seems to have followed.

All our evidence suggests that similar techniques are used on political prisoners; in a few cases of extreme bestiality, officials have been disciplined, but in general it seems that the use of torture to gain information not otherwise obtainable has the knowledge, and tacit approval, of the military authorities.

But it is important to note that allegations relate to specific sections of the army and while brutality may be fairly widespread, torture is likely to be the prerogative of those responsible for political intelligence. Since 1965, the Indonesian army has assumed responsibility for all domestic security questions, in which are included the control of subversion and in practice of political dissent. In this, it has usurped the functions of the normal judiciary, replacing statutory laws and regulations by military decisions and commands. General Sumitro, as Head of the Command for the Restoration of Security and Order — Kopkamtib — is directly responsible for all aspects of political arrest and detention, and for political intelligence. His Command's work is conducted without reference to the Ministry of Justice, the Attorney General or the civilian judicial framework. Kopkamtib powers are vested in and exercised by the normal army apparatus. In the territorial commands, Kopkamtib operations are handled by military commands called Kopkamtibda, in each of the regions special units exist to handle political intelligence and this includes the interrogation of political prisoners. The most notorious of these was the Kalong — vampire — unit in Jakarta. In 1969 or 1970, these units were reformed at the centre and the regions into Special Task Units — Satgas — operating under more tightly controlled central guidance. This administrative reorganisation of intelligence work may in part have been the result of past excesses perpetrated by officials and in part to reduce their relative independence from central intelligence supervision. There is no evidence, however, that Satgas units have been any the less prone to use torture or brutality. The gravest allegations of torture relate to interrogations by the Central Satgas Unit in Kebayoran-Lama on the outskirts of Jakarta and by the Jakarta Satgas Unit, Satgat-jaya, which operates in two Jakarta camps, one being the former Kalong camp.

This passage, written by a former prisoner, illustrates clearly the extra-legal style in which military investigations were conducted:

(Satgat-jaya) was established in 1969 or 1970 to replace

the previous operational force which had been in charge since the middle of 1966. The previous unit was known as 'Kalong' (vampire) which was its official name, and employed particularly vicious methods both as regards torture and also as regards the intensive employment of very high-ranking ex-PKI functionaries to hunt down those still at large or actively engaged in underground activities ... For some time the most powerful figure at the Command was a man named Atjep, presumably a civilian for he never wore uniform and did not seem to have a military rank. He is extremely well-known as a top interrogator, perhaps the most brutal of all, though he usually relies on his subordinates to do the actual torturing ... His methods and perhaps also his successes frequently arouse strong opposition within the Kodam itself and he was on two occasions ... actually placed under detention for particularly brutal treatment of detainees. But he has always managed to weather such storms and emerge again in full strength. He obviously has top-level backing and I have been told that he is a special favorite of General ...

At one time Kalong was almost completely dominated by two ex-PKI leading functionaries, Burhanuddin and Sampir. These two persons had been in positions at the PKI Central Secretariat which gave them very intimate knowledge of the activities of a very large number of people in the PKI and they shamelessly utilised all this knowledge, and appeared to be determined not to be outdone in brutality by persons within the army. But one gets the impression that towards the end of Kalong's existence, the methods they used there were being increasingly criticised within Kodam.

This report is of the situation in Jakarta, but allegations of severe torture have been received from East Kalimantan, Sumatra (Padang) and West Irian, and there is no reason to suppose that the pattern established in these places is not a national one. A letter which was written by 800 prisoners in Balikpapan, Kalimantan, in January 1972 states: 'We all have suffered from extensive interrogation and investigation far exceeding the bounds of humane treatment.' It continues:

'We have been pushed into self-dug pits covered at the bottom with glass splinters. We have been given electric shocks and cigarettes have been used to burn us . . . There are some among us who have been shot through the mouth.' The report from West Irian, which concerns Indonesian attempts to force the cultural development of the Dani people, is supported by a first-hand statement and photographic material.

Although, as we have seen, torture in criminal cases can on occasion be brought to light in a civilian court, redress in political cases has been neither sought nor obtained through normal judicial processes. In a handful of cases where prisoners have appeared before a military court, a plea of torture has been dismissed uninvestigated. However, were this situation changed — and there is no prospect of it — the statistics make clear the slim chance of redress. The *official* total for those arrested *and released* from detention between 1965 and 1972 is 502,000; in the same period fewer than 350 appeared before or had access to any form of military or civilian court.

Pakistan

During the civil war in East Pakistan (as it then was) which together with the war between India and Pakistan led to the establishment of the independent People's Republic of Bangladesh, the Pakistan Army committed 'terrible crimes against the population', as the International Commission of Jurists in Geneva has put it. It became clear in the autumn of 1971 that the Pakistan Army and the *razakars* (civilian militia recruited from East Pakistan) let loose a virtual reign of terror, allegedly in reprisal against guerrilla activities, but also, it would seem, because of the contempt in which the predominantly Punjabi Army from West Pakistan held the people of East Bengal.

Since (West) Pakistan returned to parliamentary rule in 1972, one particular incident has focussed attention on the issue of torture. On 18 July 1972, *The Times* of London reported that the government had confirmed in the National Assembly that 'instruments of torture' were being purchased by the Pakistan Military Attache in the United States. The

Minister of Labour said that his government was not the author of the deal, responsibility for which lay with the former regime of Yahya Khan. He added that the Bhutto government learned of the affair only through a press report from Washington and immediately sent out orders to stop it. The 'instruments' were said to include equipment for brainwashing, lie detection and torture of detainees. According to another press report, the Minister disclaimed responsibility, while simultaneously maintaining that 'everyone used these gadgets'. In June 1973, it was reported from Karachi that electric shock machinery existed inside the prisons and had been seen by detainees, but that there was no evidence of its use.

The Philippines

Since the imposition of martial law in September 1972, Amnesty has collected a number of general reports alleging the use of torture by the Army and, especially, the police. The Philippines Constabulary and the Anti-Narcotics Unit have been named. One allegation relates to the death by drug poisoning of Likiosa Hilao, a student, in Camp Crame on 7 April 1973 two days after her arrest supposedly for a narcotics offence; it is an extremely well documented and publicised case. Amnesty has asked the Ministry of Defence for the findings of an official enquiry into the conduct of the Philippines Constabulary officer named as responsible. Information from private sources suggests that while third-degree methods have been used on a number of detainees arrested for political reasons, this is rare in the case of prisoners from elite social backgrounds.

The Philippines is a signatory to the United Nations International Covenant on Civil and Political Rights and so has accepted in principle its absolute proscription of torture, and cruel, inhuman or degrading treatment even in time of public emergency (Article 7). Although the legally binding step of ratification has not yet been taken, the 1973 Constitution states (Article 2, Section 3) that 'the generally accepted principles of international law' are adopted as 'part of the law of the land'; this implies the administration's continued adherence to Article 7 of the Covenant, even during martial law. However, those now detained under martial law have no recourse to the civilian courts and Proclamation 1081 specifically excludes the Courts from deciding the 'validity, legality or constitutionality of any decree, order or acts issued, promulgated or performed by the President'.

Sri Lanka

Sri Lanka is a constitutional democracy in which human rights have been traditionally safeguarded by a strong and independent judiciary. The present United Front government, a socialist-Marxist coalition, came to power in May 1970 through free elections. In April 1971, an armed revolt was organised by the Janatha Peramuna Vimukti, a mass Marxist-Leninist youth movement which had turned to violence in a vain attempt to accelerate the creation of a fully socialist state. An emergency was declared, the revolt was defeated after heavy fighting and 18,000 people were detained of whom perhaps one third still remain in custody.

Under the Emergency Regulations, normal civil liberties are drastically curtailed. Public meetings are proscribed, *habeas corpus* is suspended and the armed forces and police have virtually unlimited powers of detention, search and arrest; one highly controversial regulation empowers the army and police to dispose of dead bodies without the presence of relatives or friends. Two emergency provisions have become statutory law. Under the 1972 criminal Justice Commissions Act, a confession made to the police is now admissible as evidence in court, while the 1973 Press Council Act makes newspapers subject to official control on sensitive public issues. Although these measures limit the powers of the judiciary, there is no evidence to suggest that its independence has been reduced.

Complaints about police misconduct were made in criminal cases for some time before 1971, and in 1965, the Police Commission was appointed by the United National Party to enquire, *inter alia*, into the discipline of the police force. Its Chairman was a former Chief Justice and his final report was sharply critical. It concluded that torture had on occasion taken place, recommended a change in the 'rude and militaristic attitude that is characteristic of a Police Station' and advised the establishment of a quick and effective complaints machinery. The Report was published soon after the present government came to office in 1970 and can therefore be said to represent their view.

Since April 1971, Amnesty has received reports of torture and brutality relating to two distinct periods: the three months from April to July when fighting was in progress and most arrests were made, and the time since August 1971. There is no doubt that grave and widespread atrocities were perpetrated by government forces in their attempts to gain information which would identify JVP supporters. This is not disputed by the government and in July 1971 Mrs Bandaranaike, the Prime Minister, told Parliament: 'I do not condone any excesses committed by the Security Forces and in the instances where there has been actual proof, investigations have been ordered and some of these are now proceeding and the persons concerned, if found guilty, will be dealt with in accordance with the law.'

But very few prosecutions have been brought and no formal enquiry has taken place. In one notorious case, where two soldiers are charged with the rape, sexual assault and savage murder of a 19-year-old girl at Kataragama on 16 April 1971, no final judgment has yet been given, although the accused have been committed for trial in the Galle Assize Court. Other allegations relating to April, May and June describe crude physical methods such as beating, the infliction of burns and sexual assault.

An Amnesty delegate who visited Sri Lanka in September 1971 reported allegations of one instance where a man was hung upside down from a tree outside the Ambalangoda police station and partially burned alive by a fire lit on the ground underneath him. His report commented: 'The delay in returning to (legal) normality may be attributable, to an extent, to fear of reprisals against the police and armed forces for the horrible crimes undoubtedly perpetrated ... during the "insurrection".'

Since August, 1971, there are fewer allegations, but reliable sources report that maltreatment in police stations continues and that the 1972 change in the law on confessions has acted as encouragement to police to extract statements from newly arrested JVP suspects. In cases now before the courts, several policemen face charges of murder and assault.

Vietnam

The conflict in Vietnam has engendered a large number of torture allegations; and there can be no doubt that a very large number of Vietnamese civilian and military detainees in the South and a small number of American prisoners of war in North Vietnam have been subjected to torture during the past ten years.

(a) North Vietnam and the Provisional Revolutionary Government

Information about the treatment of prisoners held in North Vietnam or by the Provisional Revolutionary Government (PRG) in the south is exceptionally difficult to verify. The lists of prisoners prepared by both sides in the south as a result of the January 1973 peace agreement show the pronounced discrepancies between claims about even the number of these prisoners. The PRG claimed at the time to have in detention 200 civilian prisoners; the Saigon administration challenged that figure and responded that the PRG held or had deported to the North or had executed at least 49,000 civilians. Claims about the treatment of these prisoners and of those in North Vietnam are equally difficult to assess. 'Of course we have political prisoners,' one official in the North was quoted as saying recently. 'What country doesn't? But we treat them properly, unlike the Saigon regime!' It has been argued in return by the Saigon administration (as well as by more impartial observers) that the PRG and its military arm, the National Liberation Front (NLF), hold few prisoners in the south because they execute their captives.

The most substantial allegations of torture against the North Vietnamese and the PRG stem from the imprisonment of captured American military personnel, mostly pilots, some of whom were shot down in 1965 and did not return home until 1973. According to the prisoners themselves, the alleged torture stopped in the autumn of 1969, perhaps in response to the halt in the American bombing at that time. Those American pilots captured after the resumption of bombing raids late in 1971 have not alleged systematic mistreatment.

Both the North Vietnamese and the American governments recognised the value of these prisoners of war as propaganda, and consequently the publicity that surrounded both their detention and their release makes it difficult to assess fairly many of the claims and counter-claims about their treatment while in the prisons of North Vietnam or of the PRG in the south. The North Vietnamese apparently believed that confessions of remorse by American pilots in captivity would help dissuade the American public from continuing the war, and before the autumn of 1969 it appears that the captors spent considerable energy in wringing such confessions from their captives. Those prisoners of war who suffered most were those who refused most firmly to reconsider and regret their previous military actions.

President Nixon's administration identified itself closely with the suffering of the prisoners of war, and when the prisoners were released as a result of the January 1973 peace agreement, the administration and the Pentagon arranged for national tours for forty returning prisoners who gave news conferences and public re-enactments of their ordeals. Despite the fact that much of the publicity surrounding their allegations has been theatrical and politically motivated, the substance of their statements is accepted by Amnesty International as true.

Hanoi, however, has vigorously denied that it 'manhandled' American prisoners. According to a commentary by the North Vietnamese news agency at the beginning of April 1973, 'the pilots of United States piratic planes who bombed North Vietnam were criminals'. Nevertheless, the commentary continued, in keeping with humanitarian policy and for the sake of friendship with the American people, the Hanoi Government treated them well.

The commentary quoted Colonel John Ord, who was in charge of the American hospital at Clark Air Base in the Philippines, as saying of the first batch of returned prisoners: 'The condition of the men is really good. That applies to their mental, physical and dental conditions. In all areas their condition is found to be good.' Hanoi's argument is not convincing in that three and a half years had elapsed between the last use of torture and the return of the victims to the United States. That a man was relatively healthy in 1973 does not prove that he was not tortured in 1969.

Indeed, later medical and psychiatric reports indicate some lasting disabilities among the almost 600 returned prisoners. One former prisoner's suicide is directly attributable to the traumas of his captivity, and such physical damage as that done to Commander Robert H. Shumaker is not uncommon: 'To keep me from screaming [while being tortured], they had a rag on a long metal rod that they shoved down my throat... They did some damage to the extent that I have a little trouble swallowing now. They did some nerve damage.'

A senior American diplomat, Mr Philip Manhard, spent most of four and a half years in solitary confinement. Navy Captain James A. Mulligan, who was captured in March 1966, spent 26 months in solitary confinement and 16 months in leg irons. Shackles were a common feature of imprisonment prior to 1969. The Geneva Convention No. III (1949) Relative to the Treatment of Prisoners of War prescribes that the time of solitary confinement for any prisoner of war must not exceed 30 days on the grounds that such treatment can cause severe psychological damage. Furthermore, the Convention expressly forbids the use of torture or coercion to obtain information: 'No physical or mental torture, nor any form of coercion, may be inflicted on prisones or war to secure from them information of any kind whatever. Prisoners of war who refuse to answer may not be threatened, insulted, or exposed to unpleasant or disadvantageous treatment of any kind' (Art. 17 (4)).

The method of torture most often described by the freed prisoners was the trussing and stretching of the body into painfully abnormal positions. A man's wrists and elbows were firmly bound behind his back with a long nylon rope that was then pulled upward until his arms were raised and his head was forced downward between his shackled legs. This action was usually executed by a guard who placed his foot between the prisoner's shoulder blades in order to pull the rope with greater force.

Medical attention for pilots captured by the NLF in the south appears to have been particularly inadequate. Major Floyd Kushner, a US Army doctor, has testified that for his own wounds, including a bullet in the shoulder, he was given no anaesthesia and that he was prevented by the NLF from treating his wounded fellow prisoners, ten of whom died.

The fact that Major Kushner remains a strong critic of his own government's role in the war makes it difficult to challenge the credibility of his allegations against the NLF.

A few pilots have said that they were rescued from angry villagers (whose villages lay beneath the bombs) by North Vietnamese or NLF soldiers. In this regard at least, some prisoners were protected by their captors. That does not alter the fact, however, that torture was systematic in the prisons until 1969. According to a survey taken by the prisoners themselves while still in captivity (and thus not a product of later propaganda), more than 90% of the approximately 350 prisoners captured during or before 1969 were tortured. Amnesty International believes there is sufficient evidence to indicate that systematic torture was an administrative policy.

(b) South Vietnam

In South Vietnam — or more specifically, those areas of South Vietnam controlled by the government in Saigon, rather than the Provisional Revolutionary Government of the National Liberation Front — torture appears to have been commonest in the many interrogation centres throughout the country. Some of these centres belong to police stations, as in the National Police Headquarters in Saigon, where the interrogation centre apparently holds more than two thousand people, but most of them are attached to provincial prisons. People suspected of having any connection with the National Liberation Front, captured either by the army or paramilitary security forces in the field or by the ordinary or special police in the urban areas, are taken to these centres for intensive questioning.

A large number of those brought in for interrogation have been detained under the Phoenix Program, devised in the late 1960s for 'rooting out the Vietcong "infrastructure".' According to an official US estimate, more than 20,000 suspected members of the National Liberation Front were killed as a result of Phoenix Program operations from 1968 until May 1971. Several ex-US Army intelligence operators have testified to the extensive use of torture and murder of suspects under the Program. Phoenix has continued in operation since the January 1973 Ceasefire and Peace Agreement.

Torture is also widespread in prisons administered in

Saigon. Such treatment seems to result partly from efforts to suppress prisoners rioting or protesting for better conditions, and partly from an attempt to 'rehabilitate' suspected Communists and other political dissidents through punitive discipline and the use of what can only be described as terror tactics. This is particularly true of prisoners held on Con Son Island off the south-east coast of South Vietnam. Appalling conditions prevail; beatings and other forms of torture are commonplace; and as part of what appears to be a sustained campaign to break morale, several hundred or the ten thousand or more prisoners held there are permanently shackled into disciplinary 'cages', so that they emerge with atrophied legs and in an advanced stage of physical and psychological degeneration — if they emerge at all.

In a report on political prisoners in South Vietnam published in July 1973, Amnesty International quoted at length from one of the most recent non-partisan statements on the use of torture on detainees, a British television interview with two Quaker doctors working in the city of Quang Ngai in the north-east of South Vietnam. They had been looking after a hospital ward full of civilian prisoners brought from the interrogation centre attached to Quang Ngai provincial prison. The television team asked the doctors:

Q: *In what capacity were you working in the hospital?*
A: We worked in a rehabilitation programme at the hospital and many of the prisoners that we have seen on the prisoner ward have . . . various ailments, some ailments that we attribute to torturing. We've seen people with paralysis . . . and people that have been beaten on the head, causing a brain haemorrhage and paralysis to one side or other of the body.

Q: *How recently have people been admitted after they've been tortured?*
A: People come to the prisoner ward at the hospital often immediately after they've been tortured . . . there are times when the prison officials are afraid that they might die in the interrogation centre, and they would prefer not to have a dead body at the interrogation centre, that they would have to get rid of, and thus they allow the prisoner to come to the hospital. But often people only come for a

long enough period of time, so that they would pass through what would be considered a critical point, and then they would be brought back to the interrogation.

Q: *Can you both describe the kind of state people are in, when they leave the interrogation centre ...*

A: It varies considerably, but I have seen as recently as 3 months ago, two people that were suffering from nerve damage, because they'd been beaten so badly, and covered with black and blue marks, vomiting blood, and perhaps blood coming out of their ears and noses; two of these people died on the prisoner ward, and never made it back to the interrogation centre. The torture that we see the results of most frequently, is the torture that results from people having been given electricity, they usually attach the electrical wires to people's toes, or fingers, or sensitive parts of their body. People say that they go unconscious when they're given the shock, and then when they recover consciousness, this will be repeated three or four times, and then the person will be allowed to rest for a certain period of time, perhaps to think about it, and to dread its happening again, and then it will be repeated once or twice more. After that until the interrogator is satisfied that the prisoner is innocent or in fact needs other types of torture.

Q: *Through your experience, would you say that the majority of people who enter that prison ward have been tortured?*

A: I would say that perhaps half the people that have entered the prison ward, have expressed to us directly that they had been tortured. I think many prisoners do not feel free to express whether they have been tortured or not, after all we are Americans, we could be CIA, they do not always trust us ...

Q: *How aware do you think are the US authorities in your province of what is going on at this prison?*

A: We've talked to the US authorities during our two-year stay, and we have talked to them about the fact that various prisoners have been tortured, they have never flatly denied this ... I think that they were very aware of this torturing going on. Also we know that the CIA does advise and support the interrogation centre ...

Q: *Since the cease-fire has torture been going on?*

A: We've only asked other prisoners, if there has been torturing going on, and they have told us that it hasn't let up at all.

The report also listed some of the more important previous torture allegations made in South Vietnam, a selection of which are given below:

17 June 1969: United States Study Team on Religious and Political Freedom in South Vietnam, just back from South Vietnam, reported that 'the sheer weight of witnesses' statements' on torture 'seemed overwhelming and conclusive to Team members'. The Report went on to describe different methods of torture in detail. The Report was published in the US Congressional Record on 17 June 1969.

17 June 1970: Fifteen students held press conference in Saigon at which they showed marks of torture and made a number of detailed torture allegations. They had been arrested, interrogated and brought to trial before a military court in the spring, but the Supreme Court later quashed their convictions and had the students released.

2 December 1970: Former US Army Intelligence operators in South Vietnam (including Stephen Noetzel, Edward Murphy and K. Barton Osborn), described to a war veterans' enquiry how NLF suspects were tortured and assassinated, and how Vietnamese agents who had possibly been compromised were 'terminated with prejudice'.

13 August 1972: The *New York Times* published a special report by Sydney H. Schanberg in Saigon detailing torture allegations. Schanberg quoted the Saigon police motto, 'Khong, danh cho co' ('If they are not guilty, beat them until they are').

October 1972: The Vietnamese Community in Paris published the document 'The Situation in the Prison of Chi Hoa', based on information smuggled out by inmates. Details of corruption, ill-treatment, drug-trading, imprisonment of children and inadequate food and medical facilities. Names of several 'trustee' prisoners known for their brutality were given. In August the Community had published 'Cry of Alarm', a collection of documents on prisons, including specific cases of torture and ill-treatment, initially compiled by the Committee Campaigning for Improvement of the Prison System in Saigon.

25 December 1972: *Time* magazine reported that torture of civilian prisoners was widespread. Cited such practices as inserting rubber sticks into women's vaginas, electricity and dropping lime into tiger cages.

29 December 1972: Two Frenchmen, André Menras and Jean-Pierre Debris, were released from Chi Hoa. They detailed torture procedures and alleged that torture during interrogation was a standard practice. During interviews with Amnesty International, they gave a series of instances in which various tortures had been used on specific detainees, both in interrogation centres and inside Chi Hoa itself (in particular in the so-called 'cinema room').

The report concluded:

> Of the various forms of torture, beating appears to be the most common. It is generally done with wooden sticks or clubs. The blows are applied to the back and to the bony parts of the legs, to the hands and in a particularly painful form, to the elevated soles of the feet when the body is in a prone position. Beating of the genitals also occurs.
>
> A particularly damaging form of beating is when prisoners are immersed in tanks of water which are then beaten with sticks on the outside. The resulting reverberations, while leaving no marks, can cause severe internal injury.
>
> In another type of water torture a soaked cloth is placed over the nose and mouth of a prisoner tied back on a bench. The cloth is removed the last minute before the victim chokes to death and is then re-applied. Alternatively, water — salty or soapy — is forced into the victim's mouth and nose until it is absorbed into the lungs and stomach, which are then beaten. Prison guards are said to call this 'taking the submarine'.
>
> In another procedure the victim is hung by rope or wire from his toes or feet and beaten. This is sometimes called 'the plane ride'. Electricity and sexual torture are also often used in a variety of ways, especially on women.

Victims are tortured to discover their innocence or guilt, and then to extract information, not simply to extract information after guilt has been established.

It is clear, moreover, that the brutalising effects of the Vietnam war have become so entrenched that some of the time the use of torture during interrogation is no longer even motivated by a desire to gather 'intelligence'. An administration defending itself against what it or its major ally construes to be an insurrectionary movement may regrettably find it hard to resist the expedient of torture in its efforts to crush its elusive opponent; but there can be no doubt that torture is now widely used in the areas controlled by the Saigon government not only as an instrument of intimidation but as an end in itself. Torture has become a standard part of the interrogation not only of NLF suspects, but also a wide range of non-Communist political dissidents; and, as we can confirm from expressions like 'Khong, danh cho co', it is applied with an extraordinary degree of cynicism.

Although United States officials have tacitly admitted, or refused to deny, that torture is used during interrogation, Saigon government spokesmen have frequently sought to dismiss those who have alleged its prevalence. In an interview on American television in spring 1973, for example, South Vietnamese President Nguyen Van Thieu dismissed the two Frenchmen André Menras and Jean-Pierre Debris as 'big liars'. When asked about prisoners crippled from being held in tiger cages in Con Son prison he explained that 'In every prison in Vietnam we have a doctor, we have a dispensary... We have not done anything which could be the origin of that kind of sickness'.

WESTERN EUROPE

The concept of human rights — the protection of the individual, embodied in the law of the country, against the power of the state — developed in the specific European political context. Nevertheless, it was in the same context, in this century, that political persecution on a large scale developed. Ideologies replaced religion as the driving force:

the instruments of repression and intimidation of the citizen by the state were developed alongside the ideological conflict.

Western Europe, as a result mainly of the war and the abuse of power by Hitler, and, more remotely, by Stalin, has witnessed a growing concern, since 1945, with the protection of human rights. The Human Rights Commission and the Court of the Council of Europe, whose work is discussed in Section 2, may be regarded as the embodiment of this concern. At the present time, however, inhuman treatment, sometimes amounting to torture, is noted especially in those countries of western Europe where authoritarian governments are in power, and in areas where violence is triggered off by political motives.

In two countries — Greece and the United Kingdom — allegations of torture have been investigated by various commissions of enquiry, and those instances are discussed in Section 2 above. The situations in Spain, Portugal and Turkey, which have not been so investigated, are described here as well as an instance of simulated torture, which occurred in the course of NATO exercises in Belgium in November 1971, and apparently in the UK in spring 1973.

Belgium

During the NATO exercises in November 1971, which involved troops from the United States, the United Kingdom, the Netherlands and Belgium, six Belgian commandos 'captured' a dozen Belgian 'enemy' and tortured them for twenty-four hours to get information about other units in the military exercise. The torture, which included beatings, exposure to cold and electroshock, was stopped when a major heard about it from a doctor. The six were brought to trial before a military tribunal in Liège in November 1972. During the trial a defence witness testified that NATO armies gave training in resistance to torture as well as learning about torture techniques. The defendants were found guilty of assault, in committing violent acts, out of all proportion to normal military conduct, that contravened human rights. They were given suspended prison sentences ranging from sixteen days to five months. Amnesty International's inquiries to NATO with respect to its training procedures and their consistency with human rights conventions received the following response:

1 March 1973

Dear Mr Secretary General:

Your letter of 14 December 1972 concerning the incident which occurred in the course of a NATO exercise in November 1971 has received my very particular attention.

With regard to the principles advocated by NATO with respect to the training of national forces, it can be unequivocally stated that they are in no way in conflict with the Geneva Convention. They expressly provide that prisoners are not to be made to suffer any physical indignity, and they prohibit any treatment that might infringe upon their integrity.

Within NATO, the basic and advanced training of the NATO forces is and continues to be a national responsibility. Further, the London Agreement of 19 June 1951, on the status of these forces, establishes the respective rights of the sending and receiving states to exercise penal and disciplinary jurisdiction over the members of their forces, which the internal laws of these countries confer upon them.

In consequence, it is the sovereign and sole responsibility of the national authorities who hold jurisdiction over the members of their forces to decide upon and take such disciplinary measures and legal proceedings as provided for under their national laws and regulations and as are dictated by the offenses of which these authorities have cognizance. This is what was done in the instance to which your letter refers; the offenders were legally tried and convicted by a national court martial: I assume you are aware that the individual determined to be primarily responsible for the incident was given a sentence close to the maximum provided by Belgian law for the offences for which he was judged.

The fact that the men responsible for the incident were brought before a court martial seems to me indicative of a determination on the part of member nations of NATO to enforce obedience to the principles of the international conventions to which your letter refers.

Sincerely,

(signed) A.J. GOODPASTER
General, United States Army
Supreme Allied Commander

Cyprus

During the summer of 1973 Amnesty International received substantial allegations of torture against the government of President Archbishop Makarios. The victims of the alleged torture were persons accused of belonging to the illegal EOKA B movement, whose expressed purpose was to end the independence of Cyprus in favour of the policy of *enosis*, political union with Greece. Several agencies of the Makarios government were accused of torture, the primary one being the Auxiliary Police, a unit that was organised in response to the threat from the EOKA B movement and was responsible directly to Archbishop Makarios.

These allegations were investigated and found to be credible by a British lawyer representing the International Commission of Jurists who visited Cyprus in August 1973 and received written statements concerning 40 people who were allegedly tortured. Victims were allegedly subjected to severe beating, enforced standing, burning with cigarettes, and hooding as well as threats to shoot or poison the prisoner, to destroy his property, or to injure members of his family. Protests were lodged with Archbishop Makarios by the International Court of Justice and Amnesty International, and for a few months the practice of torture appeared to decline.

Torture in Cyprus should be seen within the context of a traditional respect for legal procedure and of an independent judiciary and legal profession. The Human Rights Committee of the Nicosia Bar Council called on the government early in July 1974 to cease its continuing use of torture. Several judges tried to protect detainees who were brought before them in a broken condition by requiring the police to bring the detainees to court every day; one judge denounced from the bench the treatment of detainees by the security forces. At least two lawyers who defended opponents of the government also claim to have been tortured.

In mid-July 1974 a military coup overthrew the government of Archbishop Makarios and temporarily installed as president Nikos Sampson, a companion-in-arms of the late General Grivas and a leader of the EOKA B movement. The leaders of the coup recognised the advantage of using the issue of torture as a political weapon at home and abroad, and they gave effective publicity to the allegations against the previous government.

After the Turkish invasion of Cyprus and the replacement of Mr Sampson by Glafkos Clerides, Amnesty International urged the new government to investigate past abuses and to re-establish the rule of law by returning the process of interrogation to the authority of the courts and the legal system.

Portugal

The military coup of 25 April 1974 overthrew a regime that had practised torture for 40 years. Portugal presents a unique opportunity for the study of the institutions of torture over several decades from the time that a single German Gestapo agent helped establish the predecessor of the DGS (the security police) until the recent arrest of many of the thousands of DGS agents and informers. That history is yet to be written, but the Portuguese provisional government is not unmindful of its responsibilities to rehabilitate the victims, to prosecute the torturers, and to provide the world with an account of this dark period of Portugal's history.

The general nature of the worst allegations against the previous regime has now been verified beyond question. Under the rule of Dr Antonio de Oliveiro Salazar and that of his successor, Professor Marcello Caetano, the practice of torture was a routine occurrence. The most common motive for torture was the desire to obtain confessions from and information on potential subversives. The state was unwilling to tolerate any political activity which it saw as posing a threat to itself, and therefore any group or individual which did so ran the risk of being ill-treated: trade unionists, journalists, students, demonstrators and members of clandestine political groups were among the most vulnerable. Most of the torture occurred in the DGS headquarters in Lisbon and more recently in the new DGS centre in a wing of Caxias prison.

The DGS was responsible for handling crimes of a political nature: since 1945 its predecessor PIDE, and then the DGS, were responsible for all pre-trial proceedings where political charges were being brought. Under Dr Caetano PIDE became the DGS in 1969; the Decree Law (368/72) of 30 September 1972 broadened its powers. Article 8 of this now defunct law states: 'The function attributed by law to the judge during investigations, relating to the interrogation of the accused, the validity and upholding of arrests and decisions on granting of bail will be carried out by the Director-General, chief inspectors, section heads and assistant chief inspectors.' The Law provided for the authorisation of the security police to order an arrest without any intervention from the Courts, and the personnel of the DGS were entitled to special bonuses for 'technical competence'.

The principal methods of torture were enforced standing and the deprivation of sleep for an extended period of time: for some prisoners it was as much as fourteen days. During this period the guards were changed frequently — every two or three hours — and prisoners were kept awake by being ruthlessly slapped, beaten, kicked, and having water poured over them; reprisals were also threatened against their families.

Immediately after the April 1974 coup investigators found evidence in the prisons, including tape recorders, to substantiate the allegations of former prisoners that recordings of the voices of relatives were played during sessions of torture in order to put further pressure on prisoners to talk. Prisoners were told that they were hearing the screams of tortured relatives. Guards standing outside the prisoner's room would read from scripts of gibberish to effect a fear of madness on the sleepless prisoner. The use of loud electronic noises, recordings of moans and screams of pain were part of a well-orchestrated cacophony of physical and psychological abuse. The rooms in the new wing of the prison at Caxias were equipped with the means to expose a prisoner to extreme changes of temperature, once again in an effort to disorient the mind.

The allegations of torture have been taken very seriously by the new provisional government and by several professional associations. The government has given official sanction to the National Commission of Help for Political Prisoners (CNSPP) that is compiling testimonies of hundreds of victims of torture. A specialised team of researchers (medical, psychological, and sociological), supervised by Dr Afonso de Albuquerque, plans to examine victims of torture with the aim of diagnosing and treating the effects of torture. The *Ordem dos Advogados* (Bar Association) has appointed a group of its lawyers to determine the legal regulations by which torturers can be tried; in some ways they must chart a new course in criminal law, and they face some of the same problems that confronted the prosecutors at the Nuremburg Trials after the Second World War. The Portuguese Medical Association has expelled seven doctors, including three psychiatrists, for their assistance in the practice of torture. The clearest indication of the provisional government's determination to proceed with the cases against the torturers is the appointment by the junta of one of its own members, Admiral Rosa Coutinho, as the head of a department to compile dossiers for the prosecution of former DGS agents.

Portugal's overseas territories

In the overseas territories — Angola, Mozambique, Guinea-Bissau and the Cape Verde Islands — the security measures in effect under the old regime appeared to be harsher than those applied in metropolitan Portugal. The DGS might, by virtue of Decree Law (239/72) of 18 July 1972, imprison anyone who had acted in a way 'contrary to the territorial integrity of the nation' for up to six years without judicial control. This measure affected especially advocates of self-determination for the overseas territories and meant that they might be kept in administrative detention for a maximum of six years.

Portuguese Guinea (Guinea-Bissau)

Ever since its inception in 1961, Amnesty International has received allegations of torture from Guinea-Bissau. The torture techniques described have always been primarily physical, and such has been the intensity of the reported maltreatment that there have been numerous accounts of deaths as a result of torture. Although torture is said to be most frequently used during interrogation, it evidently is used in prisons and camps long after the initial stages of detention. The authorities who were accused were usually PIDE/DGS personnel, but soldiers have also been implicated. The evidence is mainly available in papers and affidavits submitted to the UN by PAIGC, the African Party for the Independence of Guinea and Cape Verde, the major liberation movement which claims to control about two thirds of the territory of the Province.

Cape Verde Islands

The islands are the site of two prison camps, one on the Ilha das Galinhas, and the Tarrafal camp (now called Campo de Chao Bom) on Santiago Island. Conditions in these camps are appalling and allegations of forced labour, sadism, torture and murder have emanated from them; many Angolans are detained there.

Angola

Allegations of torture, maltreatment and inhuman and degrading conditions of detention are frequent. There were numerous arrests in 1969-70, and Amnesty International has some names of a group of 36 people, mostly students, all of whom alleged that they were severely tortured before being deported to Campo de Chao Bom and eight years' administrative detention. The torture methods described were primarily physical, and included deprivation of sleep, food and water. The allegations date from the year 1969 until now (summer 1973) and most of them have been reported in the Report of the *ad hoc* Working Group of the Commission of Human Rights of the United Nations, New York, February 1973.

Mozambique

There have been allegations of large-scale torture and massacres (including old women and small babies) made against the Portuguese army and the DCS. Torture evidently occurs most frequently during interrogation. There have been detailed descriptions of primarily physical methods more varied and sophisticated than in the rest of Portuguese Africa. They include electroshock and the use of drugs described as disturbing the nervous system. Several deaths as a direct result of torture have been reported. Christian missionaries have alleged that thousands of Africans have been tortured and many more imprisoned. The most frequently mentioned prisons used for political prisoners and guerillas are the prison at Vila Cabral, the penitentiary at Lourenço Marques, the prison at Machava, the Pinto Teixeira Cabane camp in Mabalane (2,000 political prisoners) and a prison camp in Ibo (1,000 political prisoners). Prison conditions are allegedly appalling and maltreatment so severe that many deaths, caused by police violence, have been reported.

Spain

Amnesty's documentation on alleged torture in Spain covers — with few exceptions — the whole of the past decade. The material itself consists of victims' testimonies (many in the form of formal complaints to the courts); lawyers' statements; protests and petitions signed by Spanish churchmen, intellectuals and professionals; reports of trial observers; and official transcripts of court decisions on torture denunciations. All evidence indicates that torture is used in police stations, principally in order to extract information and obtain confessions from detainees, and that this practice is widespread, regular and virtually unrestricted. It covers beating of all parts of the body, including the testicles, the water-torture, running the gauntlet, death threats, night-and-day interrogations, solitary confinement without food, bed or blankets, witnessing the beatings of others, etc.

Most torture victims can be identified with one of three groups, each of which is considered to be a threat to the regime: workers, students and Basque nationalists. Furthermore, the allegations increase in intensity when opposition pressure from any of these groups becomes greater, particularly in the case of the Basques. Of the two States of Exception which have been declared in recent years, the first came in 1968 as a result of the assassination of a police chief in the Basque Country; and the second, in December 1970 at the time of the Burgos Court Martial of sixteen Basque nationalists accused of the killing. Both emergencies involved the suspension for six to nine months of Article 18 of the Charter of the Spanish People (which provides that all detainees must be freed or turned over to the judicial authorities within 72 hours of arrest). Under such circumstances, torture and the threat of remaining indefinitely in the hands of the police are also used as a means of intimidating the opposion: a large number of those detained for months after the Burgos Court Martial were eventually released without charges.

More recently, the killing of a policeman during a May Day political demonstration in Madrid in 1973 provoked an extreme right-wing backlash and so enraged the police force that they organised anti-government marches demanding stronger 'law and order' measures. Subsequent arrests of young students and workers were accompanied by fresh reports of especially brutal police torture, allegedly in revenge for the murder. The situation in Police headquarters was described by lawyers as 'absolutely chaotic, with the police completely beyond control'.

The paramilitary police (*Guardia Civil*), the armed police (*Policia Armada*) and the security police (*Brigada Politico-Social*) all figure prominently in torture allegations. Ultimately responsible to the Minister of the Interior, the police are empowered to hold a detainee for up to 72 hours before passing him on to either the judicial or the military authorities to be indicted. It is not, however, unusual — notably, but not only during States of Exception — for detainees to be released on bail by the courts and then re-arrested (or 'retained') by the police for further interrogation and torture. Lawyers protested in connection with the May Day arrests, for example, that although their clients were officially under the jurisdiction of the military tribunal which would try them, they had been transferred from prison back to the police station with the full knowledge, if not authorisation, of the military judge.

While the judiciary cannot be said officially to condone the practice of torture, trial judges as a rule do not allow defendants to mention the circumstances under which their confessions were taken, in spite of the fact that the confession is often the only piece of evidence produced by the public prosecutor. One lawyer defending a student detained during the 1971 State of Exception was himself indicted for contempt of court and 'insults to the Spanish nation' because he insisted during the trial on referring to the torture undergone by his client. Torture victims are often reluctant to submit complaints to a judge for fear of intimidation, and the majority of formal denunciations considered by the courts are dismissed for 'lack of evidence'. At three separate hearings reported in the Spanish press, judges acquitted police inspectors accused of causing bodily harm to workers arrested at the time of the El Ferrol shipyard strike (March 1972) and the Vigo Citroen strike (September 1972); in each case, the injuries sustained by the prisoners were confirmed by medical reports, but the court maintained that the guilt of the police had not been established.

Amnesty International knows of three occasions on which torture charges brought against individual policemen were actually upheld by the courts: Two police inspectors were sentenced to 15 days' imprisonment each in San Sebastian for having struck a lawyer as they arrested him (March 1970); another two inspectors were given 3-day sentences in Santander for having beaten workers detained the previous February (June 1970); and one police officer was condemned to 6 days' imprisonment in Bilbao for having tortured two students (March 1972).

Protests against torture practices and demands for investigations have been made repeatedly to the Spanish government throughout the past ten years. In October 1963, 102 intellectuals sent a letter to the Mininster of Information and Tourism alleging the torture of miners arrested after a large-scale strike in Asturias. More than 1,000 professionals, intellectuals and artists in January 1969 presented the Minister of the Interior with 31 pages of testimony about police torture of political prisoners during the previous year.

In September 1969 the International Confederation of Free Trade Unions wrote to the Minister of Justice to demand an inquiry into reports of tortures which had been inflicted on workers and students that Spring (during and after the State of Exception). The Secretary General of Amnesty International travelled to Madrid in December 1970 to appeal for a commutation of the death sentences passed at the Burgos Court Martial and for a thorough public investigation into allegations that the sixteen Basques on trial had been severely tortured. In February 1971 over 100 Madrid lawyers submitted a petition to the Supreme Court protesting against the ill-treatment of students detained during the 1971 State of Exception. Several months afterwards, the Bishop of Granada and the Auxiliary Bishop of Pamplona publicly denounced the torture of prisoners in their diocese, which the latter stated 'I have seen with my own eyes...' Early in June 1973, 200 lawyers, doctors and university professors again called for a public inquiry, this time into the alleged torture of those arrested after May Day in Madrid.

The government's initial reaction to most allegations is to attribute them to propagandists intent on spreading groundless rumours abroad in an effort to discredit the regime. Official spokesmen also argue that prisoners often inflict bruises and wounds upon themselves in order to claim that they have been tortured; or that individual policemen naturally have to defend themselves from captured, but still dangerous, terrorists. It is affirmed that torture as a systematic practice does not exist in Spain, but that isolated instances of police ill-treatment are investigated. Moreover, every Spaniard has the right to bring a complaint against a public official in the event of abuse of authority, and such complaints should be made directly to a court: general denunciations by bishops or any other public figures, according to the government, achieved nothing in themselves and only served to stir up unrest.

Turkey

Martial law was imposed in eleven of Turkey's sixty-seven provinces in March 1971; it was terminated in the last two remaining provinces (Istanbul and Ankara) in September

1973 before the general election of October 1973 that signalled the return to civilian rule. During the period of military rule there were many allegations that political prisoners were being tortured. Minutely detailed statements written by men and women who claimed to have been victims and witnesses of torture appeared in European newspapers after being smuggled out of Turkish prisons. Some released prisoners also made similar allegations.

In January 1972 Muir Hunter, an eminent English lawyer, went to Turkey as Amnesty International's representative to talk with the Minister of Justice about the allegations of torture, and about other matters of interest to Amnesty. In May 1972 Mr Hunter produced the document 'An Examination of the Allegations of the Torture of Prisoners in Turkey', which was sent to the Council of Europe and to the Turkish authorities. After a careful analysis of the material available to him, which included statements by persons who alleged they had been tortured and statements naming other persons allegedly tortured, Mr Hunter concluded: 'There appears to be a strong *prima facie* case for investigating the allegations of torture, brutality and threats in the treatment of prisoners in Turkey.'

In their reply to Mr Hunter's document the Turkish government stated '... categorically that no ill-treatment whatsoever is inflicted during the questioning, nor is there any implement or device designed to serve this purpose. Besides, there are no places, such as chambers of torture or operation rooms, as mentioned in the allegations. It is, therefore, evident that there cannot be any question of investigating non-existent places and devices.'

In November 1972 Mr Hunter returned to Turkey, this time as the leader of an Amnesty International mission to inquire into allegations of torture; he was accompanied by Sir Osmond Williams, Vice-Chairman of Amnesty International's British Section, and by Mrs Hunter, both of whom are magistrates. The Turkish authorities had agreed in advance that the mission should be allowed to visit prisons and to talk to prisoners, defence lawyers and released prisoners. Nevertheless, the mission did not meet with the cooperation from the Turkish authorities which they had been led to expect, and they were able to interview only one prisoner. Although this prisoner, a medical student, had not herself been tortured, she had attended to the wounds of other prisoners, including her husband, whom she alleged had been tortured. In their report the mission stated:

> In our opinion, Ilkay Demir was a truthful witness, both as to what she had experienced herself and as to what she had learned from other prisoners. Having regard to her obvious commitment to their cause, we cannot exclude the possibility that she may have slightly exaggerated her account of their experiences, but we accept the substance of what she said as correct.

Numerous foreign journalists and parliamentarians continued to expose torture in Turkey — so much so that the government was put on the defensive before the Council of Europe. On 12 December 1972 the London *Sunday Times* reported that its investigators in Turkey had found that 'there is a weight of evidence supporting the allegations which cannot be dismissed'. Mr Pieter Dankert, a Dutch member of parliament and a delegate to the Consultative Assembly of the Council of Europe, visited Turkey in February/March 1973 on a private fact-finding mission and reported: '... I have not the slightest doubt that torture on a rather large scale has taken place.' Early in 1973 a British television team went to Turkey unofficially to film interviews with victims and witnesses of torture; articulate professional people, including a psychiatrist, lawyers, and a former public prosecutor, gave testimony. A similar film was made for Swedish TV. The British film was subsequently shown to delegates to the Council of Europe despite the attempt by the Turkish authorities to prevent the showing.

The allegations and impartial investigations provided a convincingly consistent picture. The places where torture is alleged to have taken place, the names and descriptions of the torturers, and the methods used occurred again and again. In December 1972 the Turkish Foreign Minister appeared before the Political Committee of the Council of Europe and argued that all the allegations had been fully investigated and were unfounded.

The general election of October 1973 brought a change in

official policy. One allegation of torture dates from just four days before the election. No political party gained a majority of seats in the 450-member National Assembly, and for several months a coalition government could not be formed. Civilian rule continued despite the perilous political crises that was the longest in the history of Turkish democracy.

In November 1973 the Ankara left-wing newspaper *Yeni Halkci* began the serialised publication of 20 affidavits from female prisoners. Among them was the statement by Ayse Semra Eker, aged 23, that opens this book. The victims claimed to have been forced to sign false confessions about their supposed activities in left-wing organisations. They said their torturers were members of the Turkish military secret police and a military 'counter-guerrilla organisation' (which was never acknowledged by the government to exist). According to the affidavits, majors and colonels as well as civilian police were present during sessions of torture.

The most common technique of torture was 'falanga' (beating on the soles of the feet with hard rods). A strain of sexual sadism in the torturers is also evident from the numerous allegations that truncheons and electric prods were inserted into the anuses or vaginas of victims. Some prisoners claimed that relatives and friends had been tortured in order to exact information or a confession from the prisoner.

Under increasing pressure from the political opposition, the acting Prime Minister, Naim Talu, announced in November 1973 that the government would investigate the allegations: officials of the Justice, Interior, and Defence Ministries were appointed as well as members from the secret police to carry out the investigation. Mr Talu rejected the proposal to appoint an impartial investigative commission on the grounds that it would imply that the state was weak if it could not properly investigate itself. It was not surprising that when the findings were reported in January 1974, the governmental agencies were cleared of all charges. Amnesty International responded to this official apologia, saying that the government's self-vindication 'demonstrates the necessity of conducting completely independent inquiries'. Amnesty International called on the government to submit its findings to the Human Rights Commission of the Council of Europe for an independent evaluation.

The lengthy political crisis ended in January when a coalition government was formed between the left-centre Republican Peoples Party and the right-wing Islamic nationalists, the National Salvation Party. The new Prime Minister was Mr Bulent Ecevit of the RPP, who had been the first Turkish politician to charge publicly that torture was being used. He soon pushed through Parliament an amnesty bill that had been a part of his party's election program the preceding October. Designed to free all political and criminal offenders, the bill was abridged by parliament when 20 members of the NSP refused to support the section granting freedom to political prisoners. In May 1974 approximately 46,000 criminals left Turkish prisons but over 1,000 political prisoners were kept in detention. The RPP then argued before the Constitutional Court that the exclusion of political prisoners from the amnesty was illegal. They won their case, and in July 1974 the political prisoners who were not accused of acts of violence went free.

A serious problem regarding torture remains. Although the central civilian government under Mr Ecevit has demonstrated a will to end torture, the government has sometimes been unable to control individual police and military commanders. Before the majority of political prisoners were released, there were numerous allegations of irregular but frequent brutality in the prisons during 1974. The most widely publicised incident occurred at Mamak Military Prison, Ankara, on 31 May 1974, when military guards assaulted and severely injured about a dozen handcuffed political prisoners who were being taken to court for trial. An Amnesty International delegate who visited Turkey in July (after the release of these same prisoners) learned that three men accused of perpetrating the incident at Mamak had been moderately disciplined: one doctor temporarily had his license revoked; according to the prison authorities, two military officers were transferred (although several prisoners said that the officers were moved from inside to outside the prison).

At the time of this writing Amnesty International is aware of, but cannot assess, charges against the Turkish Armed Forces that stem from the Turkish invasion of Cyprus in July 1974 and from the detention of Greek Cypriot civilians and military personnel. Several times United Nations relief convoys were denied access to these detainees.

EASTERN EUROPE AND THE SOVIET UNION

Since the death of Stalin, attitudes towards torture have considerably changed in Eastern Europe and the Soviet Union. Until then, the use of torture had been condoned and encouraged in Russia and also in the countries of eastern Europe. Indeed, one of the few extant directives from a national authority on the use of torture came from Stalin. His Central Committee circular telegramme in code to the secretaries of Party Committees and to the heads of the NKVD organisation of 20 January 1939 formally confirmed the use of torture: 'The Party Central Committee explains that application of methods of physical pressure in NKVD practice is permissible from 1937 on, in accordance with permission of the Party Central Committee... It is known that all bourgeois intelligence services use methods of physical influence against the representatives of socialist proletariat and that they use them in the most scandalous forms. The question arises as to why the socialist intelligence service should be more humanitarian against the mad agents of the bourgeoisie, against the deadly enemies of the working class and of the collective farm workers. The Party Central Committee considers that physical pressure should still be used obligatorily, as an exception applicable to known and obstinate enemies of the people, as a method both justifiable and appropriate' (The Secret Speech by Krushchev to the 20th Party Congress in Moscow, 1956).

Krushchev's speech to the 20th Party Congress, and the uprising in Hungary in 1956, marked a watershed. The crimes committed under Stalin were revealed; the concept of 'socialist legality' — adherence to the letter of the law — was developed, so as to make life safer and more stable for the rulers and the ruled. Though prison conditions and the rights of the prisoners detained on political charges in Eastern Europe and the Soviet Union may still be in many cases unsatisfactory, torture as a government-sanctioned, Stalinist practice has ceased. With a few exceptions (see below) no reports on the use of torture in Eastern Europe have been reaching the outside world in the past decade. With the exception of Yugoslavia, all the Communist countries of Eastern Europe have clauses in their constitutions guaranteeing the inviolability of the person, and thus prohibit the use of torture. Nevertheless the rights guaranteed in the constitution are not always enjoyed in practice. This is partly the outcome of authoritarian governments limiting the exercise of civil rights. It should, however, be added that the Communist governments have always placed a higher priority on economic advancement than on the protection of the rights of the individual.

Albania, Hungary, Poland, Czechoslovakia

Amnesty International has received no allegation of torture from Hungary, Poland or Czechoslovakia in the past ten years. In the case of Albania, allegations of torture were made, but were neither investigated nor confirmed. They concerned some of the prisoners who had been arrested for Yugoslav sympathies when Albania broke with President Tito in 1948, for sympathies with Krushchev's drive against Stalinism after 1956, and, finally, for pro-Moscow attitudes when Albania moved from the Russian to the Chinese side, during the Sino-Soviet dispute, in 1961. The paucity of information on the treatment of political prisoners in Albania has been somewhat relieved by the 1962 Report to the Consultative Assembly of the Council of Europe (Doc. 1943), which stated that some 25,000-30,000 men and women were held in Albanian camps and prisons; four years later, the Free Albania Committee in New York alleged that 16,000 prisoners were still held, 5,600 of them in labour camps.

German Democratic Republic

In the German Democratic Republic, it was estimated, in 1960, that there were about 12,000 political prisoners. An amnesty in October 1964 released some 10,000 prisoners held on both criminal and political charges. In 1966, it was thought that 6,000-8,000 political prisoners was a realistic estimate. In the course of the second major amnesty which lasted from November 1972 till January 1973, about 31,000 prisoners of both kinds were released, 2,000 of them to the West.

The flow of people and information has therefore been reasonably good, and many former political prisoners now living in the West have sent reports to Amnesty and other organisations in recent years about their treatment during interrogation and in prison. In two instances, Amnesty International has received allegations in the form of personal statements of extreme brutality, by the warders, during pre-trial detention. In one of the statements made in January 1973, referring to an incident early in 1971, it is said that '... during my unjust arrest I did not eat or drink for 43 days. For 124 days I was imprisoned in a dark room. There I was, among other things, crucified to iron bars for ten days (with cuffs on hands and feet). Once I was beaten and ill-treated, so that I lost a lot of blood and collapsed in the pool of blood. I believed that I was going to die and wrote with my blood the words "Liberty, justice and humanity" on the walls of the cell. Then I lost consciousness.'

Though Amnesty International has not conducted an investigation into these allegations, they clearly relate to acts of brutality in particular prisons or by one particular person: treatment of prisoners varies from one institution to another, and appears to depend on the warders themselves. They are mostly recruited from the police force.

Romania

In Romania, until the amnesty in 1964, interrogation methods in the period between arrest and trial appear to have been intended to elicit a statement admitting participation in activities aimed at the security of the state, as well as implicating other people in such activity. It was alleged that during the period before 1964 physical and psychological torture had been used, and that a number of people had died as a result of torture. Since then, however, Amnesty International has received no further allegations of torture from Romania.

USSR

The Constitution of the USSR, presently under revision, guarantees basic civil and political rights. In order to adhere to the principle of socialist legality, the Penal Code has been amended during the 1960s to restrict the rights guaranteed by the Constitution. The authorities, through the KGB, the security police, are thus able to arrest, charge and convict political and religious dissidents through normal legal procedures. The decision to bring a detainee to trial assures a guilty verdict: an acquittal in the case of a political charge has never been known to Amnesty.

The chief source of information on political imprisonment in the USSR for Amnesty is *samizdat* publications (unofficially produced and distributed manuscripts), the most important of these being the *Chronicle of Current Events*, the bi-monthly human rights journal which appeared regularly for four years (1968-72). The documentation is detailed with many accurate references and has been corroborated by recent emigrés to the West. The accuracy of the material has never been questioned by the Soviet authorities themselves. Amnesty accepts its authenticity.

According to this information, the physical conditions of pre-trial detention are extremely poor. The prisoner is also held in complete isolation without any contact with the outside world, except in special cases, and subjected to extensive interrogation. The limit of detention is nine months, but this can be extended indefinitely, apparently by decrees (unpublished) of the Presidium of the Supreme Soviet. The verdict is a foregone conclusion, and defence lawyers, who must in practice, though not in law, have special permits in order to act in cases of political charges, are, with a few notable exceptions, reluctant to conduct a vigorous defence. Their clients are often advised to plead guilty and to base their defence on an appeal for a mild sentence. Although there have been allegations of physical and mental brutality, physical torture as an administrative practice does not appear to occur in the prisons.

The conditions in the labour camps vary in accordance with the different camp regimes laid down by law. Political prisoners are in most cases sentenced to imprisonment under the two harshest regimes, strict and special. Although conditions in all regimes are generally very bad, in the strict and special regimes the worst factor is the constant hunger: prisoners are kept on a starvation diet while being required to do hard physical labour and to fulfil their work norms. Punishment for a prisoner can also take the form of a reduction in his diet. These circumstances combined with the total inadequacy of medical treatment have led to the death of several inmates, and there are also instances of suicide and self-mutilation by desperate prisoners. As hunger is thus used as a deliberate instrument to destroy the physical and psychological morale of the prisoner, the diet may be considered to be a form of torture. (This problem will be dealt with in full in a report by Peter Reddaway for the International Committee for the Defence of Human Rights in the USSR, Brussels. Early in 1973 the same author and the same Institute published a preliminary report entitled 'The Forced Labour Camps in the USSR Today: An Unrecognised Example of Modern Inhumanity'.) According to information from the sources referred to above, torture does represent a component of the treatment of political prisoners detained in prison psychiatric hospitals for indeterminate periods. The psychological and physical treatment they receive in these institutions appears to constitute torture as an administrative practice. The psychiatric confinement of dissenters was widely practised in the early 1950s, after which a government commission investigated the problem and called for radical re-organisation. Since 1965, however, there has been increasing evidence of the re-emergence of this practice.

The main administrative instrument in this practice is the Serbsky Institute of Forensic Psychiatry in Moscow. Although it is officially administered by the Ministry of Health, the director (Dr G.V. Morozov), Professor D.R. Lunts, and other of the doctors are widely believed to take orders from the KGB (the Soviet security police). The prison mental hospitals come under the jurisdiction of the Ministry of Internal Affairs; there has been a small number of dissenters interned in ordinary mental hospitals, which come under the Ministry of Health. At the moment there are 46 cases of political prisoners in mental hospitals known to Amnesty. These are in special psychiatric hospitals in

Moscow, Leningrad, Chernyakhovsk, Oryol, Kazan, Dnepropetrovsk and Sychovka; there is now a move to transfer political prisoners to more remote places so that they will have even less contact with relatives and the outside world.

There are two legal procedures for forcible commission to psychiatric hospitals. The Directives on Immediate Hospitalisation issued in 1961 allow for the immediate commitment of a person under civil law, without the consent of patient or relatives, on the basis of the 'social change of the sick person'. This has been used against a small number of dissenters in recent years. The more common procedure is that under criminal law: the person is arrested by the KGB and interrogated for a particular crime, most likely anti-Soviet activity. If the KGB wish to avoid an open trial, perhaps because the prisoner is extremely articulate and would conduct a spirited self-defence, or because his trial might provoke demonstrations, the detainee is sent for diagnosis, usually to the Serbsky Institute. His past is investigated for any indication of psychiatric illness, and his friends and relatives are questioned about his behaviour. Then the court, at a closed trial, at which even the defendant is unable to be present, endorses the Institute's recommendations. Once committed, the patient is examined every six months by a commission, but the recommendations of experts outside the Serbsky Institute are often over-ruled by the courts.

The advantages to the State in committing dissenters to special or prison mental hospitals were pointed out by the Moscow based Action Group for the Defence of Human Rights in the USSR. This method: (1) guarantees the complete secrecy of the trial and deprives the accused of the opportunity to defend himself personally in court; (2) permits the most thorough isolation of troublesome persons without limitation of the period of isolation; (3) allows the use of medical methods of influencing the minds of dissenters; and (4) discredits these people and their ideas. When the Soviet authorities have been approached about this question by Amnesty groups and Western psychiatrists, they have maintained that the detained are all in need of treatment. However, a number of diagnostic reports have been studied by Western clinical psychiatrists and experts in forensic psychiatry, and their conclusion is that there are no apparent clinical bases for the diagnoses of schizophrenia and other mental disorders. In the Soviet Union itself, where doctors have produced evidence of psychiatric normalcy, these recommendations are always overruled and the diagnosis of the Serbsky Institute is accepted. There is evidence that dissenting voices within the Soviet psychiatric profession are intimidated or suppressed: in 1972, a Kiev psychiatrist who criticised the diagnosis of a political dissident was sentenced to seven years' strict regime in a labour camp and three years' exile. The diagnosis of mental illness coincides with the expression of ideological and political dissent; it is made clear to the patient himself that in order to be 'cured' he must renounce his political convictions.

Information on the conditions in the mental hospitals is available from reports in the *Chronicle of Current Events*, through letters from inmates and from the testimony of former patients. The political prisoners are kept in crowded wards with insane inmates, where they are constantly exposed to violent and aggressive patients, or in solitary confinement. Beatings and humiliations are frequent; the staff are often recruited from the police and patient population. The worst aspect of the treatment received in mental hospitals is, according to the political prisoners themselves, the use of drugs. These include aminazin (chlorpromazine/largactil), which causes depression and rigours; sulfazine (1% sterile solution of purified sulphur in peach kernel oil), which causes the temperature to rise to 40°C — this results in local reactions, such as abscesses, and rheumatism of the joints, headaches and weakness; haloperidol (Haloperidol/Serenace); triftazin (Trifluoperazine/Stelazine) and other drugs. The administration of these drugs is accompanied by threats that their intellectual and creative powers will be taken from them by the other types of punishment which the prisoner might receive on some pretext. In the 'roll-up' the patient is rolled from head to foot in wet canvas so tightly that it is difficult for him to breathe. As it dries, the canvas becomes even tighter. Patients are also strapped to their beds for several days without any provision for sanitation. Medical treatment for those in need has also been reported by former inmates of the asylums to be quite inadequate.

THE AMERICAS

In Latin America — though generalisations about such a large area tend to disguise differences as between particular countries — police brutality and harsh prison conditions have long been a traditional and largely accepted part of the social structure. Peasants, when detained by the local police, could expect to be beaten; and conditions have been little better in the national and urban prisons. Nevertheless, there is a marked difference between traditional brutality, stemming from historical conditions, and the systematic torture which has spread to many Latin American countries within the past decade. Costa Rica is the only country in Latin America from which Amnesty International has received no torture allegations of any kind within the past year. In Argentina, Bolivia, Brazil, Colombia, Mexico, Paraguay, Uruguay and Venezuela, there have been demands for national or international investigations into allegations of torture. In some other countries (as, for instance, the Dominican Republic, Guatemala and Haiti) the institutional violence and high incidence of political assassinations has tended to overshadow the problem of torture.

Latin American constitutions contain ample safeguards against the use of torture. Almost every constitution has a clause condemning the use of cruel or degrading treatment, while the majority of constitutions mention specifically the illegality of torture. There are also hypothetical safeguards within the provisions of international organisations (as the Organisation of American States), although at the time of writing only two countries (Costa Rica and Colombia) have ratified the Inter-American Convention of Human Rights. Yet within the past few years, few Latin American governments have paid more than lip service to their constitutions. Almost every country has experienced either an 'unconstitutional' military government or a state of siege or emergency during this period. Other countries, such as Cuba, have governments that tolerate no political opposition. Countries which claim to be constitutional democracies have specially trained security forces to combat organised 'subversion'.

It is possible to analyse the chain of events that have led to increased intervention of the military in civilian life, and a subsequent increase in the use of torture. Gross inequalities of land and income distribution have given rise to militant opposition. To counter this the military budget, often sponsored by generous US aid programmes, has grown substantially within the past decade. Some of the aid funds have been used to modernise the technical equipment of the police, the army and the special security forces.

In reading this report, it is essential to emphasise that we are frequently dealing with allegations that we have had little opportunity to investigate in detail. This applies both to the administrative practice (ie. where almost *anyone* can expect to be tortured immediately upon detention) and countries where torture may be considered exceptional. In addition, we emphasise where allegations are too few or too general to merit a firm statement. We also mention cases where there have been enquiries into the use of torture, by either governmental or non-governmental bodies.

Much has been written recently about the 'internationalisation' of torture methods, with frequent reference to Latin America. Allegations have ranged from claims that Brazilian and US personnel are present at torture sessions in Latin American countries (as Bolivia, Paraguay and Uruguay) to claims that there are special 'torture schools' in Brazil attended by security personnel from other Latin American countries, and claims that torture equipment is imported directly from other countries. Owing to the very general nature of such allegations, and the lack of specific evidence, Amnesty International is unable to make any definitive comment on them. It has, however, been frequently reported that the USA has financed and organised anti-subversive training courses for Latin American police units in Panama. It is also known that, despite amply documented denunciations made by a number of organisations including the US Catholic Conference and members of Congress, the US Government has never publicly condemned the use of torture in either Brazil or Uruguay. In financing and equipping the police and armies of governments that have used torture, it can be argued that the USA bears a contributory responsibility for the methods used by those governments.

The United States

The Eighth Amendment to the Constitution of the United States of America provides that 'cruel and unusual punishments (shall not) be inflicted'. The use of torture in any phase of the criminal process is illegal and there is no evidence of any authoritatively sanctioned pattern of violations of this law. But allegations of police brutality or harsh treatment of prisoners by prison guards abound. The veracity of some of these allegations must be presumed. Certainly, Amnesty has evidence that some of its own adopted prisoners have been subjected to harsh and brutal treatment by the guards of the prisons where they have been detained.

Thus Martin Sostre, convicted of the illegal sale of heroin and still in prison, despite the recantation of the chief witness against him and the suspension and indictment, on drug charges, of the chief police witness against him, has been subjected to degrading anal searches both before and *after* such searches were declared unconstitutional in a court case brought by Sostre against New York State. In the latter case, his refusal to submit to such a search and his resistance to it has resulted in his being charged with the felony of assaulting prison officers. In principle, he could sue the officers for such assault, but it is very difficult, in the setting of a prison, to discharge the heavy burden of proof that a convicted criminal must shoulder to be believed against officers of the state.

In the case of black prisoners, there is sometimes a racial component to such treatment. On one occasion, for example, a fight broke out in the prison yard of the US Penitentiary of Terre Haute, Indiana, between two inmates, one black and one white. Only the black inmate was led away to be disciplined. A crowd of 200 blacks gathered to protest. Among them was an Amnesty prisoner, Arthur Banks Burghardt, a black, activist playwright who had received a savage five-year sentence for refusal of induction into the armed forces. After the protest, he was summoned to the office of the prison warden and refused to go. The guards used rubber truncheons and chemical spray on him. He was charged with assault of the guards.

The tendency of the authorities to believe and support government employees as against detainees no doubt provides an incentive to such (mis)behaviour. Also, the practice of isolating 'troublemakers' in segregated units (solitary confinement, the 'hole' etc.) can have lasting psychological effects on those so confined. Both Sostre and Burghardt have been subjected to the 'hole'.

It should not be forgotten that the attitude of the political authorities may set the tone for the kind of 'discipline' meted out in prisons. In this connection, the Report of the McKay Commission on the 1971 massacre at New York's Attica prison may painfully be recalled. There was a riot against what the report called the 'petty humiliations and racism that characterise prison life'. (Most of the inmates are blacks or Puerto Ricans.) Despite pleas, the Governor of New York State refused to make an appearance. The subsequent police assault on the prison left 10 guards and 33, mostly minority group, inmates dead — killed by the police. It was, said the report, 'the worst bloodletting of Americans by Americans since the Civil War'. No killings were committed by the prisoners. Yet after the assault the prisoners were subjected to 'vengeful reprisals' by the prison authorities, according to the report. The report recommended that the whole criminal justice system be 'purged of racism' and 'restructured to eliminate the strained and dishonest scenes now played out daily in our courtrooms'.

Particularly disturbing are reports of the involvement of American troops in direct torture during the Indochina war. The pattern of an officially approved standard of criminal behaviour appears. On this, see the section on Vietnam.

Nevertheless, it should be emphasised that judicial remedies exist for complaints against inhuman or degrading treatment, even though their effectiveness may sometimes make them appear illusory to the complainants. It would be incorrect to suggest that there is an administrative practice of torture by the law enforcement authorities of the United States within their own domestic jurisdiction.

Argentina

Amnesty International has received no allegations of torture from Argentina since the government of President Campora took over in May 1973. This section concentrates on allegations of torture that have reached us during the previous military governments.

Information about widespread and sophisticated torture methods in Argentina has been collected by international organisations including the World Council of Churches and the International Commission of Jurists. A delegate for the World Council of Churches, who visited Argentina at the end of 1972, stated that it was now taken for granted that torture was the first stage in all interrogations. Evidence has also been collected and divulged by several Argentine organisations, including federations of lawyers, doctors and psychiatrists, and members of the Church. There have been numerous allegations in the press, and even the most conservative newspapers have expressed their scepticism at repeated governmental promises to investigate allegations of torture.

Though torture has been denounced in Argentina for many years, it appears that systematic torture has increased rapidly during the military governments of the past decade. As in other countries, a vast campaign against the several guerrilla movements can be considered the fundamental cause. However, though guerrillas and guerrilla suspects may have been the chief targets, torture appears to have been used indiscriminately against political and common prisoners from all sectors in attempts to extract confessions. Allegations of types of torture are many and varied. According to the documentation received by Amnesty International alone, as many as 73 different methods of torture have been used within the past ten years. The most common methods are the *picana* — electric prod — (which the Argentine Police apparently claim to have invented), the 'telephone' (consisting of beating from behind, and beating on both ears, thus causing temporary or permanent deafness) and also a version of the notorious *pau de arara* or parrot perch (a combination of hanging, near-drowning in filthy water, and multiple electric shocks).

Almost all branches of the Federal and Provincial police, the armed forces and the special security forces have been implicated in torture, not to mention many paramilitary groups which have acted with the alleged complicity of the government. The complicity of many doctors during interrogation has also been mentioned. It would be impossible to define any one branch as the most culpable, although the massacre of 16 captured guerrillas at the naval base in Trelew in 1972 helped to give the navy a reputation for extreme brutality. Some of the most serious allegations have been made against a *loggia* (Secret Society) called the Halcones, formed from a group of cadets from the Military College, School of Aeronautics and Naval Military School. The Halcones, led and organised by high-ranking military officers, were reputed to have some of the most refined torture equipment in the world.

Officially, the Argentina government had consistently denied the existence of torture. Unofficially, it appears that governmental reactions were somewhat more equivocal when government members were confronted by well-informed lawyers and journalists. The Minister for the Interior was quoted as saying that tortures, though existent, were not sufficient to constitute a system. No governmental, police or military organisation ever responded to the demands for investigations that were so frequent during the military government of General Lanusse.

Bolivia

Since the government of General Hugo Banzer Suarez came to power after the military coup of August 1971, a campaign of systematic terror has been launched against left-wing, particularly Communist, opponents of the regime. An estimated 2000 political prisoners have been detained at one time or other since the coup, and a further 5000 have been forced into exile.

There have been numerous allegations of torture. Early in 1973, 99 members of the Bolivian Church published a document entitled 'Evangelism and Violence' denouncing the 'physical and morally degrading tortures, including the rape of some women prisoners, as a systematic means of forcing declarations or so as to satisfy sadistic instincts'. In May 1973 the Bolivian Catholic Church's Commission for Justice and Peace issued a document stating that about 20 people had died in prison as a result of maltreatment, and named several of those who had died. International associations, including the International Association for Democratic Lawyers, have publicly condemned torture and arbitrary assassinations in Bolivia.

An anonymous document smuggled out of Bolivia in 1972 (believed by Amnesty International to be impartial and accurate, because of its close correspondence with other information that has reached us) denounced the use of several types of torture, similar to those so common in Brazil.

According to the information from this and other documents, most tortures are carried out shortly after arrest, in the DIC (Departmento de Investigaciones Criminales) in La Paz, and in the buildings of the Ministry of the Interior itself: also in the so-called Security Houses (Casas de Seguridad) which are often private houses rented directly by the Ministry of the Interior for the purpose of torture. High-ranking officers of the Ministry of the Interior are reported to have personally assisted at torture sessions.

Prisoners have also been beaten to death in Achocalla and other prisons, notably in the town of Santa Cruz. While torture has generally been used to extract information and confessions, prisoners have also been beaten to death from the desire to eliminate political opponents of the regime (particularly members of the National Liberation Army). Other prisoners have been machine-gunned to death.

In 1972 and 1973 a number of torture testimonies have appeared in the international press in both North and South America and in Europe. Amnesty International has frequently received letters denouncing the use of torture, and Amnesty representatives have interviewed ex-prisoners who have shown marks which are apparently the result of tortures.

The Bolivian government has denied the use of torture as administrative practice. Nevertheless when Colonel Andres Selich died after brutal treatment at the hands of his interrogators in May 1973, the Minister of the Interior admitted that he was beaten to death by his guards (*Presencia*, May 1973). Initially, the Minister of the Interior issued a statement admitting the true circumstances, and immediately tendered his resignation. Both statements were reported in the Bolivian newspaper *Presencia*. The Bolivian government is to hold an official enquiry into the circumstance of Selich's death. Prominent Bolivian citizens, including members of the Bolivian Commission for Justice and Peace, have demanded similar enquiries into the cases of the many other individuals who allegedly died after torture.

Brazil

Following the 1964 coup which brought the present military regime to power, Amnesty International received countless reports of the torture of political prisoners in Brazil. Reports escalated after the enactment of Institutional Act No. 5 in 1968, which severely curtailed remaining civil liberties in Brazil and strengthened the penalties for those accused of crimes against the very braodly defined 'national security'.

Items received included letters and affidavits from several sources in Brazil, testimony from ex-political prisoners in exile, and repeated reports by the Brazilian and international press that torture had been used. These reports, unofficial visits to Brazil by Amnesty sympathisers, and also statements by innumerable international and church organisations such as the Brazilian Council of Bishops, the International Commission of Jurists, and the Organisation of American States,* led Amnesty to attempt to arrange a mission to Brazil to investigate allegations of torture. Approaches to the Brazilian Embassy in London were made over a period of two years; despite these approaches, official permission to carry out an on-the-spot investigation was not granted.

Consequently, in 1972 Amnesty prepared and published the document *Report on Allegations of Torture in Brazil* based on material available in Europe and North America

---

* The OAS stated in May 1971 that 'because of the difficulties that have hindered examination of this case, it has not been possible to obtain absolutely conclusive proof of the truth or untruth of the acts reported in the denunciations (of torture). However, the evidence collected in this case leads to the persuasive presumption that in Brazil serious cases of torture, abuse and maltreatment have occurred to persons of both sexes while they were deprived of their liberty.'

including depositions and letters from prisoners subjected to torture, accounts by eye-witnesses, lawyers, journalists, churchmen and press reports. The documents cited clear evidence that at least one prisoner (Odijas Carvalho de Souza) was beaten to death; it cited manifold types of torture including physical, mental and sexual abuse (with prisoners often being forced to watch the torture of friends and family members).

The report was supplemented by an appendix listing the names of 1081 persons reported to have been tortured, with cross-references to indicate the multiple sources of information. A second appendix listing the names of 472 persons allegedly responsible for torture was separately published for confidential submission to the Brazilian government, other government officials and selected international organisations. Despite our official submission of the report and its appendices to the Brazilian government before publication, the only response was a new press law forbidding publication of Amnesty statements on Brazil, and the government made no move towards instituting an enquiry into the allegations.

Since the publication of the report in September 1972 we have received several further allegations and a number of new testimonies have been collected in Chile. During 1973, Brazilian Church officials have been particularly outspoken in denouncing the torture and unexplained deaths of political prisoners.

We can say that torture is widespread and that it can be said to constitute administrative practice. It appears to be used in the majority of interrogations, even against people detained for a short period of time or 'rounded up' in 'sweep' arrests and held because they lacked the necessary identification papers. Motives appear to be the extraction of information and confessions, and intimidation of potential dissidents. Though it has often been claimed that torture takes place under the least stable regimes, the recent escalation of torture in Brazil appears to belie this; the systematisation of torture seems to reflect the Brazilian authorities' desire to quell what they see as a constant threat from international and internal 'subversion'.

Torture is carried out by a number of branches of the

armed forces (Army, Navy and Air Force) all of which have their own interrogation centres; and by various political police and interrogation bodies directed by the Department for Public Safety in each federal state. The state bodies are in turn responsible to the National Secretary for Public Safety. Special security units, incorporating federal military personnel along with police officials, have been formed to crush guerrilla groups – the most notorious being Operacao Bandeirantes in São Paolo, which has allegedly been infiltrated by the right-wing terrorist organisation, the 'Commando to hunt Communists' (CCC).

Prisoners can pass through several stages of interrogation, and may be tortured by more than one body before charges have been formulated. Once a prisoner has 'confessed' a case can be formulated against him; if he retracts the 'confession' at any stage in the judicial proceedings, he can be returned to an interrogation centre for further maltreatment. There are also reports of torture in the prisons, for the amusement of the guards, or the intimidation of those who have tried to organise protests or send out information denouncing torture.

Torture and assassinations have also been carried out by unofficial paramilitary groups formed of off-duty policemen (such as the notorious 'Death Squad'), which take it upon themselves to rid society of petty criminals and sexual deviants as well as suspected political activists.

The official position of the Brazilian government on torture has repeatedly vacillated from total denial of its existence to maintaining that, if it ever took place, it no longer occurs; to admitting that it may occur in isolated instances and is carried out by local police officers who exceed their authority. Official reports contend with ludicrous frequency that those who have died in custody were 'run down by motor vehicles', or shot while trying to escape, or died of natural causes. Protest and discussion abroad (particularly the May 1971 hearings of the United States Congressional Sub-Committee on Aid to Brazil which raised allegations of US involvement in torture) have been debated in the Brazilian parliament. Nevertheless the Brazilian government has consistently maintained that reports of torture published abroad are part of a co-ordinated campaign against Brazil. Occasionally, military officials or persons accused of torture have been dismissed, in efforts to refurbish Brazil's damaged reputation. However, dismissals are often more closely related to internal political struggles than to a genuine effort to control torture. In the two trials of alleged torturers which have taken place, top officials tend to escape condemnation or to receive lighter sentences than their subordinates. The tortures, and the very existence of the Death Squads, are officially denied by the government, although policemen have been sentenced for crimes allegedly committed by them (for example, Geraldo Georginodas Neves, a former policeman, was sentenced to 31 years imprisonment in São Paolo in May 1973, when found guilty of two 'executions' of petty criminals). At the same time Reuters estimated the number of victims of the 'non-existent' Death Squads as 1300.

Colombia

After a civil war of unprecedented violence in the 1940s and the 1950s, in which an estimated 200,000 lives were lost, Colombia has been subjected to a state of siege for almost all of the past 20 years. Special powers have been given to Security Forces (the DAS — Departamento Administrativo de Seguridad — and the F2) to combat 'subversion'. The increased activities of the three guerrilla organisations in Colombia (particularly the Ejercito de Liberacion Nacional — ELN) have been countered by severe anti-guerrilla operations.

Allegations of torture have been of two major kinds. First, several Colombian organisations and leading Colombian newspapers have denounced brutality by the local police and rural DAS against peasants, claiming that peasants have been severely beaten, have had acid poured over them, and have been threatened with execution, in attempts to extract confessions. The Asociación Nacional de Usuarios Campesinos — ANUC — has sent documents to international human rights organisations, denouncing the torture and assassination of indigenous people by the rural DAS and the armed forces. To these allegations, the Colombian government has responded that the activities of the DAS — albeit involving deaths — are the product or logical consequence of the disruption of public order in the areas concerned.

The second type of allegation has concerned systematic torture in interrogation techniques used by the DAS on political prisoners (notably those accused of having links with the Liberation Armies). In August and September 1972 Colombian newspapers (particularly *El periodico*) published a series of articles about physical and psychological tortures used by the Colombian military police and secret service. *El Periodico* published the declarations made by political prisoners then awaiting trial and provided sketches with details of torture techniques. This newspaper also published a statement by several Colombian federations denouncing the use of fifteen types of torture against the prisoners.

After this wide publicity, the defence lawyers classified the denunciations and presented a petition before the Attorney General and Colombian Congress. A Debate about Torture was held in Congress in September 1972. After hearing the allegations, the Minister of Defence denied the use of systematic torture and stated that measures would be taken against all who could be proved to have abused their authority.

Amnesty International has been able to study numerous allegations of torture in the Colombian press, and other denunciations made by Colombian prisoners. The consistency of the information received leads us to believe that refined techniques of psychological pressure have been used in attempts to extract information and confessions from guerrilla suspects.

Chile*

Amnesty International had received allegations of torture, in 1969, including the application of electric shocks during interrogation, under the government of President Eduardo Frei (1964-70).

Under the government of President Salvador Allende, which took office in 1970, two further allegations of torture

*For a further discussion of the widespread use of torture in Chile since the coup in September 1973, see the Appendix to this volume, beginning on page 243.

reached us, both documented in the Chilean press. The first denunciation was made by detained members of the National Liberation Army — ELN — and was published in the militant left-wing magazine *Punto Final* in August 1972. The prisoners are alleged to have been submitted to torture including electric shocks, physical beating and partial drowning. A further allegation reached us in February 1973 when two anti-government television workers alleged severe physical tortures in the town of Concepcion. An Amnesty member, who made an independent enquiry, stated that there was evidence of police brutality during interrogation.

Chile

On 11 September 1973, the constitutional government of President Salvador Allende was overthrown by a swift but extremely violent military coup. The coup, the first in 40 years in Chile, came after months of bitter social tension and ended a longstanding tradition of democratic government and non-intervention by the Chilean armed forces in civil and political affairs. In an atmosphere of extreme xenophobia, many thousands of foreign refugees and visitors were imprisoned or expelled; thousands of Chilean civilians lost their lives, either killed during the brief fighting, or executed without trial or after drum-head courts martial within hours of their arrest. An estimated 40,000 Chileans were detained, denounced by neighbours or professional associates, or arrested by the military merely because of the positions they held during the previous government. All pro-Allende newspapers, magazines, radios and other media were closed down; their directors were killed, imprisoned or forced to seek asylum. All political parties that had formed the Popular Unity coalition of the Allende government were outlawed; leaders and militants of these parties were subjected to immediate and bitter persecution. The Central Workers Union (*Central Unica de Trabajadores*) was immediately declared illegal, and the right to strike and the right to freedom of association were terminated. The military immediately assumed administrative powers over the universities and hospitals. Recognised Allende supporters among teachers and students were expelled from the universities, a vast number being detained. Faculties within the universities were closed down. A State of War was declared on September 22nd, drastically limiting civilian freedoms and permitting the military to arrest, interrogate, detain and judge whomsoever it wishes for as long as it wishes, in accordance with the severe penal legislation of the Code of Military Justice in Time of War.

Torture has been common practice during the interrogation of political prisoners; confessions extracted by torture have been considered as admissible evidence by the military tribunals. This widespread use of torture has been documented by a number of international organisations that have carried out investigations in Chile since the coup as well as by foreign diplomats, journalists and lawyers who have observed trials, leading members of the Chilean church, Chilean lawyers, the relatives of political prisoners and (naturally) the ex-prisoners themselves. A delegation from the International Federation of Human Rights, the International Movement of Catholic Jurists, and the International Association of Democratic Lawyers reported on 13 October 1973 that

> ... the delegation that went to Chile interviewed several persons that had been tortured, including a man with cigarette burns on his body, a woman with large blue bruises on her legs, and another woman who had been raped. Of 30 persons who told them of mistreatment of prisoners, some were victims of torture, others had witnessed torture and executions, and others gave second-hand accounts.

The Amnesty International delegation (1-8 November 1973) likewise confirmed individual cases of torture. They personally saw the marks of torture on prisoners then detained in the National Stadium of Santiago, the marks on prisoners who had recently been in the stadium, and those of one woman who had recently been released from a police station where she had been beaten and subjected to electric shocks. Her body showed the marks of recent and severe lacerations.

The Amnesty delegation was also informed by prison guards within the National Stadium that the Brazilian police had assisted in interrogations there and had also given a course in techniques of interrogation at the Ministry of Defence. One member of the delegation saw torture marks on Brazilian prisoners who alleged that they had been tortured by members of the Brazilian police. Officials at the Foreign Ministry vigorously denied that foreign interrogators had been present in Chile. This denial should be evaluated in a wider context of denials. For example, Chilean officials at the Ministry of Defence and Ministry of Interior said that only one case of torture had been brought to their attention although the delegation was informed that officials of the International Committee of the Red Cross had brought many similar cases to the ministries' notice before and during the period of the delegation's stay in Chile.

The Chicago Commission of Enquiry, which visited Chile in February 1974, talked to several prisoners in the *Estadio Chile* in Santiago who still showed the marks of torture. The Chicago Commission also testified to the brutal torture in the special interrogation camp of *Tejas Verdes* north of Santiago. The International Commission of Jurists and other visiting groups of foreign lawyers from Canada, Denmark, Belgium and Argentina, all asserted in April, May and June 1974 that torture was still commonplace during interrogation.

In Chile itself, Cardinal Raul Silva Henriquez issued a public statement in April condemning the 'physical and moral pressure used during interrogation'. His statement was based on a memorandum submitted to him by leading members of the Chilean church which gives the most detailed and accurate evidence to date of individual cases of torture in Chile. The document lists eight centres in the Province of Santiago alone where torture was proved to have taken place. Altogether, it lists 17 different places where severe torture is known to have taken place. The document lists 27 different methods used and describes over 100 cases of torture, including 16 cases where the prisoner died as a result of torture.

The report of the Human Rights Commission of the Organization of American States that was filed with the Chilean government in August 1974 makes it clear that almost a year after the coup, physical and psychological torture continues.

In the first weeks after the coup, no fewer than 45,000 people were detained for political reasons. During interrogation, the majority of the prisoners were kicked, beaten, threatened, and subjected to many kinds of physical and moral pressures. In the National Stadium of Santiago at least 50% of the prisoners were maltreated. In provincial prisons and military barracks prisoners had even less protection. Many were killed, others were forced to stand naked for hours while being continuously beaten with rifle butts. In many of the detention centres, such as the *Estadio Chile* or the boats *Lebu* and *Maipu* anchored off the coast of Valparaiso, physical abuse and physical conditions were appalling. In the first stages, methods of interrogation appear to have been similar everywhere. Prisoners were beaten incessantly by soldiers and asked such questions as 'Where are the arms? Where have you hidden the arms?' The purpose of such brutality appears to have been intimidation, rather than any genuine attempt to extract confessions on which to base criminal charges. After a few days of this treatment thousands of prisoners were released.

Though not *all* prisoners were tortured, all ran the risk of being tortured and were aware that they had no form of judicial protection during interrogation. Within a few weeks of the coup, prisoners began to be transferred from the larger detention centres (Pisagua, Quiriquina, National Stadiums of Santiago and Concepcion) to military centres and schools — 16 of whose names are known to Amnesty International — which were specifically equipped for torture. In some cases torture was used to extract information that could lead to further arrests and thus to the breakdown of the Chilean resistance; in other cases torture was used to extract written confessions that could be used as evidence against the prisoner.

Many people were tortured to death by means of endless whipping as well as beating with fists, feet and rifle butts. Prisoners were beaten on all parts of the body, including the head and sexual organs. The bodies of prisoners were found in the Rio Mapocho, sometimes disfigured beyond recognition. Two well-known cases in Santiago are those of Litre Quiroga, the ex-director of prisons under the Allende government, and Victor Jara, Chile's most popular folk-singer. Both were detained in the Estadio Chile and died as a result of torture received there. According to a recurrent report, the body of Victor Jara was found outside the Estadio Chile, his hands broken and his body badly mutilated. Litre Quiroga had been kicked and beaten in front of other prisoners for approximately 40 hours before he was removed to a special interrogation room where he met his death under unknown circumstances. In other prisons techniques were similar, the degree of brutality depending on the whims of the individual camp commander. There were many cases of burning (with acid or cigarettes), of electricity, of psychological threats including simulated executions and threats that the families of the prisoners would be tortured. At times the brutality reached animalistic levels. Prisoners have been forced to witness or participate in sexual depravities. An unknown number of women have been raped; some of them, pregnant after rape, have been refused abortions. women have had insects forced up their vaginas; pregnant women have been beaten with rifle butts until they have aborted. Prisoners have been forced to eat excrement, have been plunged endlessly into ice-cold water, have had their bones smashed, have been left to stand naked in the sun for many hours. On the boat *Esmeralda*, anchored off the shore of Valparaiso, prisoners were allegedly left naked and tied to the masts of the boat. At times prisoners were forced to witness the torture and death of others. One doctor in the prison camp of Pisagua is said to have been forced to witness the execution of fellow prisoners. Other forms of torture, such as immersion in tanks of petrol or in ice-cold water, are also known to have caused the death of political prisoners soon after the coup.

By the end of October more systematic torture for more specific purposes was used in many places of detention. In the National Stadium rooms were equipped for the application of electricity. In the stadium and in military barracks throughout Chile prisoners were hooded during interrogation for prolonged periods; electricity became a regular tool; female prisoners were subjected to frequent sexual abuse during interrogation.

In recent months the methods of torture have tended to become more uniform. All prisoners have been hooded during interrogation, both to hide the identity of the torturer and to increase the psychological fears of the prisoner. Psychological torture appears to have become more prominent. Prisoners have been threatened that they would be thrown from windows if they did not make the required confessions. They have been subjected to screams in adjacent cells (either genuine sounds of torture or simulated noises to produce the effect of torture); they have been subjected to simulated executions; they have heard threats against their families, and have even been told that relatives were being tortured in adjoining cells. The most common forms of physical torture have been prolonged beating (with truncheons, fists or bags of moist material), electricity to all parts of the body, and burning with cigarettes or acid. Such physical tortures have been accompanied by the deprivation of food, drink and sleep. More primitive and brutal methods have continued to be used. On 19 December one prisoner was found dead, his testicles burned off. He had also been subjected to intensive beating and electricity. One day later another prisoner who died from torture had the marks of severe burns on the genital organs. In January 1974 a hooded prisoner was dragged with his hands bound to his feet; he too had previously been tortured with electricity.

At the end of 1973 the Junta created its own intelligence service, *Directorio Nacional de Inteligencia* — DINA — in order to coordinate the activities of the four separate intelligence services of the armed forces and police. DINA, it was decreed, would be responsible directly to the junta. Even the commanders of the provinces were unable to demand access to detention centres which were under DINA's control in their own provinces. At the beginning of 1974 it was no coincidence that the head of DINA was also the commander of *Tejas Verdes*. It is in *Tejas Verdes* that the largest number of individual cases of torture have been documented, and where there have been the most deaths as a consequence of torture. In *Tejas Verdes* a pregnant woman had electricity applied to her genitals; in *Tejas Verdes* a prisoner died after his legs had been broken and his genital organs had been burned; in *Tejas Verdes* prisoners had been detained for periods of up to 21 days of such repeated sessions of torture.

As a result of international pressure and publicity and of

overtures to the Interior Minister from concerned lawyers and church officials in Chile, *Tejas Verdes* and a number of interrogation centres in Santiago have now been closed. Torture nevertheless continues, and the judicial process provides no safeguards for the victims. This last fact is clear from the report of Dr Horst Woesner, Judge of the Federal Court of West Germany, who observed the Air Force trials on behalf of Amnesty International in May 1974. He reported that when a defence lawyer alleged that his client had been tortured, the court ruled that such allegations constituted political arguments and were therefore inadmissible. At the time of this writing, AI was still receiving reports of prisoners being subjected to electric shock treatment and psychological torture in order to extract confessions.

Many ex-prisoners and observers have alleged that the medical profession has participated directly and indirectly in the torture of political prisoners in Chile since the military coup. Allegations are of two major kinds. The most serious claim is that doctors have attended torture sessions, advising on the physical state of the interrogated. A second charge is that leading members of the medical profession have been aware that the torture of political prisoners has taken place within the Santiago Military Hospital itself, and have at times had the opportunity to visit those prisoners who had been subjected to torture. There appears to be, at the very least, some truth in these allegations. There is considerable evidence that doctors were present during the torture of prisoners in the National Stadium. One doctor who was himself a prisoner for many weeks in the stadium (who was not himself tortured but received statements from a number of prisoners who had been tortured) has asserted that doctors were often present at the sessions.

On the second point, the complicity of some members of the medical profession 'by silence', there can be little doubt. Many prisoners have been treated in military hospitals after suffering torture. One doctor, the former director of the National Health Service for the zones of Cautin and Malleco, died from post-operational anaemia after doctors had operated to repair severe internal lesions caused by torture. Despite their awareness that torture is being used, none of the doctors in positions of responsibility have publicly acknowledged what they have seen.

In quantitative terms the worst period of torture may have passed in Chile. In qualitative terms, the situation must be considered as grave as ever. At the beginning of 1974, General Pinochet is known to have circularised military camp commanders, informing them that reprisals would be taken if the extensive use of torture was not controlled. While attempts may have been made to stem the flow of torture, no steps have been taken to alter the arbitrary powers of those intelligence and security services which have been trained in the use of sophisticated torture techniques (with the aid of Brazilian experts) in their task of eradicating political opposition in Chile.

Cuba

International organisations such as the Inter-American Commission of Human Rights (of the OAS) and the International Commission of Jurists have published reports on Cuba since Castro came to power, including sections on prison conditions and the treatment of prisoners. The ICJ report *Cuba and the Rule of Law*, has mentioned allegations of psychological pressures on prisoners and their families. The IACHR has published two reports on the 'Situation of Political Prisoners and their Families in Cuba'. The information has been gathered from allegations made by Cuban prisoners and their families. In these reports there is a wealth of allegations of physical and psychological torture, executions and simulated executions of prisoners, and inhuman prison conditions. Most of the allegations are gathered from the early 1960s, although the most recent report (of April 1970) includes allegations made up to 1969. Prisoners have alleged that, when they refused to accept the ideological rehabilitation courses imposed by the Cuban government, they were subjected to manifold tortures. The report concluded that the situation of political prisoners in Cuba displayed serious characteristics incompatible with the UN Declaration of Human Rights.

As the Cuban government has consistently refused to accept an international commission of enquiry, it has been impossible to check these allegations. From reports received through usually reliable sources Amnesty International believes that, while there have been strong indications of the torture and assassination of prisoners during the early years of the Castro regime (particularly during the mass arrests of CIA suspects at the time of the Bay of Pigs invasion) conditions have improved at least since 1968. Nevertheless there are still indications that psychological pressures are used in order to break the will of political detainees. Suspected political opponents are handed over to the 'G-2' political police, and may be detained for over a year until they sign confessions (allegedly extracted by psychological torture) that they have committed crimes against the State (usually that of being a CIA agent in the service of North Americans).

Two recent allegations of torture have been given wide publicity. One is that of Pedro Luis Boitel, who died in Castillo-del-Principe prison after a long hunger strike, allegedly after torture by prison guards. The second instance is that of Herberto Padilla, the Cuban poet who was arrested in 1972 and released after 'confessing' to counter-revolutionary ideology. Many western observers assumed that the confession had been extracted from him by psychological pressure and 'brainwashing'. Amnesty International has received no allegations of torture in Cuba during 1973.

Dominican Republic

Information that has reached Amnesty International from many sources suggests that the most elementary human rights have consistently been violated in the Dominican Republic. Although the regime of President Balaguer (president since 1966) is nominally a constitutional democracy, there are clear signs that all political opposition has been bitterly suppressed. After guerrilla invasion in February 1973, an estimated 1500 people were detained, many of them held incommunicado for long periods.

Most of the allegations received in the past have concerned the numerous political assassinations carried out by Death Squads (such as the notorious *La Banda*) that have been openly tolerated and supported by the National Police. In 1970 it was alleged that there was one death or 'disappearance' every

34 hours. There are also allegations that prisoners have died after beatings in the Penitentiary of La Victoria (where political prisoners are usually detained) and the prison of San Francisco de Macoris. Severe physical tortures have been alleged in the Palacio Policial in Santo Domingo (the Servicio Secreto of the national police being held responsible). In these quarters, prisoners have claimed that they were kept naked in filthy underground cells.

In 1971 a Dominican newspaper *El Nacional* published a series of articles about torture in the prisons, asserting that the allegations had been proved beyond doubt. At the end of 1972 a member of a human rights committee, who denounced the torture of political prisoners, was summarily deported from the country. Amnesty has also received photographs of prisoners with severe lesions, allegedly the result of torture. It appears that, while torture techniques such as consistent beatings and nocturnal interrogations have been used by the Servicio Secreto to extract confessions, in the national prison sheer brutality is common practice, often merely to intimidate prisoners.

High-ranking officers in the national police force have frequently been accused of complicity in, and responsibility for, torture. Although the government has never accepted responsibility, a Chief of Police was dismissed in 1971 after accusations had been made against him of cruelty to political prisoners and responsibility for the operations of the Death Squads.

Ecuador

Ecuador has been ruled by a military government since the successful coup of General Guillermo Rodriguez Lara in February 1972. In July 1972, by the Decreto Supremo No. 618, Special Tribunals were set up to judge several types of offence including those of political subversion. Comprising two military judges and one civilian, these Tribunals have been condemned by prominent lawyers and high church officials as not impartial, and in direct contravention of the Universal Declaration of Human Rights.

It has been widely alleged in Ecuador that political prisoners have had confessions extracted from them under torture before they were sentenced by the tribunal. Amnesty has received a testimony from one prisoner, read in the presence of his lawyer, denouncing extreme physical tortures that drove him to the verge of suicide. In November 1972 the Rector of the Central University of Ecuador sent cables to the International Red Cross and the United Nations Human Rights Commission demanding that an international commission should investigate allegations of torture against political prisoners. In May 1973 the National Association of Ecuadorian Law Schools addressed a letter to the national press asserting that the sentences passed on political prisoners by the Tribunal Especial Primero de Quito should be declared invalid, on the grounds that torture had been used to extract confessions.

Mexico

Though Mexico has a tradition of extreme political and social violence, together with intense political brutality (as witnessed in the street massacres of 1968 and 1970) it is only comparatively recently that Amnesty has received allegations of systematic torture carried out by institutions that are responsible to governmental ministries.

Within the past year, we have received allegations of torture contained in letters from prisoners and ex-prisoners (some of them published by the Church both within and outside Mexico). One prominent Church member recently stated that torture was becoming a 'social gangrene' throughout the country.

The growth of systematic torture has been seen as directly linked to the resurgence of guerrilla activities (there are now some 12 guerrilla units), particularly in the province of Guerrero. It has been observed that the Mexican army is not well-trained in counter-insurgency warfare, and has therefore resorted to the cruder technique of seizing and torturing the families of guerrillas and guerrilla suspects. One of the most serious allegations was published in February 1973 when 29 peasants (originally accused of belonging to guerrilla bands) were released after their families had proved their innocence. Though all 29 had previously signed statements admitting their guilt, they later stated that the confessions had been extracted by torture.

Political prisoners, in statements to the Mexican press,

have asserted that torture is carried out in the main interrogation centre, Campo Militar No. 1, by agents of the Direccion Federal de Seguridad which is responsible directly to the Secretary of Government. In an article in the opposition magazine *Porque* in October 1971, one prisoner accused the Secretary of National Defence of complicity in turning the prison into a torture camp. There is no evidence that torture has been used extensively in the main political prison Lecumberri. However, after the death of a prisoner under mysterious circumstances in 1972, the Director of Lecumberri was accused of complicity in torture and homicide.

According to some sources, women have been subjected primarily to mental cruelty, while men, particularly in the military interrogation centre, have suffered the physical tortures so common in Latin America.

In addition to the use of torture during official interrogations, the Mexican press has published reports of paramilitary groups detaining left-wing sympathisers (recently two priests) and subjecting them to severe tortures, including electric shocks; then releasing them. This is a clear use of torture as intimidation.

Paraguay

Paraguay is ruled under a state of siege, declared by Alfredo Stroessner when he came to power in 1954, and renewed every 90 days since then to combat what is officially described as a continuing Communist threat.

In 1966 Amnesty International published a report on prison conditions in Paraguay. The author spent three weeks in Paraguay, interviewing leaders of the three main opposition parties, as well as lawyers, journalists, priests, social workers and persons concerned with the welfare of prisoners. He found that 'there is no doubt at all that torture has been a usual means of extracting confessions, and very often a means of extracting money, from prisoners'. The report noted that torture, often resulting in the death of the prisoners concerned, was carried on in the presence of top Paraguayan police officials. The author also pointed out that the 'medieval' conditions under which the political prisoners were held in small groups of five or ten in cells in numerous *Comisarias* (Police Stations in Asuncion) in themselves led to physical deterioration of the detainees.

The 1966 report took care, however, to place the situation of the political prisoners in proper historical perspective, noting that the continuing disrespect for human rights in Paraguay should be viewed against a background of 150 years of absolute rule by dictator presidents, almost all of whom have seized power in uprisings supported by the army. Although the Constitution does contain certain safeguards of human rights, chronic poverty and lack of educational facilities in the country mean that the down-trodden peasants have little concept of their supposed rights to protection from physical brutality, and from the inhumane prison conditions under which political prisoners are held.

Between the years 1969 and 1971 an Amnesty sympathiser, resident in Paraguay, carried out his own investigation of the situation of political prisoners in Paraguay, and found that much the same conditions continued to prevail. A new report, published by Amnesty International in October 1971, was based on interviews with all sectors in Paraguay including the families of prisoners.

Both Amnesty reports and material received more recently – including reports in Paraguay and abroad, individual denunciations of torture by Paraguayan church figures, and testimonies submitted by released Amnesty prisoners of conscience – not only note continuing torture, but also mention the deaths of persons not formally arrested. Their bound and torture-marked bodies are thrown into the Paraguay and Parana rivers, and are reported with photographs in the Argentinian and Uruguayan newspapers when they wash up on the opposite shore.

In Paraguay, motives for torture are varied since charges of Communism are often used as an excuse for arrest and maltreatment in order to dispose of rivals. The most extreme opponents of the regime are summarily disposed of, so that those who are tortured do not usually represent violent opposition, but may simply be the relatives of suspects or persons whom the government deems it desirable to intimidate. As noted, torture may be used to extract money from the victim.

As regards technique and organisation, the system of torture and repressions is far less sophisticated than that of neighbouring Brazil; yet it is extremely effective in a country like Paraguay with its history of dictatorship, low educational levels and small-town atmosphere.

Torture usually takes place immediately after arrest, during the interrogation stages. Both the Ministry of the Interior and the Department of Crimes and Vigilance in Asuncion carry out torture in their respective centres. Techniques seem to concentrate on physical brutality, although sexual abuse of women prisoners takes place within the Comisarias, and families are also threatened. Torture is frequently witnessed by Army Generals and by a prominent political figure, and is carried out by teams whose members include the mentally deficient and the sexually disturbed.

Once the prisoners have been removed to the Comisarias, conditions vary from police station to police station, with local police chiefs responsible for the treatment given to their own prisoners.

Officially, the government claims that there are no political prisoners, but that those held are rather delinquents responsible for violent acts. The 'violent acts' are never explained, and only two political prisoners have ever been brought to trial. The press is not permitted to engage in open debate on such issues as torture; and although General Stroessner has said that he considers the American Ambassador to be an ex-officio member of his Cabinet, the US has never officially acknowledged or taken steps to prevent the use of torture by a government which appears to be very much within its sphere of influence.

Peru

Police brutality during interrogation of common and political prisoners has allegedly been common practice in Peru for many years. Within the past year, some Peruvian papers have published reports of brutal treatment, after which prisoners have needed hospital care for bruises, broken bones etc.

In 1970 there was a general amnesty for political prisoners, involving many people who had been detained since the early 1960s. Since then, however, there have been new political detentions, mainly involving leaders of labour syndicates and extreme left-wing political parties.

In 1972 Amnesty received personal reports of the severe torture of imprisoned members of the Partido Vanguardia Revolucionaria, in attempts to persuade the prisoners to confess to crimes which they maintain they did not commit. Since May 1973 Amnesty has received allegations of systematic torture of labour leaders, teachers and intellectuals opposed to the government. Allegations stem from conversations with the families of prisoners, and the testimony of the prisoners themselves. After a wave of political strikes in May 1973, over 200 people were detained and taken to the state security division of the Policia de Investigaciones de Peru in Lima for interrogation. There, the prisoners claim to have been subjected to severe physical tortures. The prisoners also report that they were subsequently taken to the Operations Room of the 'Criminal Brigade' headquarters, which is specially equipped for the use of torture.

Although Amnesty has received very few allegations, it appears from the nature of the evidence available that some of these torture techniques (such as near-drowning) are common practice during interrogation of all kinds of prisoners. There is no reason to believe that torture is carried out after the interrogation stage.

We are not aware of any official position taken by the Peruvian government with regard to the use of torture.

Uruguay

Uruguay has traditionally been a country where the rule of law and respect for human rights has prevailed. However, a crisis within the national economy since the mid 1950s has caused serious structural problems which in the early 1960s led to the formation of the urban guerrilla movement, the Tupamaros.

The attempts to control this guerrilla movement and to control civil unrest by force have resulted in an increasing use of torture, which now appears to have become accepted routine procedure after the arrest of a Tupamaro suspect or sympathiser. The purpose of this torture is to extract confessions and to make the prisoner disclose the names of other members of the organisation. Large numbers of citizens who have in no way been involved in violent political opposition have also become victims of arrest and subsequent torture.

An Amnesty delegate, after a visit to Uruguay in 1969, concluded that maltreatment was more common in police quarters than in military barracks, where prisoners were usually treated adequately. Since then, the Armed Forces have become more directly involved in both the political life of the country and counter-insurgency operations and there have been an increasing number of allegations of systematic torture under interrogation in military barracks. However, it is believed that the extent and seriousness of the torture varies considerably from barracks to barracks, depending on the officer in charge. Some officers are reported to be totally opposed to the practice of torture.

As early as 1970' a multi-party Commission of Enquiry, appointed by the Uruguayan Senate, concluded that 'the application of inhumane treatment and torture to persons arrested by the Montevideo Police is common practice'.

The large number of allegations subsequently received from the Uruguayan press and other national bodies – medical, parliamentary, political – corroborated by a few medical affidavits, lead to the conclusion that torture has become even more of an administrative practice. The continued state of emergency and suspension of individual guarantees has allowed prisoners to be held incommunicado for days, weeks and even longer. Naturally, this is the period when most of the maltreatment occurs. Responsibility rests with the Fuerzas Conjuntas (Police and Armed Forces) and, ultimately, the Ministry of Defence.

Methods of torture are similar to those used in other Latin American countries. Blindfolding and hooding the prisoner from the moment of arrest, thus preventing the torturer from being recognised, appear to be routine procedure. Among torture methods that appear to be widely practised, one might mention *el planton* (where the prisoner is kept standing, legs apart, for many hours or even days) and *el submarino* (where the prisoner is roped to a plank before being submerged in water).

In the Uruguayan parliament serious denunciations of torture have persistently been made. One senator also brought to the knowledge of parliament a taped confession by a leading member of the Uruguayan Death Squad. It should however be said that the tape was made while he was held by a group of guerrillas, and probably subject to pressure.

Allegations of torture received by Amnesty now number several hundred cases. There are strong indications that several deaths are the result of torture, while heart-failure has been given as the official cause. Luis Batalla died in a military barracks in May 1972, under extremely suspicious circumstances.

A year later, in another military barracks, Oscar Felipe Fernandez Mendieta died a few hours after his arrest. His medical certificate is signed by three doctors, all in the service of the police or armed forces. The result of their autopsy was heart failure. A subsequent examination of the body by three other doctors showed that the head and the thorax areas were covered with bruises, and the wrists and ankles were badly cut.

Reports allege that advisers from the US and Brazil are training Uruguayan police in counter-insurgency techniques, including methods of torture.

The Uruguayan government has not denied the existence of torture. In 1969 an Amnesty delegate reported that some policemen had been prosecuted on charges of maltreating prisoners; in June 1970, however, the Parliamentary Commission of Enquiry pointed out that some of these officers were still active in the police force. Although some investigations have been ordered into allegations of torture, there has been no serious attempt to curb the practice. Military leaders apparently feel that torture, though regrettable when practised against people later recognised as innocent, is necessitated by the present political circumstances.

Venezuela

During the past year, Amnesty International has received allegations of torture from the Venezuelan press and from individuals who have interviewed political prisoners. In addition a great many political opponents have disappeared under strange circumstances, some while actually under detention. Tortures are allegedly carried out under the supervision of high-ranking officers of the SIFA (Servicio de Inteligencia de las Fuerzas Militares) usually in the so-called 'anti-guerrilla camps' (the most notorious of these being TO4, Cocollar, and TO5, Yumare). There have also been allegations made against the police intelligence units.

In TO5, according to the testimonies we have received, tortures have included: electric shocks through the use of a field telephone, prolonged periods of exposure in a 'tiger-hole', beatings, burnings and simulated executions. Many prisoners are alleged to have died in TO5 Yumare. The tortured people are almost invariably guerrilla suspects. The torturers are military personnel, while it has been reported that 'torture specialists' are sometimes called in from Caracas.

The frequent allegations of torture in Venezuela have given rise to an official inquiry in Congress. After a Commission had investigated the existence of tortures in Yumare, a book was written about conditions in this camp. Continued allegations have led to further calls for official inquiries.

Central America

Costa Rica

Costa Rica has a good reputation in the field of human rights and is the only Latin American country from which Amnesty International has received no allegations of torture.

El Salvador

Amnesty International has little documented information on the existence of torture in the Central American republics, *El Salvador, Honduras* and *Panama*. However, from the allegations received it appears that brutality and maltreatment are more common than systematic and refined methods of torture. Some allegations resemble those received from Guatemala and Nicaragua (see below), such as disappearances and assassinations for political reasons.

The disposal of bodies by throwing them into the sea or into the craters of the volcanoes is a recurrent allegation in Guatemala. In Nicaragua a statement in 1967 indicates this procedure was used to dispose of the body of a prisoner who died in detention following severe torture. In the past year Amnesty International has received allegations of torture in El Salvador on two occasions, July 1972 and February 1973, when a considerable number of students, workers and teachers were arrested for political reasons. Private sources and newspapers report that the torture took place immediately after arrest in order to extract confessions, and was carried out by the Guardia Nacional.

Amnesty appealed to the President to make an impartial investigation but has had no information on the result. Further allegations of torture of members of the Christian Democrat Party led the Congress of El Salvador, in June 1973, to vote for a parliamentary investigation into the methods used by police during interrogation.

Honduras

Amnesty has received no specific allegations of torture in Honduras but we have been informed that brutal treatment is common after arrest.

Panama

The most serious allegations of torture in Panama date from before 1970, when some prisoners are alleged to have died in detention in the penitentiary island of Coiba and in the Carcer Modelo in Panama. The official version of their death as accidental conflicts with statements made by fellow prisoners and press. The bodies are reported not to have been returned to their families. It is also alleged that police were involved in the disappearance in 1971 of a young Colombian priest working among peasants in Panama. There have been recent allegations that one prisoner's confession was extracted under torture in 1972.

Guatemala

For many years, the characteristic feature of Guatemalan political life has been the large number of disappearances of Guatemalan citizens. Amnesty International has an incomplete list of over 300 persons who were reported to have disappeared over a period of 18 months. The information comes from the national and international press, universities and trade-union organisations and private sources.

Dead bodies have been found regularly by the roadside, in deep ravines, or near volcanoes. It is alleged that the bodies are transported by helicopter and thrown into the sea or the crater of the volcanoes, sometimes missing the target. It is invariably reported in the Guatemalan press that they show signs of having been tortured and mutilated before death. It is not known whether the victims are interrogated before being killed or whether the torture forms part of the assassination.

There are strong indications that these abductions are made by terrorist groups of a Death Squad type, including off-duty policemen and military elements among their members. Many of those who disappeared were seized as guerrilla suspects. However, the practice has reached such proportions that the victim may be anyone with known or suspected left-wing sympathies, or even petty criminals.

This practice can be seen as a consequence of the massive anti-guerrilla operations of the 1960s led by the Colonel who later became President of Guatemala. The uncurbed rate of disappearance points to tacit governmental approval and the unofficial involvement of the authorities. The body chiefly responsible is the Policia Judicial (secret police).

The government denies responsibility, and claims that the assassinations are the work of rival gangs. When people disappear, the official explanation is that they have secretly left the country on their own initiative. Investigations ordered by the authorities have, as far as is known, never led to any definitive statements.

Nicaragua

In 1968 an Amnesty delegate wrote a report on the treatment of prisoners in Nicaragua that was presented to the International Conference on Torture, Inhuman and Degrading Treatment held in Stockholm the same year. He wrote: 'Nicaragua has been under the effective jurisdiction of the Somoza family, father and sons, since the early 1930s.

This jurisdiction has been maintained with the aid of violence and terror, including the use of torture on political prisoners.' The specific instances of violence detailed by the report gave an indication of the means generally employed by the Somoza family to maintain their government.

Much of the torture is reported to take place in the Presidential palace itself and in the quarters of the National Guard. A respected newspaperman told how he was made to squat for periods of many hours until he collapsed, and was kept with a bright electric light shining within ten centimetres of his eyes. Other prisoners, with hands and feet manacled, were subjected to near-drowning. Others were caged up in close proximity with cages of wild animals, in the Presidential garden.

The report covers a period from 1956 to 1968. Although Amnesty has not subsequently received specific information, press reports do not indicate any change in governmental policy towards political opponents. The country is now ruled by a triumvirate, but the effective power lies with General Anastasio Somoza, now serving as head of the National Guard.

The current detention system recalls South African practice and is a form of mental torture: when a prisoner has served the six months without trial provided for by law, he is allowed out of prison — only to be re-arrested immediately.

Haiti

Under the dictatorial rule of Dr Duvalier (1957-71) political prisoners in Haiti were subject to arbitrary detentions without recourse to any judicial machinery. Despite concerted efforts to improve Haiti's image abroad after Dr Duvalier's death, the only significant change has been a more open conflict between the contestants within the old power structure.

It has long been known that torture is common practice in Haiti but as there is no judicial machinery, nor a free press, nor prison-visits by family or lawyer, few details have been available. As a result of this repressive climate the few prisoners who have been released have been reluctant to speak, even in exile, for fear of retaliation against their families.

Although the death of a prisoner is not announced even to his family, it is known that the death rate in Haitian prisons is high, due to maltreatment and prison conditions that can be described as a daily torture. Prisoners are reported to have been kept naked in underground dungeons for years, in complete darkness. Mutilation, castration, starvation, introduction of a hot iron in the anus, are methods of torture denounced by prisoners who have recently been released and exiled.

Torture is practised in an attempt to identify any sign of political dissent, and to deter any active opposition. Personal enmity and revenge may also be factors behind maltreatment.

Haiti has long been ruled by individuals rather than institutions, and several of these individuals bear personal responsibility for torture. Duvalier's private security force, the Tonton Macoutes (bogey men) played an important part in the repressive machinery and are reported to have used torture. High-ranking military officials and government ministers have also been implicated.

THE MIDDLE EAST

Although the concept of human rights in the European sense is largely unknown in the Arab World, the protection of the individual — the orphan, the widow, the sick and the aged — has always been provided for and protected under Islamic law. In some Arab countries all justice is administered according to Islamic law, together with traditionally accepted local common law or tribal custom. Where the principles of Islamic law do not explicitly cover a particular situation, the law is administered according to Koranic interpretation and analogy. Corporal punishment, routine ill-treatment and execution are part of this accepted practice; and political crimes are still very largely seen within the context of tribal feuds and are dealt with in the traditional way.

In other Arab countries there exist, alongside the Islamic courts, secular courts based on Western codes of law and these have a wide jurisdiction in civil and criminal matters, while Islamic courts deal purely with personal status matters – marriage, divorce, inheritance etc. In some countries Islamic and secular courts have been amalgamated.

Since the growth of Arab nationalism over the past few decades, and with it the continuing struggle for power between rival factions, internal security has become a fundamental requirement for a country's political stability. And, with worldwide interest and involvement in local Arab politics since the discovery of oil, interested countries outside the Middle East have been instrumental in strengthening police forces, organising state security systems, and introducing new interrogation methods and sophisticated torture techniques.

Despite the provision in many of the constitutions for the protection of the human person from ill-treatment, torture is widely used as a means of interrogation – to extract information and to elicit confessions for use in court and as a method of public persuasion – and as a means of intimidation.

What is not known is to what extent the use of torture in any one country is an administrative policy, and how much the result of individual initiative on the part of prison officers. No country will admit that it is guilty of torturing prisoners. On the other hand, no enquiries or investigations are known to have been made by the authorities concerned.

The difficulties involved in collecting evidence of the use of torture in the Middle East are great: first, because of the acceptance as customary practice of what to Western eyes would be regarded as ill-treatment; secondly, because the intimidating use of torture in a country and the fear of retaliation prevents people from approaching international organisations such as Amnesty; and thirdly, because much of the information that Amnesty has received is questionable, coming as it does from exile groups who are involved in a political struggle against the government concerned.

The following report should be viewed in this context, and the extent of the information on any one country should in no way indicate the extent of the use of torture in that particular country. The fact that a few countries have been omitted – and these are Kuwait, Jordan, Libya, Lebanon, Yemen Arab Republic – is not an indication that torture is not practised there, or that Amnesty has received no allegations of torture, but rather that the evidence is slender. Only in the case of Israel and the Aden Protectorate (now the People's Democratic Republic of Yemen) has Amnesty International investigated and published reports on its findings.

It should be remembered that the legal systems of Iran and Israel are different from the Arab states, and while the availability of documentation on Israel is high — owing to the open nature of the political system of the country — information on the use of torture in Iran is much more difficult to obtain.

Bahrain

An affidavit obtained in 1969 from a former prisoner described his treatment and that of his fellow prisoners in Jidda Island prison during two detention periods from 1964-8. The detainees were trade unionists, strikers, demonstrators and people who opposed the regime, and they all suffered from the appalling prison conditions and diet. The torture inflicted by prison guards was both physical and mental, as prolonged periods of absolute solitary confinement had a serious psychological effect. The author of the affidavit said that, in June 1968, having been beaten by two guards, he was tortured by an intelligence officer and two local policemen during interrogation and, like his fellow detainees, never charged or brought to trial.

All the allegations of ill-treatment date from pre-independence days, though we have reason to believe that the situation with regard to the use of torture has in no way changed since the gaining of independence in 1971.

Egypt

Until the late 1960s the maltreatment and torture of political prisoners was said to have been almost a matter of routine. During 1966 four separate groups of alleged plotters accused of planning to overthrow President Nasser, were arrested — the numbers were estimated at between 4,000 and 20,000. Many were rumoured to have been subjected to the most appalling tortures, and the French newspaper *L'Observateur* reported that one detainee, Salah Khalifa, a nuclear physicist, went insane after torture which included the application of metal bands progressively tightened around the skull.

After the 1967 war with Israel there were reports of Jews having been arrested and maltreated. In January 1973, a book was published describing the experiences of Yair Dori, an Israeli, who was captured by Egyptian soldiers in May 1970 during a raid across the Suez Canal. He was released eleven months later after suffering brutal torture.

However, recent allegations of torture during interrogation appear to be a new departure on the part of the present regime. Despite declared intentions of following a policy of increased liberalisation, Sadat has been consolidating his control over internal and external security, thereby strengthening his own position, which he sees threatened by the growing criticism and restiveness of the country's educated circles. Student unrest at the end of 1972 and the beginning of 1973 was forcefully repressed, and many arrests were made. The French newspaper *Le Monde* reported in April 1973 that twenty-two women, comprising students and intellectuals, held at Barrages near Cairo, had been maltreated; and in May that Nabil Sohi, a left-wing militant, was in a mental hospital at Abbassieh after having been severely tortured, though this allegation was denied by a spokesman for the Egyptian government.

Iran

Iran is a constitutional monarchy. Parliament is theoretically sovereign, but in practice the Crown is the sole source of authority. The Shah is also commander-in-chief of the army. Because of this, opposition within the country and outside is concentrated on criticism of the Shah and his policies.

Some political prisoners may not be members of any political group, illegal or otherwise, but may have simply been associated with a group of friends who discussed politics. In the past few years there has been some guerrilla activity, which has provoked extremely repressive measures by the authorities. In 1969 Iran acted as the host to a large international conference on human rights, but a concern for human rights appears not to be reflected at all in its domestic practice.

It is alleged that torture of political prisoners during interrogation has been established practice in Iran for many years. The earliest detailed statement of torture known to Amnesty is dated 23 December 1963 and describes torture alleged to have occurred on 17 December 1963. However, opponents of the Iranian regime allege that torture has been taking place since the overthrow of Mossadegh in 1953.

The Iranian government has consistently denied that torture is used, but as no systematic inquiry has ever been made into the allegations, their validity can only be judged by a study of the available material. Amnesty has only one signed statement alleging torture; most of the available information about torture is contained in the reports of observers who have attended trials of political prisoners in Iran. Nearly all of these prisoners have retracted their confessions in court on the grounds that they were made under torture and therefore are not valid. Allegations relate to the period of pre-trial custody, which may be several months. During this time, investigation of alleged political crimes and the preparation of the files on the basis of which trials are conducted, is carried out by SAVAK, the intelligence and security organisation.

M. Nuri Albala, an observer who attended a trial in January/February 1972, reported that one of the defendants, who was executed subsequently, 'suddenly pulled off his sweater in front of everyone and showed me appalling burns on his stomach and his back; they appeared to be several months old'. Other defendants at the same trial alleged torture and stated that one of their number was unable to walk due to having been tortured; another was alleged to have died in the torture room. M. Albala concluded: 'The length of time that a prisoner can be held in custody before trial is unlimited, SAVAK is completely free and can do as it pleases during this time; it does not hesitate to use torture, sometimes leading to death, on the persons it has under its control'.

Other observers have mentioned allegations of torture in their reports; some have concluded on the basis of what they heard and saw in court that the torture had occurred; others have stated that they had no way of checking the validity of the allegations and must therefore suspend judgment. Apart from these reports, information about torture has been smuggled out of prisons and published outside Iran. In February 1972 a detailed account of torture, written by an escaped political prisoner from Iran, was published in *Le Monde* and subsequently elsewhere. He described the methods of torture used in general and then proceeded to particular cases of which he was an eyewitness.

Many methods of torture are alleged to be in use, including both physical and psychological, but those which are mentioned most frequently are: beating of the feet, weighted handcuffs, insertion of electric cosh or bottle into the rectum, and placing the prisoner on an electric grill which is then heated. The last method is alleged to have paralysed some of those subjected to it, so that they were unable to walk, but could only move about by crawling on all fours. Investigation of these cases would be handicapped by the fact that the alleged victims have been executed.

From February 1972 until June 1973, no observers or foreign journalists were allowed to attend trials of political prisoners in Iran. Very little information is available, but as far as is known all these trials were completely closed to the public. Many resulted in executions. For this reason there is hardly any recent information about torture in Iran, although opposition groups outside Iran allege that the torture of political prisoners has continued. A French lawyer, Francoise Rozelaar-Vigier, who went to Iran in December 1972 with the intention of observing a trial for the International Association of Democratic Lawyers, was deliberately misled by the Iranian authorities and told that no trials were imminent, although, as she subsequently learned, a trial was in progress while she was in Teheran. In connection with this trial it has been alleged that at least one of the defendants was tortured and has since been executed.

Taking into account the constant factors in all the allegations over the past ten years, together with the details supplied, which include descriptions of methods, names of torturers, places and times, it can be concluded that enough *prima facie* evidence of torture exists to warrant a properly constituted inquiry.

Iraq

Since 1963, there has been a continuous struggle for power between the moderate and extreme wings of the Baath Party, accompanied by purges, repression and physical elimination of all opposition to the existing regime. Such opposition continues to come from the left-wing Baathists, Communists, the Kurds, the Shiites, religious leaders and scholars. The 'National Security', in combination with the secret police and the intelligence service, is responsible for supressing all dissent and has effective authority to apprehend, detain, torture, and even assassinate; neither the laws made by the Baath Party officials nor even the most elementary formalities are respected.

Amnesty International has received general allegations of torture as an administrative practice in Iraq for many years, but only since 1968 has the information been of a specific nature, consisting of quoted statements, lists of names, description of physical techniques used, and case histories provided for the most part by political or religious groups outside Iraq who have contact with the victims. For example, other Communist parties in the Middle East have reported on the ill-treatment suffered by Iraqi Communists.

Interrogation usually takes place in Kasr al-Nihaya prison in Baghdad — although other detention centres have been used — where detainees are tortured to reveal information about fellow dissidents, to renounce their political beliefs, and pledge to refrain from further involvement in political activities; some victims are released after a month, clearly in order to intimidate and deter other dissidents. Torture techniques are known to be brutal, including bodily disfigurement and injury inflicted by knives and sharp instruments, causing permanent physical and psychological effects, and in many cases resulting in death. Amnesty International has the names of 18 men who have died as a result of torture. In one case — that of a Kurd — the photographs of the corpse and a physician's post-mortem report reveal lesions that are consistent with reports of torture techniques used by the Iraqi authorities. The latter admitted in 1970 that three men had died in Kasr al Nihaya, but rather than disciplining the individuals responsible, they offered financial compensation to the families.

Sixty additional named cases and 40 unnamed victims have been reported on in the past five years — students, workers, teachers, communists and peasants. A former Prime Minister, Abdul Rahman al-Bazzaz, was said to have had his arms and legs broken and to have lost an eye while in detention before his secret trial in 1968; when he was released after a year his left side was paralysed.

The Jews, of whom only about 450 remain, out of a community of 130,000 twenty years ago, have been severely repressed in Iraq. Certainly, after the Arab Israeli war in 1967, the situation of the Jews worsened: small groups of Jews were arrested and tortured for a few days while questioned about their connections with Israel and Zionism, and released after payment of a fine by the community. A Western observer reported to the Israeli newspaper *Haaretz* in June 1971 that an 11-year-old girl had confessed to membership of a 'Zionist imperialist spy ring' after three days of torture and rape. Recent reports allege that 20 Jews who have disappeared since November of 1972 have died from torture during interrogations made by the Secret Police.

Israel

In April 1970 Amnesty published a report on the treatment of certain prisoners under interrogation in Israel. The material which formed the basis of this report had been collected in the course of three separate visits to Israel by Amnesty representatives between December 1968 and January 1970; it included statements from people who alleged torture, photographs and medical evidence. The statements contained detailed information about the places where torture was alleged to have taken place, and the descriptions and names — or pseudonyms — of the alleged torturers. Most allegations referred to the period during which the prisoner was held for investigation and interrogation, before being brought to court or admitted to administrative detention.

Methods of torture alleged to have been used include the following: electric shocks applied to the genitals and other parts of the body, suspension by handcuffs, beating, kicking and punching of all parts of the body, and the burning of the body with cigarette stubs. It has also been alleged that dogs have been set on prisoners.

Amnesty submitted an early version of the report to the Israeli government in April 1969, recommending that, as there was *prima facie* evidence of maltreatment of some persons detained by them, the government should establish a commission of enquiry to consider such evidence, preferably including persons nominated by outside international organisations such as the International Commission of Jurists, the International Committee of the Red Cross or Amnesty International. In their reply to the Amnesty report the Israeli government stated that after 'meticulous examination . . . of the material available . . .' they concluded '. . . that there is no substance in the allegations mentioned in the Report and its Appendices'. They also stated: 'It is well-known that Israel is a state in which Rule of Law prevails. Every complaint of abuse by government authorities submitted by any individual is investigated; where *prima facie* evidence justifying such a complaint is available, the government itself institutes legal proceedings against the possible perpetrators. Detailed and elaborate regulations govern the treatment of all prisoners, and ensure the full protection of their rights. There is constant supervision and surveillance over the actual execution of these regulations. Legal aid to all prisoners is provided as a matter of right and course, and at the expense of the state, where necessary. Every prisoner enjoys free access to judicial bodies and is guaranteed judicial hearing. The independence of Israel courts of law is universally recognised.'

In Amnesty's view a detailed examination of the Israeli government's reply did not provide a basis for a satisfactory refutation of the allegations. Negotiations with the government continued, and in January 1970 three representatives of Amnesty visited Jordan and Israel to enquire further into the allegations. They collected additional statements and reported: 'Our considered opinion is that a *prima facie* case of ill-treatment of prisoners during interrogation by the Israeli authorities has been made and that a full investigation is therefore warranted.'

Late in January 1970 Amnesty received a memorandum

from the Ministry of Foreign Affairs in Israel in which it was stated that '... motivated by the sincere desire to ascertain whatever truth there may be in the complaints mentioned above, the Government of Israel has decided to grant the complainants, now present in enemy states, the requisite permits to enter Israel-held territories so that they may be able to lodge their complaints in accordance with existing legal procedures. Should the complainants so desire, they will further be permitted to appoint local lawyers of their choice to assist them in the submission of complaints or evidence. The government of Israel would, of course, assure the safety of the complainants during the entire period of their presence in Israel-controlled territory and guarantee their right to leave.'

In further correspondence with the Israeli authorities Amnesty tried to establish what were the 'existing legal procedures' referred to, but no satisfactory answer was forthcoming. It was felt that for many reasons the Israeli offer would not fulfil the demands of the situation; many of the complainants refused to recognise the validity of Israeli jurisdiction over the territory and it was also thought that the normal legal processes would stretch over a period of years and therefore a commission of enquiry was desirable in order to establish as soon as possible the truth, or otherwise, of the allegations.

In March 1970 the International Executive Committee of Amnesty International came to the conclusion that the Israeli government had no intention of establishing a commission of enquiry and that Amnesty should, therefore, publish a report based on the available material. It was made clear in this report that '... Amnesty restricts itself to claiming that the serious nature of these allegations warrants immediate inquiry so that their truth can be tested and the practice of torture, if it exists, can be brought immediately to an end.'

Delegates of the International Committee of the Red Cross have visited prisons in Israel and the occupied areas since the end of the June 1967 conflict, but in accordance with their usual practice the reports of delegates have not been published. In the *International Review of the Red Cross*, September 1970, it was stated: 'During the visits delegates have sometimes met detainees whose bodies showed traces of, according to the prisoners, ill-treatment during interrogation. In keeping with the ICRC general practice, each case was brought to the attention of the military authorities so that they could investigate whether detainees' allegations were correct and if so, punish those guilty, as required by the Geneva Convention and national legislation.'

The activities of the United Nations regarding Israeli practices affecting the human rights of the population of the occupied territories are dealt with in Section 2 of this report.

From the publication of its report in April 1970 until late in 1971, Amnesty received no allegations of torture which were regarded as being substantial enough to warrant further action. In January 1972 three specific reports of ill-treatment of Arab detainees were referred to the Israeli ambassador in London. In March Amnesty was informed officially that these cases had been investigated and that the torture allegations were unfounded. The prisoners had been released.

During 1972 allegations of ill-treatment of Arabs during interrogations were reported from time to time by the Israel League for Human and Civil Rights. The number of detailed allegations increased in December 1972 and January 1973 with the arrest of at least 40 people, including Israeli Jews, in connection with a Syrian-operated espionage and sabotage ring. Official complaints of torture were made in the names of some of those detained, by their lawyers, and a Communist Knesset (Parliament) member also complained officially, as well as to the press and to Amnesty, about the ill-treatment of his son, one of the six Jews arrested. The charges of torture were officially denied by the police, but as far as is known, no formal investigation of these allegations has been carried out.

For torture allegations after the 1973 war, see p. 239.

Oman

Most reports of torture come from the Popular Front for the Liberation of Oman and the Arabian Gulf (PFLOAG), whose guerrilla activities in the province of Dhofar pose the major challenge to the regime. One report stated that fourteen Dhofaris arrested on 17 June 1965 were tortured for two days during interrogation at Salalah and were then transferred to Bait al Falaj, where they were periodically questioned and tortured for six months.

Other allegations concern religious leaders of the Ibadi sect of Islam – to which the majority of Omanis belong – who hold the view that the head of a Muslim state should be an elected Imam. Amnesty received a report in 1969 that Al Jabiri and a judge, Zaid Ibn Saif, were, in 1963, repeatedly subjected to severe maltreatment. Al Jabiri was tortured on a machine made out of garage equipment normally used for raising up cars, but fitted with a flat wooden top on which he was laid; the machine was raised so that he was pressed against the roof, and left for long periods in considerable pain. They were both tortured so that their confessions and a renunciation of their beliefs might be used as a method of public persuasion.

The PFLOAG allegations, despite their undeniable bias, should be taken seriously in view of reliable information that has been received, especially on general prison conditions. The Omani authorities have not instigated any investigations into these reports, and have forbidden the Red Cross and Red Crescent to enter the country.

People's Democratic Republic of Yemen

At the end of 1963, violence erupted against the British presence in the Aden Protectorate, and a state of emergency was proclaimed, permitting indefinite detention without trial. Amnesty International sent an observer to Aden in the summer of 1966 to investigate allegations that local British authorities were using physical violence to extort confessions. He was not allowed to visit detention centres nor to interview the detainees, and the High Commissioner categorically denied there was ill-treatment and torture in British interrogation centres. Ex-detainees and relatives of those still detained at the time of the observer's visit complained that torture was practised at the interrogation centre, and a number of sworn affidavits were obtained which supported the charges of torture.

Subsequently, an investigation was undertaken by Mr Roderic Bowen QC on behalf of the government (*The Bowen Report*, 14 November, 1966, Cmnd. 3165) which indicated that late in 1965 reports of allegations of physical maltreatment and requests for their investigation had come to the High Commissioner's office. The Director of Health had sent the following memorandum to the Deputy High Commissioner on 14 November 1965: 'The injuries sustained by the detainees brought from the Interrogation Centre indicate that their interrogation was assisted by physical violence ... I should be grateful if the allegations of physical violence which were substantiated by bruises and torn eardrums etc., could be investigated.' Mr Bowen concluded in his report that 'there was a most regrettable failure to deal expeditiously and adequately with the allegations of cruelty which were made in respect of the Interrogation Centre'.

Amnesty's findings in Aden were finally confirmed when, in 1972, military interrogation procedures in Northern Ireland were under consideration, and Lord Gardiner in his Minority Report said: 'These procedures of interrogation in depth, namely hooding, a noise machine, wall-standing and deprivation of diet and sleep ... had been for some time orally taught for use in emergency conditions, in Colonial-type situations, at an army intelligence centre in England. They had been used in Aden, although surprisingly, it does not appear from the report of Mr Roderic Bowen, QC, on Interrogation in Aden that he ever discovered that these interrogation procedures were used there.' (*Report of the Committee of Privy Counsellors appointed to consider authorised procedures for the interrogation of persons suspected of terrorism*, March 1973, Cmnd. 4901).

Since the establishment of the People's Democratic Republic of Yemen in 1967 the more widely publicised method of dealing with political dissidents appears to be summary execution, although occasional allegations of torture have been received. One such allegation, from a reliable source, reported that Anwer Ramsu, a former Minister of Finance, was sentenced to death in December 1971 after conviction for bribery and embezzling, but died a few hours before his execution as a result of the tortures he had suffered.

Saudi Arabia

Amnesty International has recently received allegations of torture in Saudi Arabia which, although they have in no way been investigated, are serious enough to warrant inclusion in this Report. There is well-substantiated information about traditional punishments meted out to criminal and political offenders, such as public floggings and executions, or cutting off a hand or foot as punishment for theft. It seems reasonable to assume, therefore, that torture and the casual ill-treatment of prisoners is commonplace. What is not known is how widespread or how systematic is its use.

Most of the reports of torture received by Amnesty International have related to the period after 1969 and concern those arrested for plotting to overthrow the government. Among the alleged victims are air force and army officers as well as government officials, students, workers, etc. Amnesty International has the names of nine who are reported to have died as a result of torture.

The Saudi Intelligence Bureau, which together with the Ministry of Interior is responsible for arrests and interrogation, is staffed largely by non-Saudi Arabs, and there are indications that since 1969 American advisers and torture equipment have been imported. It is alleged that whereas torture techniques before 1969 were crude, resulting frequently and quickly in death, American advisers have introduced more sophisticated methods of psychological interrogation and torture, such as very long periods of solitary confinement, sometimes with only the Koran to read. However, other alleged techniques include a machine for the pressing of weight on the head or chest, electric shocks and the alternation of extreme temperatures in order to disorient the mind.

The bodies of prisoners who have died as a result of torture are usually returned to the families concerned, with the explanation that death was due to illness. Marks on the body, however, have borne witness to the infliction of torture.

In line with public executions and floggings, the torture of prisoners would appear to be as much a method of intimidation, deterrence and punishment, as a means of eliciting information.

Syria

Until recently, imprisonment and torture was a routine occurrence for critics and opposers of the regime: seventeen former-ministers who were arrested after the coup in 1970, are alleged to have been tortured and for some time were detained at the Military Hospital at Al Mezze in Damascus. Three of them are said to have sustained skull fractures causing nervous complaints, another has a paralysed arm and another has lost the sight of one eye. They are now in Palmyre prison in the desert, still uncharged and untried. In 1970 several members of the Communist party, at that time a rival political grouping, but now part of the newly-formed National Front, were reported to have been arrested and tortured, in some cases resulting in death: one leading party official was kidnapped, tortured and returned to his family in a coffin. However, Amnesty International has received fewer allegations in the last three years, which is perhaps a reflection of the present regime's confidence in its position after three years in power.

Other allegations concern minority groups. The Kurdish community of half a million people, repressed for many years, have been subjected to imprisonment and ill-treatment in their struggle to regain their national rights. Jews have also been maltreated. At the end of November 1971, an Amnesty International member had an interview with, and received an affidavit from, a Jew who had escaped from Syria. He stated that it was routine for Syrian Jews to be arrested, maltreated and tortured, and that he himself had been imprisoned with his father and brother, and all had been subjected to physical and sexual tortures from the effects of which they were still suffering. In June 1973, three Israeli pilots, repatriated after three years' imprisonment in Syria, told the press that they had been held under extremely harsh conditions, and that two of them had had beatings and electric shocks and had been caned on the soles of their feet. They also alleged that, when the Israelis reminded their captors of the Geneva

Convention on the treatment of prisoners of war, they had replied that it did not apply to Jews.

* * *

One group of allegations related to both Syria and Israel stems from the October 1973 war in the Middle East and the treatment of prisoners of war by the belligerents. Properly speaking, the treatment of wartime prisoners falls under the authority of the International Committee of the Red Cross rather than within the mandate of Amnesty International. Nevertheless, torture under any circumstances is the concern of AI, and the allegations should be mentioned here.

Shortly after the conclusion of all-out warfare, the Israeli government charged both the Egyptian and the Syrian governments with responsibility for the torture of Israeli prisoners of war; counter-allegations were issued against the Israelis by both the Egyptians and the Syrians. Within a few months the Egyptians and the Israelis exchanged prisoners, and except for a few notices in the press, the issue was not raised officially by either government, apparently because neither government wished to endanger the pending agreement for military disengagement.

Israel continued to press, however, for investigations into the treatment of its military personnel who were being held in Syria. After the two countries exchanged prisoners in June 1974, the Israeli government claimed that each of its 67 men had been tortured by such methods as severe beating, electric shock, and starvation. Some Israeli pilots claimed that their ears had been beaten so that they would be prevented from flying combat missions in the future. The Syrian government replied that many of its military personnel had suffered psychological torture in Israel as well as inadequate medical attention from Israeli military doctors. One Syrian pilot alleged that his legs had been unnecessarily amputated by Israeli doctors. These allegations will be the subject of an Amnesty International investigation.

Conclusions

At present there exist few effective ways of stopping torture. We have seen that only in the case of Greece was proof of torture authoritatively established by an intergovernmental judicial enquiry. The Compton and the Amnesty International investigations in Northern Ireland coincided in their description of facts though they differed in the conclusions they reached. South Africa and Brazil have received much international attention, but their governments have instituted no special internal enquiry to examine the use of torture, and sharply opposed any suggestion of an enquiry from the outside. Amnesty International has also investigated complaints from Aden and Israel. In none of these cases, apart from Greece, did the international enquiries receive cooperation from the local authorities.

We have described the situation in those countries where enquiries of one kind or another have been instituted. We have also attempted to describe many other situations. We are fully aware of the deficiencies of our information and of the difficulties in evaluating it. There is at present no central repository for torture complaints.

We have also noted, in the Report, certain new developments. In the first place sophisticated methods of torture are being introduced in many countries. Interrogation techniques are being constantly refined. But torture is not being used for the extraction of information alone. It is also used for the control of political dissent. Often, the two main impulses are combined in one appalling practice.

There also exists evidence that the practice of torture is becoming internationalised. Experts and their training, as well as torture equipment, are provided by one government for use in another state. Internally, responsibility for the use of torture is being broadened, involving other authorities than the police or security police. The trend seems to be towards duplication, or in some cases displacement, of the police by the military forces, and by the army in particular. Special units are used not only in situations of war, in an occupied territory: the case of Vietnam is referred to in this Report. The practice has also been applied in countries which are not at war and which, in some cases, have no broadly based domestic insurgencies to cope with. For instance, in Uruguay, Brazil, Indonesia, Greece and Turkey, the military are torturing civilians for reasons of domestic politics. This development reflects the growing involvement of the military in politics, and the increasing number of military regimes, as well as the development of various counterinsurgency theories by military experts.

The responsibility for torture is, however, no longer confined to governments. Allegations of ill-treatment and brutality, amounting to torture, have been made against several opposition movements which use violence and, from time to time, hold prisoners or hostages. Though this is a comparatively recent development, it is a serious one. There is no redress of any kind for the victim. It contributes to the escalation of violence. In such confrontation between the forces of the government and the forces of the opposition, the individual remains totally unprotected.

Torture can occur in any society. Certain indications have emerged from this study as to the situations where torture is likely to occur. For instance, it is misleading to suggest that poverty causes and wealth prevents torture. Torture exists in situations of sharp conflict.

The legal situation — the observance or the disregard of the due processes of law — appears to be more directly relevant. Special powers acts; martial law; state of siege or of exception: wherever the rule of law has been suspended, the torturer finds it easy to move in. When the citizen has a free access to *habeas corpus*, to legal aid, to a free press, he is better protected. It is not impossible for the state to torture him: but it is much more difficult.

Experimental psychiatric and psychological evidence points to the fact that the potential to torture is present in man, and that only institutional, legal or religious restraints put on him provide assurance that this potential will not be used. The decision, on the other hand, by the state to use the potential has frequently been accompanied by campaigns aimed to isolate a group of individuals and put them firmly beyond the pale of humanity. The ideological conflicts of the twentieth century have facilitated such campaigns. Racial minorities, class enemies, and 'enemies of the people' of various kinds are specially vulnerable.

It is therefore the suspension of the rule of law, often accompanied by putting a specific group of individuals beyond the limits of a society, which seems to create the matrix for the growth of torture.

It is directly linked to politics, as governments may see the use of torture as necessary for their survival. It is also the most sensitive of all political issues. Though a state may admit that it holds political prisoners, it will never admit that it uses torture. The confrontation between the individual and the limitless power of the state, between the torturer and his victim, takes place in the darkest recess of political power.

So far, little attempt has been made to define, and finally to eradicate, the use of torture. The main purpose of this Report is to contribute to public awareness and increase resistance to the practice of torture. We have noted that national remedies, whenever they are available, can be effective. In international law, the doctrine of individual responsibility was firmly laid down a long time ago, at Nuremberg. Now the international community has to try to work out effective remedies for the prevention of torture.

Appendix: Special Report on Chile by Rose Styron

[*Publisher's note:* This appendix on Chile was written by Rose Styron, a member of the board of the American section of Amnesty International. She visited Chile in February 1974 and has written this appendix for the American edition of *Report on Torture* in view of the extensive interest of the American public in the involvement of the United States government in Chile, both before and after the September 1973 coup d'état that replaced the legally elected government of Dr. Salvador Allende and his Popular Unity party with a dictatorial military junta. She writes as a private citizen and journalist. A substantially different version of this article appeared in the May 30, 1974, edition of *The New York Review of Books*.

Interested readers are referred to "Chile: An Amnesty International Report," an extensive investigation by the AI research staff in London that reports in great detail on the matter of political prisoners and torture under the junta. It is available for $2.10 directly from Amnesty International, 200 West 72nd Street, New York, New York 10024. Another invaluable source of information is *Chile: Under Military Rule,* "a dossier of documents and analyses compiled by the staff of IDOC/International Documentation with the special assistance of guest editor Gary MacEoin," available for $4.95 directly from IDOC/North America, 235 East 49th Street, New York, New York 10017.]

Chile since the right-wing military coup of September 1973 has been an occupied country. The Commander of the Army, president of the junta, and now President of Chile, is Augusto Pinochet. Pinochet rose to prominence toward the end of Salvador Allende's troubled presidency when, in August 1973, the respected General Carlos Prats resigned as Commander, hoping to avoid civil war. (Prats went to

Argentina, where he was subsequently killed by a bomb planted in his car.) Officially, Chile is in an extended State of Siege, operating under the laws of a State of War. During the long series of court trials in 1974 (most of them closed), the State of War was interpreted by the ruling junta as retroactive to June 29, when a small coup was aborted, or to March, when President Allende showed renewed popularity in congressional elections and plans for his overthrow began to be put into effect.

Sixteen months after the coup, the only law in Chile remains military law. Congress, the Constitution, all political parties, unions, and the authority of civilian courts have been eliminated. Media censorship (or self-censorship) is almost total. The right to assembly is denied. Justice, by North American standards, has disappeared. Yet the idea of legality, ingrained during decades of Chilean democracy, continues to nag those in power. On November 14, 1973, the Chilean Supreme Court announced with formality that it "would lack jurisdiction and competence for the duration" and issued this decree:

> ... from the moment in which a general in command of the army is appointed to take action against a foreign enemy or organized rebel forces ... this commander shall have jurisdiction to punish personally, and without any form of trial, all abuses which in his opinion do not constitute a criminal offense. To order the formation of Courts Martial to try them. To approve, revoke, or modify the sentences ...

Pinochet has used the Supreme Court's decree to full advantage. He has made it clear that it would be at least five years before his country would be ready for elections and democratic rule. In his first anniversary speech he concluded that "the recess for political parties can only be responsibly lifted when a new generation of Chileans with healthy civic and patriotic habits can take over the leadership of public life." A number of former political leaders who encouraged the military to abandon its tradition of non-partisan loyalty (thus to betray Allende) have expressed surprise that, with the coup complete, Pinochet still finds the taste of power delicious, that he still sees "the mentally deranged citizens who keep resisting" as a threat, that he does not turn the reins of government over to an experienced civilian.

On March 30, 1974, there was a new announcement: Pinochet had been given unequivocal authority to seize and detain any minor for an indefinite length of time without charges or explanation. This meant that a fifteen-year-old boy, Adelberto Muñoz Meza, kidnapped by the military earlier and held incommunicado for a month (immobilized upright between fences night and day) because at eleven he had joined a pro-Allende demonstration, at twelve thrown stones at a vehicle, and at thirteen learned karate, could now legally be judged a threat to the state and confined indefinitely to places of detention and torture.

Countless adolescents are among the political prisoners held in jails and camps throughout Chile. Mexico's daily *Excelsior* described a medieval scene in which a fifteen-year-old girl was kept nude in a cell, her body smeared with excrement and covered with rats, and one in which a sixteen-year-old boy was closed up in a box for fifteen days, food occasionally being pushed in through a small hole. A fourteen-year-old has been given sodium pentothal daily under severe interrogation. Another fourteen-year-old collapsed from the pain of electroshock administered for hours to her eyes and hands. A pregnant seventeen-year-old, who heard on the radio that police wanted to talk to her, reported and was subjected to clubbing and electroshock on her uterus, which caused brain damage to the baby she bore. In November 1974 the International Commission of Jurists, its members back from Chile, stated that the junta was planning to establish work camps for more than 600,000 juveniles whose parents had been supporters of Allende. A subsequent letter from Santiago indicates that the first new camp is on an island and that children more likely to be politically aware are being enrolled. A woman filing a writ of habeas corpus for her thirteen-year-old son states, "My home was invaded . . . they made me surrender Patricio . . . dragged him from bed, struck him, dragged him away . . . said they would give him back to me when he was older and re-educated. I have not seen him since."

Long before March 30, Pinochet had been delegating similar authority over Chile's adult inhabitants to Army, Navy, Air Force, and police officers *(carabineros),* and to a new instrument of terror, the paramilitary DINA (Dirección de Inteligencia Nacional). The last, a plainclothes apparatus under Pinochet's direct control, was set up in December 1973. DINA is apparently modeled on the Death Squad in Brazil, whose military regime Pinochet has praised for its "free enterprise and domestic discipline."

Indeed, several of DINA's leaders, ex-members of the tough right-wing *Patria y Libertad* (Fatherland-and-Freedom Party), were trained in Brazil. Others were apprenticed to Brazilians invited by the junta to give courses within Chile to the military and police. Among the Brazilian instructors were those fresh from intelligence schools in the United States and the Panama Canal Zone. They were given a free hand in Santiago with their own nationals, 250 of whom lodged complaints of torture.

DINA was used first in cases where the government wished to avoid legal inquiries about missing persons. (Over 1,900 writs of habeas corpus were filed, in vain, in 1974.) The four other intelligence services are now under DINA's firm control. DINA specialties, besides surprise individual arrests (the tales of waiting for the ominous knock on the door at night remind one of Stalin's Russia), are invading factories, classrooms, restaurants, and homes without a warrant, wreaking select destruction, and hauling away the assembled—insulted, battered, and blindfolded. Their vehicles are unmarked. Their decisions are independent, arbitrary. Their initial places of interrogation and torture, unseen by the hooded, bound victims, are numerous houses in and around Santiago. They are nicknamed "The House of Terror," "The House of Bells" (church bells can be heard from Calle Londres 38), "The Palace of Laughter." The most infamous interrogation center was a high-security camp called Tejas Verdes. Official visitors to the Santiago stadiums and other facilities organized for detention, among them former United States Ambassador Ralph Dungan, reported that young men newly transferred from Tejas Verdes showed the marks of having been hung up by the wrists, stretched on a rack, bound pretzel-fashion for electroshock, subjected to something called the "plastic-bag treatment," having instruments jammed under their nails, and so forth. Visitors to the women's jail describe girls who arrive with their hair pulled out, genitals and nipples destroyed, mice inserted in their vaginas, and evidence of savage beatings and rape. In response to international publicity, Tejas Verdes was reportedly closed down last summer. However, by October, Amnesty International was again receiving calls about victims thought to have been taken there. One was a young psychiatrist, Katia Reszczynski, who, prior to her arrest on September 17, 1974, had been working for the Committee for Cooperation and Peace, a group of church leaders in constant danger because they collect information on those who have disappeared, and try to provide legal and financial aid to prisoners and refugees and their destitute, demoralized families.

When DINA is rumored to be on the prowl, fearful Chileans hide. Almost everyone has reason to fear, for DINA makes mistakes. A group of right-wing youths whose midnight party prompted annoyed neighbors to call the police found themselves jailed, incommunicado, for over a week until their parents located them. Two other young men, brothers who voted against Allende—one actually spent those years at a U.S. business school—were thrown into a truck and taken to a DINA torture center for days and nights of hideous interrogation. "This is a dictatorship!" shouted a torturer. "There are no human rights! We are establishing fascism. There is only Pinochet and us!" Surviving electroshock sessions, the American-educated brother was reduced to weeping when he saw a fifty-five-year-old man whose legs had been torn open and back muscles pulled out by shock spasms. "How can our country do this to us?" he cried. The weeping fits continued long after his release.

Since the coup, Amnesty International has been receiving almost daily reports of disappearances, of summary executions and arranged deaths, of brutal physical and psychological torture in camps and prisons, of government by intimidation. AI's sources have included, along with refugees and diplomats, the Organization of American States and the

International Commission of Jurists, Chilean and North American clergy, the Women's International League for Peace and Freedom, the American Federation of Scientists, international organizations which sent delegates to Chile on fact-finding missions, journalists, the U.N. High Commissioner for Refugees (whose deputy set up sanctuaries in Chile and worked for the release of thousands), and AI's own two commissions. Although the junta rejected the first commission's January 1974 report as "biased and superficial," the eyewitnesses to torture multiplied. AI's second commission, in Chile November 1–8, 1974, noted that in current trials a lawyer may not mention his client's torture; it is "inadmissible political argument." By now, types of torture are so standardized that they are referred to by nickname: "El Condor," "El Tirabuzón," "El Ulpo," "La Campana," and so on. Former U.S. Attorney General Ramsey Clark and West German judge Horst Woesner managed to attend the Air Force trials of May 1974. Clark called them a "charade." Woesner commented on the widespread evidence of continued, sophisticated, systematic torture. Testimony has been presented at Helsinki and Rome, and is being prepared for a conference in Mexico City (at President Luis Echeverría's invitation) in February 1975. All of it repudiates the widely reported statements of the junta and its appointees:

> "The junta has governed since September 11th in an atmosphere of absolute peace and normality"—p. 5, *The White Book,* in which the junta justifies seizing power.
>
> "The situation in Chile is absolutely normal"—Pinochet, September 18, 1973.
>
> "No execution or torture has taken place in Chile"—Raúl Bazán, Ambassador to the U.N., September 19, 1973.
>
> "In Chile there have been no prisoners; they have only been taken to a precinct where they have been treated as genuine human beings, while investigations have been made to see if they have committed a criminal act which should be tried by the tribunals"—*El Mercurio,* quoting the Chilean section of the I.C.J., February 17, 1974.
>
> "The last execution took place December 19th and no more are planned"—Bazán, February 25, 1974.

In Washington, Ambassador Walter Heitmann, answering questions on the Today show a year after the coup, strongly reaffirmed the junta's innocence in violating human rights.

Chile and its current voices are of particular concern to members of the American section of Amnesty International because, unlike the Soviet Union and its satellites, Chile is squarely in the American sphere of influence. By September 1974, when *The Washington Post* noted that Chile had hired the J. Walter Thompson advertising agency to spruce up its image, and Heitmann had employed a former vice president of Anaconda Copper as liaison with Congress, it was evident that North America was in for a program of junta propaganda. The Thompson firm registered itself as a lobbyist for Chile, and promised to advise its new employers "on reporting more effectively and fully to the media." Thus, each time Pinochet announced that he would release a hundred prisoners, Americans heard about it. We did not hear about promises reneged upon or new prisoners taken. *Corriere della Sera, Le Monde,* and *The Manchester Guardian* had made it their practice to weigh Chilean announcements, but the U.S. press, when it wrote of Chile at all, usually reflected U.S. naïveté or U.S. foreign policy. Jonathan Kandell and *The New York Times* had not yet been kicked out of Santiago for straight reporting on the dictatorship, nor had Joseph Novitski of *The Washington Post*. Everett Martin had not written his new, vivid Chile pieces for *The Wall Street Journal* (a year earlier, Martin himself had presented persuasively the conservative businessman's viewpoint), and Seymour Hersh had only begun his detailed series on our secret policies, citing Henry Kissinger's rebuke to Ambassador David Popper for "interfering" when Popper initiated a discussion on torture with Chilean military officials. Clearly, Tad Szulc's early piece (October 21, 1973) on U.S. infiltration of Chilean political parties and its $400,000 contribution to the anti-Allende press in 1970 (acknowledged by C.I.A. Director William Colby and his assistant at a House Subcommittee on Inter-American Affairs hearing) had been forgotten, and *Time*'s report of feasting roadside truck-owners saying their banquet in the midst of the strike was provided by the C.I.A., discounted.

When Roger Plant came from Amnesty International's London Secretariat in September to publicize AI's *Chile Report,* only *El Mercurio* in Santiago gave play to U.N. press-conference questions asked him about Nazis in Chile. Plant correctly declined to answer on the grounds that he could not substantiate the facts, but reports of direct Nazi influence (not simply Germanic military training) keep cropping up. The most persistent report concerns Walter Rauff, once head of the SS in Milan. An American AI member, captured and tortured by the Nazis for her part in the Italian Resistance, remembers her friends' cruel deaths at his hands. Rauff, convicted at Nuremberg of mass murder—he devised the mobile gas chambers—escaped to Chile. West Germany has failed in its repeated attempts to extradite him. *El Mercurio* says he is raising cattle in Punta Arenas. But the rumors are that he is directing Pinochet's prison system, running DINA, and planning the work camps for children. Prisoners from Dawson Island, near Punta Arenas, say Rauff planned their special ordeals. Why have major United States newspapers and newscasters not investigated these and other stories told by exiled Chileans? As late as November 1974, when Hortensia Allende and Moy Toha, the eloquent widows of the President of Chile and his Minister of Defense, came to New York to speak and answer questions, it was difficult to get media coverage.

Controversy will continue over the causes of Allende's fall: his misplaced trust in the military; his lack of economic expertise; his determination to reform society along Marxist lines, utilizing established laws and a coalition government instead of a confrontation with the powerful right; the punitive financial and trade blockade initiated by President Richard Nixon when the Unidad Popular and deputies of the right voted together to nationalize copper mines; opposition, and even sabotage, by right-wing Chileans. Yet it is obvious that under Allende's democratic socialism Chile was a free society. No doctors or lawyers or artists went to jail for pursuing their professions according to their consciences. No striking workers had reprisals taken against them. No newspaper was routinely censored. Nor was there any record of a policy of brutality and illegal detention. In the year before the coup, in the days when the streets of Santiago were full of noise, when workers' celebrations and demonstrations for Allende were followed by the truck owners' strike and upper-class women marching on La Moneda banging pots and pans, when columns of leftist university students trailed protesting rightist Catholic university students shouting "Momias!" ("Reactionaries!"; literally, "mummies"), and in the nights when the pans still banging behind drawn shades made a crazy modern music, the air of freedom was unmistakable.

That air is gone. Unruly citizens no longer characterize Santiago. By September 1, 1973, it was a capital paralyzed by strikes and apprehension. The military nurtured a new xenophobia. Helicopters showered leaflets from the skies warning: "Have no compassion with foreign extremists who have come to Chile to kill Chileans . . . Denounce them to the nearest military authority." Pinochet announced that 10,000 such extremists had entered Chile and he told his troops that Chile must be protected from these monsters of the left. He convinced them that a government defense study paper was a Cuban-backed blueprint for armed revolution and that by September 19 "Plan Z" would have effected the assassination of Allende and prominent citizens of the right and imposed Communism on Chile. It was whispered to one citizen after another that he was on the "list." Young soldiers quaking with fear were sent out to raid homes, schools, and factories in search of secret arms. All dark-skinned foreigners were to be assumed to be Cuban and assiduously watched (when paranoia led to book-burning, even volumes on cubism kindled the flames). The 13,000 refugees from other tyrannies and turmoils who had sought haven in democratic Chile over the previous decade, the foreign scholars and businessmen and diplomats who had found life there so congenial, held their breath. One by one, Navy men loyal to Allende were detained and savagely treated. By dawn on September 11, scores of Army men had been shot in their quarters. Then came the midmorning explosion: rockets, tanks, guns, bloodshed. Elegant women from their balconies raised champagne toasts to the pilots who were bombing Allende's office.

Allende's last speech was broadcast at 11:15 a.m. He thanked the people of his country for their faith in him as the interpreter of their ideals and expressed his confidence that, sooner or later, highways would open for men of honor to continue construction of a new society in Chile. He beseeched his followers not to make martyrs of themselves—he would not surrender, and that was enough—and he exhorted farmers, workers, intellectuals, mothers, and the young to carry on his fight. By afternoon Allende was dead. The junta said Allende committed suicide with a gun Fidel Castro had given him. Others, noting the bullet holes in the wall behind his desk, the multiple wounds on his torso and his smashed face (his widow was not allowed to see the body prior to burial), called it murder.

After a forty-eight-hour curfew, Santiago was subject to a new order. The situation changed in every respect. *El Mercurio,* one of the few newspapers still operating, began to attack a wide range of "undesirables," including moderate Christian Democrats. Mayors and university directors and hospital administrators were replaced by military men. Of a population of 10,600,000, June 1974 estimates of executions and death-after-torture ranged from twenty to fifty thousand. Some 90,000 have been detained and interrogated for at least several days, and of the 18,000 on prison lists for January 1974, approximately 8,000 remain in January 1975. (Mrs. Allende cites the true figure as 20,000.) The number of missing is uncalculated. Three hundred thousand have lost their jobs for political reasons. Twenty-five thousand students and nearly 30 percent of the professors have been dismissed from universities. Neither they nor the fired workers whose papers are marked "activist" can find employment. Prices of food and household goods are up an average of 1300 percent since September 1973. Bread that was 5 escudos then was 140 escudos by February 1974. Even *El Mercurio* states that 20 percent of the population live in extreme poverty. With the truck owners' long strike over, farm products are again arriving in Santiago. Except for the bakeries (absenteeism and high costs have closed many), shelves are full and the bourgeoisie are more content. But the poor are starving. Beggars and young prostitutes are on the streets for the first time in years, as are silent drunks. Children, alone or in small bands, the signs of malnutrition clear, stop visitors to ask for coins. Some still search the streets and stadium entrances for their parents. There are an estimated 30,000 orphans in Chile today.

Fresh slogans on the walls of Santiago proclaim socratically: "In every Chilean there is a soldier. In every soldier, a Chilean." Soldiers appear at crossroads and at the entrances to parks, churches, restaurants. Most of them look seventeen and forlorn. Accompanied usually by a veteran officer, they stop Santiagan and visitor alike to examine papers. Woe to him who does not have them in order. If he is poor, he may be beaten on the spot. If he is a child on an errand, he may be thrashed and taken home. Citizens have disappeared altogether for lack of satisfactory identification. Their bodies float in the Mapocho River or lie bullet-ridden on its banks. Families find missing relatives in the morgue, grotesquely mutilated. Pictures smuggled out, of corpses missing eyes, noses, limbs, and genitals, are eloquent testimony to torture. Countless summary executions have been justified publicly under "la ley de fuga": killed while trying to escape. Certain members of Allende's Unidad Popular were dropped from the very helicopters that earlier had dropped propaganda leaflets. Once a person is apprehended—and this is true for all those seized because of their political sympathies or moral convictions, for being community leaders (doctors, civil servants, educators, labor organizers) suspected of holding antigovernment beliefs, or for daring to protest conditions under the new regime, or being a relative or a friend of a protester, or simply for being in the wrong place at the wrong time—interrogation and tailored torture are routine. The victim is held incommunicado for days, weeks, months. He may then be released and cautioned to say that he was well treated (a paper attesting this must usually be signed). Or he may remain in prison, be brought to trial, or be killed. Dragnets for political suspects plague the *poblaciones* (the poor districts surrounding Santiago). One morning in September 1974, 10,000 men were rounded up, 650 of them arrested and taken away. A radio voice later lyricized the people's "great admiration for the men who guard us."

The long curfew imposed at first has been cut back progressively, but violators are still subject to being shot on sight. On October 4, 1973, Santiago woke to one of its frequent earthquakes, which traditionally send everyone into the streets lest he be caught under a falling roof. The earth shook in forty separate tremors, a different kind of modern music, but no one broke curfew. There are priorities in fear.

In the strangeness of life under the military, fear is strengthened immeasurably by the new fact of torture. An anthology of torture tales is fast collecting. Their settings are interrogation centers and camps called Cerro Chena, Estadio Chile, Calle Londres, Tres Alamos, Pisagua, Capuchinos, Casa de Mujeres, El Buen Pastor, the ships *Lebu, Maipú,* and *Esmeralda,* Quiriquina and Dawson Islands, Chacobuco, and Tejas Verdes. Talcahuano Naval Base, Tacna Regiment, Ritoque, Quintero, FACH (Air Force headquarters), and a variety of military installations, municipal buildings, schools, sports arenas, and hospitals the length of Chile have been converted for detention. The protagonists of these tales are the famous, the obscure. Nor are the kin of those in high places protected: General Baeze's nephew was tortured to death; Ambassador Heitmann's niece, Ingrid Silvia Heitmann Ghiliotti, has this very month been jailed and brutalized.

Mrs. Allende reports that Senator Jorge Montes, his wife Josefina Miranda, and their two daughters Diana, aged twenty-four, and Rosa María, aged twenty-three, were arrested July 8, 1974. Montes had his teeth removed and his eardrums ruptured, his leg is paralyzed, and he has suffered massive internal bleeding. The three women were raped and beaten at the Air Force Academy of War. Diana's arm is now paralyzed.

Kandell quotes a petition of habeas corpus filed for Victor Daniel Arévalo Muñoz, twenty-six, arrested August 21 in the stall he owns at La Vega food market. His wife was arrested forty-eight hours later at home by three agents without a warrant. Her eyes were taped shut and she was driven downtown:

> "They made me walk down several stairs to a flat landing," she recounted. "There was a great number of people, whose voices I could hear, all of them apparently blind-

folded and in terrible shape. There were men and women crowded together, some against each other, others in chairs, others on the floor."

"They interrogated me," she continued, "asking about firearms and telling me that if I did not talk they would hook me to an electric machine to make me talk. Then they took me to a cell, and after a while I heard someone moaning, and I realized that it was my husband, who was in the throes of a convulsion. He was in serious condition, and his whole body felt swollen from the torture he had suffered.

"When he recovered from his convulsions I was able to speak to him and he told me that when they interrogated him they made him strip naked and then placed him on a bedspring, tied his hands and feet with wet cloth and began to apply electric current to his ears, testicles, tongue, chest, stomach, legs and the soles of his feet. Once they had finished with the electric treatments, they forced a liquid into his mouth that seared it, and then they placed an iron bar in his anus, putting it in until it drew blood, and then finally they beat him. These interrogations are repeated several times a day."

Ambassador Robert Woodward and Dr. Luis Reque, visiting Capuchinos for the O.A.S., include in their lengthy report on political prisoners this young man's history:

Detained for six months. Says that no charges against him. Has been beaten; shows marks; has three ribs broken as a result of beatings and tortures. Tortures also in hands, feet, mouth and teeth. Says was tortured in Tejas Verdes and in another place that he did not recognize, in which he was blindfolded for nine days and was again tortured with electric shock in the ears, feet and hands, razor cuts on the fingers, hands and feet. The treatment in the jail was inhuman. He remained for two months on bread and water, was tortured at nine different locations. One of them was in the Barco Lebo, in Valparaíso; on one occasion a black liquid was forced down his nose. It is his family he is worried about. He asked the Commission to do something for them if possible.

The O.A.S., a generally conservative organization which reflects U.S. foreign policy, sent investigators to Chile in the summer of 1974. Although they were denied access to five famous torture centers on the grounds that "these installations had recently been declared military areas," their report is thorough and balanced.

Eyewitnesses have described the death of Chile's renowned folk singer-composer Victor Jara: his captors led him into Estadio Chile, gave him a guitar, and commanded him to play. They smashed his fingers. When he began to sing, they beat him, again and again, till his eyes filled with blood and his genitals were "pulverized." When at last, days later, he died, they strung his body up in the foyer, then threw it out into the street. I quote half the lyrics from his last song, *Estadio Chile,* as it was read in North America by his British wife last October:

> We are five thousand
> here in this little part of the sky.
> We are five thousand,
> how many more will we be?
> In the whole city and the country
> ten thousand hands which could seed the fields,
> make run the factories.
> How much humanity
> now with pain, panic and terror?
> We are six of us,
> lost in space among the stars,
> one dead, one beaten like I never believed
> a human could be so beaten.
> The other four wanting to leave all the terror,
> one leaping into space,
> others beating their heads against the wall,
> all with gazes fixed on death.
> The military carry out their plans with precision;
> blood is medals for them,
> slaughter is the badge of heroism.*

---

*© Copyright 1975 Mighty Oak Music Ltd., London, England. TRO-CHESHIRE MUSIC, INC., New York, controls all publication rights for the U.S.A. and Canada. Used by permission.

Friends of Pauline Altamirano, wife of the leader of Allende's Socialist Party, who had escaped through Cuba though he was billed "the most wanted man in Chile," report that she was psychologically destroyed by being forced to listen to tapes she believed were of her absent children screaming. (Altamirano, reacting to the proclamation of a State of War, commented, understandably: "War against whom? Women and children?") A military officer awaiting trial in Santiago tells of being injected with drugs and convinced that a simulated voice was his son's pleading. A Señor Ayress was spiritually broken by being forced to witness the brutal beating and rape of his daughter by four soldiers in succession.

Children are used in various ways to terrorize and control adults. In March 1974 a nine-year-old girl and a four-year-old boy were reportedly tortured to death under their parents' eyes. In October, a couple and their four-year-old child were all tortured together. The woman died and her body was thrown over the wall onto the grounds of the Italian Embassy. (Italy has never recognized the junta.) The boy and his father have disappeared. The father is presumed dead. There have been dozens of documented cases of kidnappings from the *poblaciones*. The children who are fortunate enough to be returned to their parents are often severely disturbed after maltreatment. Many must be hospitalized.

A special, sophisticated form of torture for parents involves telephoned threats of kidnapping while the children are at school. For doctors, extreme sensory deprivation during months of incarceration is as effective as the ferocious physical tortures documented in the reports that Amnesty has received. For professors and artists, the effects of bizarre, excessive, inescapable light and sound, administered incommunicado, are shattering. For women, sexual degradation and the dread of bearing malformed babies is sufficient barbarity. For women, too, the responsibility for young lives can become unbearable. A secretary of Allende is haunted by the slow deaths by torture (beatings, pulling out of nails, cutting off of tongues, ears, and feet, gouging out of eyes) of two youths, "El Gordo" Toledano and Eduardo Muñoz, whom she had known well. She was made to watch their last hours of agony on a blue-lit "stage" in prison because she refused to yield information.

Torture in Chile is not isolated sadism but state policy, fashioned cleverly to create conformity by terrorization, dehumanization, and destruction of the will through prolonged, incalculable pain. Its primary aim is to extort information and to obtain "confessions" that are used against prisoners at trials.

When I was in Chile in February 1974, I was shown a crumpled piece of blue paper with minute writing, edge to edge, smuggled out of the stadium. Its author was a very young man. I quote from it here:

> On the chance that this message of agony should reach the hands of someone in my family, I am going to relate what they did to us when civilian personnel "invited" us to an interrogation which would last "two hours." We calmly climbed into two trucks, one white or cream, the other blue, if I am not mistaken. We followed streets until we reached the open country. Once there, they put adhesive tape over our eyes, and we realized that this was an abduction, and the beginning of our "calvary"...
>
> They put us into a closed truck... We traveled two or three hours. It was dark. They made us get down. I heard the sound of arms and it chilled me. I said goodbye to all my beloved ones, with my eyes full of tears. I thought they were going to kill us because they put us against some wood, with our hands up, feet behind and turned around. I didn't know what to think. My God, why are they doing this?
>
> They put us in a wooden room... They had us Friday, Saturday, Sunday with blindfolds... On Monday they took us away.
>
> In a truck 10 or 15 minutes from the encampment, they made us get down from the vehicle and they put us into a basement (we went down some stairs). We went with our heads covered and our hands tied behind us; they made us undress. They tied us and put us into cells which were noticeably narrow. Then began the inferno of terror.
>
> From the first whom they took to the torture table, we heard not shouts, but howls. My body shuddered with fear. One could hear the beating and heard the voice of the tor-

turer: "Who did it?" "Who went?" And our names were repeated, more blows, more cries and more terror. They finished with the first. We could hear his doleful moans outside . . . They took the second . . . the same cries, supplication, the same questions, and the interrogator demanded: "You, too, were in the group! Talk or you will never leave here alive!" The third was the same.

Then my turn. They tied me on top of the table, powerful lights above me. They put cables on my nude body, dampened my skin, and began to apply the current to all parts of my body. The interrogators didn't ask anything, but assured me that "I did it." I denied these monstrosities and they began to hit me in the stomach, abdomen, ribs, chest, testicles, etc., I don't know how long they beat me, but with all the blows to the chest, my throat and lungs filled and I was drowning, I was going to die. They laughed, but assured themselves that I wasn't pretending. Then they put acid between my toes, they pricked pins in me. I felt nothing. They lowered me from the table. I could now breathe. They returned us again to the cells. But not one slept with our moaning. The other prisoners cried with us. They took us the next day, and it was worse. They did things that can't be described . . . there were threats of death unless we signed what the interrogators wanted . . . no one knows anything about us, they said . . . or they just applied the tortures. We were no longer men, but shadows . . . Eight days later, we were moved from Tejas Verdes where we had been sequestered to the place where we were kept incommunicado for being "dangerous" . . . We signed the criminal declaration, forced upon us in this way, because we wanted to live and demonstrate our total innocence.

Why did they do this to us? From where comes the desire to blame us for something in which we did not participate? This is our "calvary"? Why, God, why? We have faith in justice.

Certain groups seem to have been singled out for persecution and brutal treatment, in addition to the loyal military of whom examples had to be made. Health workers, educators and students, and organized labor dominate current documentation.

We know most about the medicos: at least sixty-eight doctors have been shot or died as a result of torture and untreated wounds. Seventeen psychiatrists were murdered in various parts of Chile the first day of the coup, and psychiatrists in general have been persecuted, jailed, or kept under house arrest. Scores of nurses and medical assistants have been seized as potential threats to the junta because their communities respect them. Those who did not go out on strike with a group of right-wing medical personnel in Allende's last year became highly visible. Their own colleagues failed to defend them when they were dismissed, barred from further practice, or imprisoned. Over a thousand left the hospitals, and an undetermined number of top researchers emigrated. Silvia Morris, head nurse at the children's hospital in Valparaíso, was condemned and tortured, for no greater offense than suggesting that her small patients needed more nourishment and attention. Dr. Natacha Carrión, a respected pediatrician in Cautín province whose husband, Dr. Eduardo González, had been shot, was tortured and sentenced to three years in prison although she was in advanced pregnancy. Her crime seems to be that she treated Mapuche Indians. Dr. Danilo Bartolín, a heart surgeon, was taken to the Estadio Nacional in September 1973, whipped and tortured, and removed to the mine at Chacobuco. A colleague of his, a surgeon from Valparaíso, has arrived in Boston with his fingers cut off at the second joint.

On March 26, 1974, Amnesty International received an anguished appeal from the Chilean doctors themselves. It listed eighty-five doctors in prison. None had had concrete charges lodged against him. Nine had been condemned to death. Ten categories of torture they had endured were described. While the appeal was on its way, six more doctors were seized. This time an ad placed in *The New York Times* by American colleagues, and a committee Senator Edward Kennedy sent to Chile, helped effect the release of at least one of them, Dr. Gustavo Molina. Apolitical, but an old friend and roommate of Allende's, Molina had come out of retirement to administer the national health service. In January

1975 he was in the United States on a visit from Colombia, speaking to medical personnel here. Anthony Lewis interviewed him for *The New York Times:*

> On Jan. 8, 1974, "three gentlemen from the Air Force," as he puts it, seized him without notice in Santiago. They threw him on the floor of a station wagon with two other doctors . . . They were taken to a prison camp called Tejas Verdes and kept together in a small room. On Jan. 14 the three were taken to another place, with hoods over their heads, for questioning . . . Dr. Molina was not tortured— he attributes that to his age. His two roommates were. They were strapped under gymnastic "horses," beaten and given electroshocks. "Their lower limbs were paralyzed . . . It must be a very low current, because the paralysis lasted only four or five days. I nursed them."

Molina, whom Allende's predecessor, Eduardo Frei, called "a serious man, a respected physician, not involved in politics," told me that he was speaking out in the hope that American response might save other doctors such as Hugo Behm, Dean of the School of Public Health, arrested and tortured a year after the coup and taken to Tres Alamos, and Patricio Cid, condemned to death in May 1974, still alive but badly maltreated after he talked with California doctor Leonard Sagan, who visited Chile in June on a Federation of American Scientists trip. Condemned with Cid at the May trial was thirty-year-old Bautista von Schowen. Prior to May, AI heard that von Schowen, picked up in December 1973 after police had surrounded his parents' home for two months, had been so badly beaten, so mangled in captivity, that he had died. Then in January 1975, AI learned that he had been found in a hospital, badly paralyzed, his extremities a mass of hematomas, inarticulate, always drowsy, but alive, and still being tortured. The ferocity with which doctors were treated was probably triggered by *White Book* assertions that they were stealing supplies and equipment to set up clinics of their own, anticipating a left-wing coup. *The White Book,* on every newsstand in Santiago, contains clever photostats of "documents" to prove the necessity of the September 11 orgy of violence.

The three doctors sponsored by F.A.S. affirmed that Dr. Salvador Allende, the first president of the physicians' union, had given high priority to the quality and distribution of health services. His programs of community participation in the administration of health services to effect prevention and accelerate cure bothered many conservative doctors. Since the coup, though all but one of the eight physicians and two nurses on Allende's personal medical staff have been released (and exiled or denied the right to work), all three physicians of his Health Policy staff—Drs. Eduardo Paredes, Enrique Paris, and Jorge Klein—disappeared after their arrests. It is widely believed that they were tortured and executed. The team of visiting doctors interviewed prisoners and ex-prisoners and citizens they felt to be objective, and concluded that torture was still being practiced in a highly systematic fashion. A list of medical students arrested in 1975 has just been received.

Students and teachers are in a position comparable to that of doctors. All university rectors were fired on September 11 and replaced by military personnel. Some departments have closed; Psychology, Sociology, and Latin American History are particularly affected. Textbooks have been revised. Thousands of students are in detention. Professor Viola Muñoz (Social Anthropology, U. of Arica in northern Chile) received an arbitrary sentence of twenty-six years, exceeding that which the prosecutor asked. In Arica four students—Enzo Villanueva, Jorge Jaque, Miguel Berton, and Sergio Básquez—after seeing lawyers for a few minutes, were condemned to nineteen and a half, thirteen, twenty-five, and eighteen years for university activity. Jaque, suffering from gangrene, had to have his fingers and toes amputated as a result of torture and the denial of medication.

At the Latin American Faculty of Social Sciences (FLACSO), Luis Ramallo's best students, mostly foreign-born, were kidnapped and tortured to death though they had never been active in politics. He found them with multiple concussions and gaping chest wounds in the Santiago morgue on October 5, among 150 unidentified bodies. *Newsweek*'s John Barnes, reporting his own grim visit to the morgue the same week, was accused by the junta of "journalistic imperialism." Ramallo confirmed the horrible details, and wired UNESCO for aid in the immediate repatriation of all non-Chilean students. Even secondary schools were affected. St. George's, a large private school run by the Holy Cross order of Indiana, was taken over by the military after certain parents complained. A young teacher received a thirty-year sentence for "concientización" of his young pupils: telling them about Marx.

There has been a recent crackdown on faculty and students at Catholic University, once a stronghold of anti-Allende sentiment. Professor Herman Schwember, a mechanical engineer, was arrested on October 9, 1974, but released when Stanford University offered him a post. While he and his family prepared to leave Chile, he was suddenly seized by DINA, unofficially charged with collecting funds to aid the families of political prisoners, and taken to Tres Alamos. He is still there, being treated harshly. An eighteen-year-old prisoner who reached California says his captors threatened him with castration and a torture scene "worse than the Nazis." He was forced to beat his brother, who is now in Paris awaiting plastic surgery on his battered face.

The power base of the MIR—Movement of the Revolutionary Left, which the junta still seems to fear—was alleged to be at the University of Concepción, the most vital academic center in the south. There, six thousand of eighteen thousand students and hundreds of professors were suspended. At the Santiago branch of the University of Chile, eight thousand had to leave, as well as seventy law students and forty-four of their professors, and fifteen hundred students and a hundred teachers from its schools of art, architecture, and music. Temuco's campus was decimated by the dismissal of three hundred students, most of them Mapuche Indians accused of being extremists. They were taken en masse to the police station in Cautín province. Their heads were shaved and for fifteen days they were subjected to all manner of abuse, including electroshock. Then they were taken to another station and the process repeated. "My God," despaired one of the *carabineros*, "we are full of Marxist Indians."

The surviving supporters of MIR are being actively hunted.

When its leader Miguel Enríquez was smoked out and shot (October 5, 1974), Carmen Castillo, the woman bearing his child, was kicked, drugged, and given electroshock in the hospital to which she and the other wounded were removed. Thanks to international pressure, she was finally flown to London. There her newborn son, named Bautista, exhibited extensive brain damage and died when a few weeks old. Doctors are operating now on her crippled arm, hoping she will recover some use of it. Meanwhile, her brother, Christian Castillo, has been picked up in Santiago and has disappeared. The MIR mantle passed to Andrés Pascal Allende, who at this writing is in hiding. His mother Laura, President Allende's youngest sister, recovering from a major cancer operation, was routed from her bed by more military officers than could fit into her apartment. Andrés's sister Mariana was seized at the beach with her friends and all of them were interrogated cruelly so that Andrés would give himself up. The tactic failed. After debilitating psychological mistreatment—mock executions were the worst, she told me—Mariana was permitted exile in Mexico. Such reprieves are cause for only brief celebration. Laura describes her four months in a prison where women and their small daughters were beaten, raped, and subjected to electroshock. A hungry baby crawls through filth. A three-year-old is locked alone in a cell. And scores of new prisoners are being taken each month: Quatros Alamos and Villa Grimaldi are two torture centers opened to accommodate the victims of 1975.

Allende's government had dedicated itself to improving the lot of the poor and working classes—it had raised workers' basic pay 200 percent, improved food distribution to the poor, and begun to redistribute the wealth of the nation—and most workers, accordingly, were enthusiastic supporters of Allende. The junta was therefore especially harsh in its treatment of workers, and factories were the first places to be searched for illegal arms after the coup. In the Cevillos Cordón, many workers were killed when the factories were raided or razed. In the Sumar textile factory, bombing left at least 500 bodies. Neighborhood organizations were invaded and destroyed. The Unica de Trabajadores (Central Workers Federation) was abolished. The poor again stood on bread lines, this time under the watchful gaze of the police. Everyone was nervous. Eyewitnesses describe the arbitrary shooting of a mother whose frightened child darted out of the line, of youngsters being shot while playing ball after the early curfew, of a boy machine-gunned to death because he forgot his papers when he went to shop for his mother. In Sumar Población, sixty young men and women were taken away after the men were severely beaten and the women's breasts stabbed with bayonets. Trucks loaded with "prisoners" from the shantytowns rolled up to waste lots and stopped. As the men came off the trucks, told by the police that they were free, they were shot.

Three months after the coup, dock workers in San Antonio staged a strike. Their leaders were dragged under trucks and killed. In late November 1973, subway construction workers for Ingemetro in Santiago struck for more pay. Wages were frozen or cut back throughout industry. Pinochet had asked for a twelve-hour day, plus Saturdays, and with inflation the workers' families were on the brink of starvation. One hour after the strike began, trucks of police arrived. Each man was asked if he was going to return to work immediately. Those who were not intimidated into saying yes were herded into the trucks. As of March 1974, fourteen had not been heard of again.

With unemployment high and climbing higher, a whispered word of disagreement means firing and replacement. The identification papers of the dismissed may be marked "activist," rendering reemployment impossible. Well-paid junta "spies" sweep the floors of the factories and listen. They, too, are afraid, chiefly that they will meet with accident perpetrated by the workers, who hate them. The atmosphere is so tense, so unpleasant, that even employees who favored the take-over want to get out. While they are working, many are fearful for their families at home. In February 1974 this incident was reported to AI:

> At 10:30 a.m. on January 30, Sr. Ayress and his twenty-three-year-old daughter Luz were working in a factory when twelve armed men burst in and without identifying

themselves ransacked the building, damaging machinery, holding everyone at gunpoint. Sr. Ayress managed to leap out the window and raced to the police station to report the incident. The police told him to go back, "it's a routine intelligence operation," and he did. His reappearance surprised the raiders, who, assuming he had escaped, had sent six men to his house. Led by a bearded, sloppily dressed "foreigner," the six broke in, insulted Sra. Ayress, put a pistol to their teenaged daughter's head, mistreated the two other teenagers, frenziedly destroying things of value, and beat the wife "around the arms" so she would answer the phone normally when it rang, mentioning nothing of their presence. At 2:00 p.m. the others burst in, bringing Sr. Ayress and Luz as prisoners. After fruitless interrogating, still without identifying themselves, the twelve marched Sr. Ayress, his daughter Luz and his 15-year-old son off in unmarked station wagons. At 7:30 p.m. the mysterious bearded man, whom others in Santiago report seeing at "operations," returned, broke down the door, and while two men with machine guns stood in the hall (no one was home), he smashed dolls, a teddy bear, a child's bracelet, and stole, besides a tape recorder and camera, men's underclothes and feminine articles. Neighbors who had phoned police were told it was not a robbery, to return home. The three prisoners have not been seen since.

Months later, Luz was found and told her story in the Women's Reformatory, where she remains. She had been chained, beaten insensate, given shock, hung upside down, cut with knives and razors, sexually assaulted, caged with spiders and frightened mice which clawed her and were forced up her vagina, was compelled to witness the torture of her father and brother, was left for dead and wanted to be dead.

In the September campaign against foreigners, a number of Americans were among the 4,000 first subjected to confinement and savagery in the stadiums. Mr. and Mrs. Garrett-Schesch, sociologists from Iowa, arrived exhausted in Miami. They described the beatings, the terrifying sounds of torture and executions in the makeshift cells of Estadio Chile. Frank

Teruggi, a student from Chicago, was arrested with his roommate, David Hathaway, when police broke into their apartment the night of September 20, 1973, searching for "leftist literature." The police were clearly scared of them: "Who are you? Why are you here—to make bombs?" Early in the morning, friends reported their kidnapping to the American Embassy, where the young men were registered. Frank was not seen alive again. At 6:00 p.m. that evening his name was called out in the stadium and he was led away. His corpse, disfigured and punctured by fifteen bullets, was identified on October 2. This was only after Hathaway, angered that the U.S. Embassy had done nothing to investigate the arrest, prevent the death, or attempt to identify the body when Chilean authorities informed them they had it, insisted, after his own release on September 26, that U.S. Consul Frederick Purdy make a trip to the morgue with him. Stories of Teruggi in American newspapers prompted Professor Richard Fagen of Stanford, who had spent 1972–3 as a Ford Foundation Consultant in Santiago and had known Teruggi, Hathaway, and Charles Horman (a young filmmaker who was also killed), to call the U.S. State Department and the U.S. Embassy in Chile. Like Teruggi's family, Fagen received no information from either source. Teruggi's father made a personal trip to Santiago in February and pieced together the dreadful story. Spokesman Purdy was still polite, vague. Fagen wrote a letter to Senator Fulbright in which he stated that "the expressed hostility of the American Embassy to the Allende government extended to all members of the American community who were known to cooperate or sympathize" with the regime. He reported comments by embassy personnel that specific individuals were behaving in ways that were "against the best interests of the U.S." Words like "traitor," "Commie," and "fellow traveler" were casually attached to certain of Fagen's friends. Under Nathaniel Davis (promoted since to Director of Inter-American Affairs in Washington and now Ambassador to South Africa), the Embassy was run by Frederick Purdy, Naval Intelligence Captain Ray E. Davis, Harry W. Shlaudeman (nominated to be Ambassador to Venezuela following testimony he gave the House of Representatives on June 12, 1974, that the U.S.

had followed Kissinger's policy of non-intervention, had undertaken no significant development lending in Chile after 1968, and continued the same assistance programs in effect under the Allende regime), and, from Washington, Jack Kubisch (now ambassador to Greece). After turning away Americans such as Horman, Professor James Ritter and his seven-year-old son, a couple named Hunt and a young woman with a two-year-old, each of whom came to seek sanctuary, Shlaudeman—characterized as a hard-liner during the crushing of rebels in the Dominican Republic—was credited with the remark: "They never come to see us in normal times; now they're crawling out of the woodwork and expecting us to do things for them."

From September 7, 1973, Charles Horman, a filmmaker, was in Viña del Mar, where Allende had his seaside "palace." Ambassador Davis was in Washington talking to Kissinger and the National Security Council. At the start of the coup, sources report, American military officers spoke openly and enthusiastically to Horman about the event. On September 15, Captain Davis gave Horman a ride in his car back to Santiago. On the afternoon of the seventeenth, Horman went to the Embassy to ask for protection. He was sent to his house. Horman's wife, Joyce, was caught by the curfew in downtown Santiago and spent that night with a friend. When she returned in the morning, the house had been ransacked and Charles was missing. She went immediately to the American Embassy to report it. According to Joyce, she was turned away by embassy personnel, who suggested "Charles probably just wanted to get away from you," and to "be patient. Go home and wait. We have many problems to take care of."

The days dragged on into months. Joyce and Charles's father in New York inquired and tried to investigate on their own, to no avail. But the Chilean military had apparently told Purdy weeks before that Horman had been killed in the National Stadium. Joyce reports that Ray Davis called her to denigrate Charles, and to say, "Don't worry, you'll get over it, you're young." The family has still not been allowed to bring Charles's body to the United States. Writer Mark Harris noted indignantly that Horman's death brought no protest by the U.S. government. American citizens, if they focus on

Chile's story, will find fresh reason to worry: should their views at any time differ from the C.I.A.'s, their government may no longer hasten to protect them abroad.

In the aftermath of the coup, the American Embassy took in no refugees of any nationality. The Swedish Embassy, whose heroic Ambassador Harald Edelstam so annoyed the junta that it declared him *persona non grata*, took in everyone who came, including Americans who had been turned away from their own Embassy. Edelstam went out into the streets and hospitals to extend sanctuary and worked to get other embassies to take in the desperate when his own facilities were overflowing. Many union leaders who were not picked up the first day or two of the coup were rescued by Edelstam, who then let them in and out of asylum to rest and rescue others. As security tightened, the in-and-out habit stopped. Nine hundred and fifteen refugees were accepted in Sweden once safe-conducts had been secured. Their families are joining them now, as they learn Swedish and new trades. The Mexicans gave asylum to thousands. Once every refugee in the Mexican Embassy in Santiago had received safe passage out, President Echeverría broke off relations with the junta. The French were especially ingenious. Unable to accommodate a group of young people who wanted to come to their Embassy for asylum, partly because there was no bus to transport them safely, the Ambassador bought the building the youths were in, and ran up the French flag.

Soldiers lurked outside the windows and courtyards of the sanctuaries, with particular targets in mind. Rolando Calderón, former Minister of Agriculture, was shot in the head in the Cuban Embassy. Edelstam brought in a Swedish specialist, Dr. Ragstrom, to operate on him, but he was expelled immediately. Calderón is now recovering. A young Chilean was killed in the Argentine Embassy. Two were shot as they emptied garbage inside the gate. Jaime Faivovich, an Under-secretary of Transportation who resigned during the truckers' strike to keep peace, was wounded in April on the Mexican premises. The most-wanted refugees found themselves faced with Army men at the door, threatening to massacre their families and friends outside if they did not renounce their asylum. Many foreigners were afraid to go to embassies or to register at the U.N. refugee camps for fear of reprisals.

During the first year after the coup, France received over one thousand refugees, West Germany took one thousand, East Germany four hundred; Yugoslavia, Sweden, Holland, Poland, the U.S.S.R., Finland, Mexico, Spain, Bulgaria, Hungary, Belgium, Switzerland—governments of the left and of the right—all came through, largely due to the immediate and continuing efforts of the United Nations refugee committees. Canada took several hundred: Chileans are to be seen on the streets of downtown Toronto with placards asking help for their countrymen who have not escaped. Cuba has been a haven for those of the far left. The numbers in Peru and Argentina are large but uncounted, since so many have managed to cross the border on foot. Officially Peru and Argentina are unwilling to handle more, as refugee housing is already filled to capacity.

The United States has been noticeably reluctant to accept refugees. In February 1974 the number we had accepted under pressure was eleven; by January 1975, it was thirty-one. The few who have been released from jail and have been granted U.S. visas since have powerful American connections or are the recipients of top teaching posts, like ex-Ambassador to Washington Orlando Letelier and former Minister of Mines Sergio Bitar, who arrived in the States with the New Year. For the ordinary Chilean, even one like AI "adopted" prisoner José Verdejo Duarte, an American-trained customs inspector languishing uncharged in Arica's jail, fearing the death penalty for invented crimes, while his sister, a teacher in Connecticut, sends money and appeals to every official, there is little hope of being allowed to go anywhere. Besides AI members, how many people are working for the release of editor José Gómez López, actress Elsa Rudolphi, or widow Haydee Castro Muñoz, all imprisoned without charges, and tortured?

Thirty-six of Allende's "elite" were sent to Antarctic Dawson Island near Tierra del Fuego, after their Santiago interrogations in September 1974. Nineteen had responded to a radio request and turned themselves in to the police, rather than take refuge in the embassies that offered it. These included Carlos Jorquera, Allende's Press Secretary; university president Enrique Kirberg; Hugo Miranda, a Chilean senator for twenty-four years; Alfredo Joignant, head of the Chilean F.B.I.; Daniel Vergara, the deputy shot in the back after he tried to negotiate with soldiers in La Moneda during the coup; Luis Corvalon, Secretary of the Communist Party; Osvaldo Puccie, Anselmo Sule, Orlando Letelier, Miguel Lawner, Jorge Tapia, Pedro Ramírez, Miguel Muñoz; and José Toha, the 6'4" Minister of Defense under Allende, who, when last seen alive, was down to 112 pounds and could barely see, hear, or walk. He is dead now; the junta calls it suicide. Many Dawson prisoners arrived by boat from Valparaíso, the marks of savage beatings all too evident. Those on Dawson Island fared better than those in other detention camps, but they had to endure extreme cold and hunger, manual labor too severe for them, and total lack of medical attention. For a time Vergara's arm was in danger of amputation from gangrenous untreated wounds. The prisoners were made to run in the sand carrying heavy rocks back and forth, back and forth. One prisoner's face flushed, his eyes bulged, and his extremities swelled so with the effort that he nearly died. There was international protest, and a demand for quick open trials. The U.N. requested that conditions be improved, and specifically asked for the release of five of the prisoners. The latter request was denied, but by the time the roughest winds of May had reached the southern tip of Chile, most of Allende's associates had been removed to basement cells near Santiago, where, confined in idleness, they listened helplessly as young MIRistas screamed day and night under torture in adjoining cells. But other prisoners, including one hundred and twenty boys, stayed at Dawson. One had a Z burned into his chest. One, who survived being shot thirty-five times, was sent to a hospital due to a "nervous breakdown." Orlando Letelier reports that everyone he has seen from Dawson had been tortured.

Allende's Foreign Minister, Clodomiro Almeyda, was transferred from Dawson before the others. In February 1974 he was used as a showcase example while his successor, Admiral Ismael Huerta, was in Mexico to convince U.S. Secretary of State Henry Kissinger and the world press that Chile was back to normal with all justice and dignity preserved.

From Dawson, Almeyda was transferred to Tacna Regiment, given an officer's room, and permitted books and writing materials and visits from his family. When Huerta returned to Chile, Almeyda was removed to an undisclosed place. A month later his wife found him on the point of suicide. He had been ruthlessly starved, interrogated, and tortured.

The Dawson group eventually was sent to Ritoque, a military installation near Valparaíso, and then scattered to various centers. Since New Year's, five Dawson Island men have been released and sent to Rumania. On January 30, Santiago radio announced that the three leaders of the Radicales—Morales, Miranda, and Sule—had been tried and acquitted and would leave for Venezuela. So would former Press Secretary Jorquera, suffering the results of a nervous breakdown due to torture, and Toha's younger brother, Jaime, his hand useless from untreated bullet wounds. Intellectuals like Dr. Fernando Flores and Enrique Kirberg remain in jail, though American university posts await them. Acquittals until now have been rare.

"Public" trials proceed unpublicized in Santiago. Secret trials, with lawyers given an hour or possibly a day to meet clients and prepare their cases, condemn prisoners throughout the country. In Osorno, for example, scores of farmers and workers disappeared and were located only when their sentences were announced or their bodies were washed onto the riverbanks. California lawyer Warren Wilson, who visited the Osorno jail in November 1974, with the junta's permission, writes:

> It was painful and terribly upsetting to look at this handsome group of young men around us, obviously the flower of Chilean leadership, helplessly deteriorating in the depressingly bleak, damp cellblocks, realizing that there was no genuine legal process available to them.

Church leaders have been the citizens' best allies, but they are in danger. Cardinal Raúl Silva and the Bishops of Chile, cautious and conciliatory at first, now openly condemn the junta's "climate of fear." Spanish priest Juan Alsina is dead. Father Joel Gajardo was arrested, tortured, exiled. Methodist minister Ulysses Torres is in prison.

The government is taking reprisals against Chileans who work with the Church's Committee for Cooperation and Peace and even with the Red Cross. Dr. Hector García was killed in August 1974 because he had worked with the Red Cross and treated torture victims. New proceedings have been instituted against the detained psychiatrist Bruno García, accusing him of being "the doctor for the guerrillas."

Rumors of U.S. involvement in the coup began shortly after September 11. Three days before the coup, Ambassador Davis returned to Washington to talk with the 40 Committee, headed by Henry Kissinger. A week before, U.S. Air Force pilots visited Santiago to prepare for an aerial acrobatics show. The bombing of the Moneda on the eleventh was so accurate—inner offices were destroyed by bombs landing in inner courtyards, while the façade of the building was left intact—that observers guessed the pilots of the British Hunter (Hawker) airplanes were using U.S.-supplied "smart bombs." In the week before the coup, the unlucky Charles Horman was told by a U.S. officer in Valparaíso that he had just taken a Chilean naval officer on a "shopping spree" for equipment in the States. Between September 7 and 12, a U.S. Air Force plane, registry number 6313298, type WB 575, the weather version of the reconnaissance RB 575, flew four missions between Chile and Argentina, where twenty-two more WB 575's were based, to coordinate "weather programming." The plane is supposed to have been on a communications mission on its several stops in Chile on September 11.

Two days after the coup, Senator Edward Kennedy spoke in the Senate about Chile. The White House had denied U.S. involvement and the State Department had said that Latin America's bloodiest coup in years was "an internal matter." Kennedy now reminded that Senate that in 1971 the White House pointedly did not send the traditional congratulatory note to Allende upon his election as President; that the Nixon Administration had snubbed a personal invitation from Allende for the carrier U.S.S. *Enterprise* to dock at Valparaíso after Admiral Elmo Zumwalt's acceptance had been widely and favorably publicized in Chilean newspapers; that the White House blocked Export-Import Bank financing of new jet airliners for Chile's national airline and had dissuaded various multinational banks from advancing credit to Allende's government. Kennedy declared: "A wise Administration policy would have recognized that the Chilean experiment in socialism had been decided by the people of Chile in an election far more democratic than the charade we saw last week in Vietnam."

It is difficult to draw firm conclusions from partial evidence, evidence that by its very nature is kept secret or denied by the highest, most responsible, and prestigious leaders in the U.S. government. Americans are reluctant to admit a pattern of official deceit, and belief and rumor are often tangled.

When Allende took office, 4,374 Chilean military officers had graduated from U.S. military training programs. The United States refused to sell Allende's government 300,000 tons of desperately needed wheat, denied all other economic aid, put pressure on other nations to suspend financial and other aid, but simultaneously gave $130,000,000 in aid to the right-wing Chilean military. In the twenty years before Allende, Chile had received $175,000,000 in military aid, more than any other Latin American country except Brazil. The Pentagon had for a long time had close ties with Chile's military, especially the Navy and Air Force, and Pentagon analysts considered Chile's 90,000-member military force the best on the continent. U.S. AID gave the *carabineros* $2,500,000 during the sixties. By coincidence, large joint-hemisphere naval maneuvers were scheduled for the Pacific off Chile in September 1973, but U.S. ships (which may have been standing by to help Chilean ships) turned away upon hearing news of the coup.

In the midst of bloodshed and the junta's Reign of Terror, the White House restored to Pinochet the financial credit it had denied to Allende, granted sale of the 300,000 tons of wheat Allende had been refused only a month earlier, negotiated compensation for the American corporate property Allende had nationalized, and continued military aid to Chile at a per capita rate higher than anywhere else in the Western Hemisphere. (By contrast, citing the brutality of the junta, the British government voted to discontinue military aid to the new Chilean government; among other things, the British refused to sell spare parts to the Chilean Air Force for their British-made Hunter [Hawker] fighter bombers, the planes used to bomb the Moneda Palace. The U.S. Department of Defense, on the other hand, announced that it would sell a number of F-5 "Freedom Fighter" all-purpose fighters to Chile.)

General Pinochet angrily denied the United States had advance knowledge of the coup—"even my wife didn't know"—but *The Washington Post* said the White House learned of the planned coup the night before it happened, and the *Los Angeles Times* quoted Administration sources as saying that Chile gave Nixon forty-eight hours' notice. Columnist Jack Anderson wrote about an ITT memo describing John McCone's offer of $1,000,000 to the C.I.A. to stop Allende's election in 1970. McCone had been C.I.A. director from 1961 to 1965 and was an ITT director at the time of the offer; ITT owned the Chilean telephone system. State Department spokesman Paul Hare refused to condemn the coup, saying righteously: "President Allende upset the U.S. by nationalizing American-owned copper mines, telephone exchanges, and other properties."

Among Chileans and foreigners who survived arrest and detention after the coup, there was frequent talk of interrogators trained in torture technology at an American military base in the U.S. Canal Zone. Research by U.S. groups like the North American Congress on Latin America (NACLA) indicates that U.S. police academies and military-intelligence schools in places like Washington, D.C., and Fort Gordon, Georgia, headquarters for the U.S. Army Military Police, are training military and civilian "exchange students" from Latin America, Greece, South Vietnam, South Korea, in the latest interrogation techniques, at the same time establishing personal contacts that will be useful in the future to U.S. intelligence personnel. James Ritter, a young American physics professor who was arrested and tortured in Estadio Chile, was interrogated by a Chilean detective who said he had graduated from the International Police Academy in Washington, D.C., in 1965. "Don't try any funny stuff," he warned. "I was trained in *your* country."

After a year of fragmentary information in the U.S. press,

much of it necessarily undocumented, Seymour Hersh, writing in *The New York Times* on September 8, 1974, revealed that C.I.A. Director William E. Colby had testified in secret to a House committee in April that the Nixon Administration had authorized over $8,000,000 for covert activities in Chile between 1970 and 1973. The original authorization came from the 40 Committee. In 1969 and 1970, the United States had spent $1,000,000 to keep Allende from winning the election, and then in the fall of 1970, after the election, had spent $350,000 to persuade members of the Chilean Congress to refuse confirmation of Allende's popular election. At the end of September, in a prime-time television press conference, President Gerald Ford answered a questioner about the role of the United States in Chile:

> Question: "Under what international law do we have a right to attempt to destabilize the constitutionally elected government of another country?"
> Answer: "I am not going to pass judgment on whether it is permitted or authorized under international law. It is a recognized fact that historically as well as presently, such actions are taken in the best interest of the countries involved."

It was a startling admission for the President of the United States to make.

It thus appears that the United States government, whether directly or indirectly, whether by assisting the military or by failing to oppose it, bears some *political* responsibility for the fact that a coup d'état took place in Chile, installing in office a group of men who have systematically tortured and killed Chilean citizens. From this it follows that American citizens and American policymakers have a special *humanitarian* responsibility to assist efforts to stop the junta's policy of terror and torture. This responsibility has been recognized by Senator Edward Kennedy and others in the Congress, and it has been sensed by many American citizens, including members of the American section of Amnesty International.

The still-tangled skein of the United States in Chile is an apt and instructive example of the sorts of problems faced by organizations such as Amnesty International, which are bound, by their organizational principles and the personal principles of their members, to work within the framework of international and national laws. While the nations of the world which are directly and indirectly responsible for the torture and murder of prisoners of conscience ignore at their convenience the canon of international law forbidding such behavior, workers for AI, the United Nations, and other organizations acting on behalf of prisoners, must obey completely not only the law but the local interpretations of the law made by national governments. It has been the experience of AI that the moral authority conferred upon the organization has often enabled it to bring the pressure of international embarrassment and exposure to bear on governments that practice and condone torture and political murder. But, ultimately, Amnesty International can only influence the actions of governments; it cannot actually intervene, as, for example, the United Nations can. The case of Chile is a tragic example of the realities of international politics. In such a situation, Amnesty International can only work to uncover the facts of the situation and to publicize them as widely as possible.

Although it is vital that Amnesty International continue to collect information on the policies of all governments toward prisoners of conscience, its logical focus should be the world's great powers, the Soviet Union, the United States, and perhaps China. Their neglect in the areas of human dignity and individual rights can be argued to be a legitimization of practices followed by their many client-states in their respective spheres of interest. The extensive international network of police, military, and intelligence agencies that is trained, financed, influenced, and to a varying extent controlled by the counterpart American, Chinese, and Russian agencies provides lessons in technique and rationalization that encompass the lives of millions of citizens in many countries. For the United States, a number of Latin American governments, Greece under the colonels, Iran, South Vietnam, South Korea, and Pakistan serve as examples of American influence or control. The Soviet Union has direct influence and control over the police, intelligence, and military activities of the German

Democratic Republic, Hungary, Poland, Czechoslovakia, Bulgaria, and Rumania.

An example of Soviet intervention in the affairs of another country that has strong parallels to the involvement of the United States in the Chilean coup is the invasion of Czechoslovakia by the Soviet Union in August 1968. Fearing that the movement toward a more democratic socialism under the government of Alexander Dubček would infect the other five Warsaw Pact countries of the Soviet bloc, the Russian leadership applied pressure on Dubček during the spring of 1968, then scheduled Warsaw Pact military maneuvers in areas bordering on Czechoslovakia, finally entering Czechoslovakia in the course of the maneuvers with a joint Warsaw Pact force. This force was withdrawn following meetings between Alexei Kosygin and Dubček in August, but four days later the Soviet Army invaded and occupied Czechoslovakia. There was passive resistance on the part of many thousands of Czech civilian citizens—it was clear the Soviet leadership did not consider the Czech military to be reliable from their point of view—but the resistance ended, the Dubček government was deposed, and a government entirely consistent with Soviet objectives was reimposed on the Czech people. There were arrests and imprisonments following the change of government, but it must be noted that there were no reports of systematic, officially sanctioned torture or murder of prisoners of conscience. So far this has been reserved for dissidents inside Soviet borders.

What did result was a broad loss of freedom for the Czechoslovakian people to direct their own destiny. Members of the Czech professional and intellectual classes have been acutely aware of their loss of freedom and have noted the parallels between what happened in their country and the Chilean coup d'état. A letter from a group of Czech "former political prisoners, of the years 1969–1974," to the Union of Czechoslovak Lawyers, published in *The New York Review of Books,* October 31, 1974, made the parallels painfully clear:

> Your resolution in defense of civil rights in Chile and in opposition to the Chilean fascist junta is hypocritical, and

your voice rings false. We, Czechoslovak political prisoners in the first half of the Seventies, are indeed linked by tight bonds of solidarity and affinity or proximity in ideology and action with Chilean socialists, communists, revolutionary Marxists, diverse political orientations.

You, however, have nothing in common with them, and hypocritical words can hardly mask that. Your own task is merely to defend, through propaganda, the situation in your own country, complete with the lively trade between Czechoslovakia and the Chilean fascist junta, and with Czechoslovakia's refusal to offer political asylum to Chilean refugees.

The writers of the letter are saying clearly that imprisonment for political reasons and torture for any reason are the products of inhumane, repressive government policies, that imprisonment and torture know no ideological or religious boundaries, and that all people must struggle against fascism and terror wherever they occur.

I spent Easter of 1974 in Czechoslovakia. In Prague many persons were talking of the tragedy in Chile, comparing it to their own recent past. They had just seen TV films of a funeral in Santiago (was it Toha's?) during which angry fists were raised and anti-junta shouts heard and responses of "Presente" made when the roll of the recently killed was called.

In Prague, concerned young people asked how much resistance exists in Chile and whether its voices were heard in North America. It was difficult to answer the first: Mrs. Tohá, asked the same question when she was in New York, commented that resistance had brought about 30,000 deaths. Though the junta tries to muffle the sounds of dissent, some voices carry. Members of Congress such as Edward Kennedy, Donald Fraser, Michael Harrington, James Abourezk, Frank Church, and Jacob Javits have heard them. So have journalists like Seymour Hersh and Anthony Lewis and Tom Wicker, lawyers like Joseph Morray and Charles Porter and Warren Wilson and Peter Weiss, and a number of vocal labor leaders and professors and feminists. American women now are publicizing the plight of their Chilean sisters via radio, rally, press, and petition. But how many people listen? Young people here have not asked enough questions. Too few organizations have spoken out. If more Chileans are released from prisons on condition that they emigrate, will the United States let them enter? Today they are blocked by continuing U.S. Administration suspicion that they may be revolutionary Marxists. Senator Kennedy is leading the fight to change immigration policy, just as he persisted until military aid to Chile was cut off, and, a year ago, questioned the role of the C.I.A. there. It is a tough battle, one in which the support of citizens counts heavily.

In Prague, I heard Pablo Neruda's poetry read. Neruda "no longer exists" for Chileans. I was reminded of the article Mexican novelist Carlos Fuentes wrote on the poet's death in the aftermath of the coup and the destruction of Neruda's home. Fuentes commented that Santiago had been "made safe for supermarkets and the ITT," and asked the sad question: "Is the fortress of detente to be built on the graves of democratic socialism in Chile and Czechoslovakia?"

In Chile the reign of terror is unabated, torture one of its essential components. A recent American witness is Amy Conger, a young Chicago art instructor. For thirteen days in October 1974 she was detained by Chilean Air Force officers (the Air Force is conceded to have the most savage intelligence service). On November 27, back in America because, under threat of being taken straight to DINA's torture center or killed, she signed a statement "confessing" to knowing "subversives," Ms. Conger told Jack Anderson the following. She was brutally arrested by four men in street clothes with sub-machine guns at 7 p.m. (October 11), tightly handcuffed, and thrown into a car. Subsequently, she was flung down stairs blindfolded, questioned obscenely, deprived of sleep and water, and forced to stand for hours till she was near collapse. Thrown onto a bed, she was menaced with rape, then held in the insect-infested Air Force War Academy prison, where the unflushable toilet brimmed with blood and excrement; the guards, who kept "nervously experimenting with their sub-machine guns," played Joan Baez's *Happy Birthday*, over and over, on a cassette. At night, blindfolded, she heard prisoners scream under prolonged torture. By day, she saw two officers slugging and kicking an eighteen-year-old boy picked up with her, "heard his sharp quick screams of No! and afterwards long cries of No! like a dying animal. Finally he confessed to anything they suggested." The boy was dragged off to DINA anyway for more torture. On his return,

> his chest was covered with black and blue marks and inflamed red points, his face totally without color, white as plaster—anemic, it seems, due to blood loss. He had a deep cut about five inches long, open and unbandaged, on the inside of his left arm.
>
> Another young man returned from his trip (to the torture center) with discs broken in his spinal cord, and another in a wheelchair with a broken leg.

The President of the United States did not make a formal protest until the appearance of the newspaper stories made one advisable.

By the latter part of 1974, with wider access to information, Congress began to publicize and investigate the atrocities of contemporary Chile—fueled, of course, by the confirmation of U.S. involvement. Whereas in March 1974 the U.S. delegation to the United Nations had voted against a resolution to condemn the junta for its inhumanity, in October, after hearing a speech by Hortensia Allende and months of testimony prepared by AI and other organizations, it merely refrained altogether from voting on a similar resolution. The tally was 44–0, with Chile and the United States abstaining.

The gains are depressingly small. Yet the season is not without hope. A number of Chilean leaders are being offered permanent exile as an alternative to permanent imprisonment. This is clearly unjust punishment for patriots, but those who choose to leave may help free those who cannot, through raising international awareness and marshaling international pressure on the junta. Several universities in the United States have invited qualified Chileans to teach, and a small number are being permitted to accept the invitations. These intelligent visitors, although extremely discreet for fear their families in Chile may suffer, bear testimony to the terror in their homeland. If the new United States Attorney General, Edward Levi, ex-president of the University of Chicago, noted for his humanitarian interests, is persuaded to give parole visas to even a few hundred deserving Chileans soon, and if American citizens then welcome to their shores these refugees from tyranny and listen closely to their tales of innocence and experience, perhaps significant American voices will swell the international outcry and the day of state-sanctioned torture, in Chile and the world, will be hastened to its end.

Rose Styron

February 1975

Select Bibliography
(with special reference to Section 1)

BASTIAANS, J. *Vom Menschen in KZ und vom KZ im Menschen*, Vienna, 1971.
BASTIAANS, J. 'Over der specificiteit en de behandeling van het KZ-syndroom', *Net. Mil. Geneesk. Tijdschrift*, 1970.
BASOWITZ, H. et al. *Anxiety and Stress: An Interdisciplinary Study of a Life Situation*, New York, 1955.
BAUER, R.A. 'Brainwashing: psychology or demonology', *Journal of Social Issues*, 13, 41-7, 1957.
v. BAYER, W., HÄFNER, H. & KISKER, K.P. *Psychiatrie der Verfolgten*, Berlin, Göttingen, Heidelberg, 1964.
BEXTON, W.H., HERON, W. & SCOTT, T.H. 'Effects of decreased variation in the sensory environment', *Canadian Journal of Psychology*, 8, 70-6, 1954.
BIDERMAN, A.D. 'Communist attempts to elicit false confessions from Air Force prisoners of war', *Bulletin of New York Academy of Medicine*, 9, 33, September 1957.
BIDERMAN, A.D. 'Social-psychological needs and "involuntary" behaviour as illustrated by compliance in interrogation', repr. from *Sociometry*, 23, 2, June 1960, Bureau of Social Science Research Incorporated, Washington D.C.
BIDERMAN, A.D. & ZIMMER, H. (eds) *The Manipulation of Human Behavior*, New York, 1960.
BURNS, T. 'Friends, enemies and the polite fiction', *American Sociological Review*, 18, 654-62, 1953.
COHEN, E.A. 'Het post-concentratiekampsyndroom', *Ned. Tijdschr. v. Geneesk. Jrg.*, 113, 46, 2049-54, November 1969.
DAVIS, A. *Lectures on Liberation*, Berkeley and Los Angeles, 1969.
DEBENHAM et al. 'Treatment of war neuroses', *Lancet*, 1, 107, 1941.
DOUGLASS, F. *The Life and Times of Frederick Douglass*, London, 1962.
EITENGER, L. 'Rehabilitation of concentration camp survivors following concentration camp trauma', *Proc. 7th Int. Congr of Psychotherapy*. Wiesbaden, 1967-1969.
EITENGER, L. *Concentration Camp Survivors in Norway and Israel*, Oslo, 1964; repr. The Hague, 1972.
EITENGER, L. & STROM, A. *Mortality and Morbidity After Excessive Stress*, Oslo, 1973.
FANON, F. *The Wretched of the Earth* [*Les Damnés de la Terre*], Harmondsworth, 1967.
FARBER, I.E., HARLOW, H.F. & WEST, L.J. 'Brainwashing, conditioning and DDD', *Sociometry*, 20, 4, December 1957.
FEDERN, E. 'The endurance of torture', *Complex*, 4, 34-41, 1951.
GROUP FOR THE ADVANCEMENT OF PSYCHIATRY, 'Factors used

to increase the susceptibility of individuals to forceful indoctrination: observations and experiments', *Symposium No. 3*, New York, 1970.

GROUP FOR THE ADVANCEMENT OF PSYCHIATRY, 'Methods of forceful indoctrination: observations and interviews', New York, July 1957.

HINKLE, L.E. Jr. & WOLFF, H.G. 'Communist interrogation and indoctrination of the enemies of the state', *Arch. Neurological Psychiatry*, Chicago 76, 115-74, 1956.

KLUGE, E. 'Über die Folge schwerer Haftzeiten', *Nervenarzt* 29, 462, 1958.

KLUGE, E. 'Über den Defektcharakter von Dauerfolgen schwerer Haftzeiten', *Med. Sachverst.* 57, 185, 1961.

KLUGE, E. 'Über Ergebnisse bei der Begutachtung Verfolgter', *Nervenarzt*, 36, 321, 1965.

KLUGE, E. 'Über Defektzustände nach schweren Haftzeiten', in von Paul u. Herbert, *Psychische Spätschäden nach politischer Verfolgung*, Basel-New York 1967.

KLUGE, E. 'Chronische Schädigung durch Extrembelastungen in der Psychiatrie', *Fortschritte Der Neurologischen Psychiatrie*, 40, 1, 1972.

KORANYI, E.K. 'A theoretical review of the survivor syndrome', repr. from *Diseases of the Nervous System, GWAN*, supp. vol. 30, 115-18, February 1969.

KRAL, V.A., PAZDER, L.H. & WIGDOR, B.T. 'Long-term effects of a prolonged stress experience', *Canad. Psychiat. Ass. Journ.*, 12, 175-81, 1967.

KRYSTAL, H. *Massive Psychic Trauma*, New York, 1968.

LAING, R.D. 'The Obvious', in *To Free a Generation*, New York, 1968.

LILLY, J.C. 'Mental effects of reduction of ordinary levels of physical stimuli on intact healthy persons', *Group for Advancement of Psychiatry, Symposium No. 2, Illustrative Strategies for Research on Psychopathology in Mental Health*, New York, 1956.

LÖNNUM, A. *Helsesvikt en senfölge av krig of katastrofe*, stencilled report, 1969, translated into English at the request of the Norw. Ass. of Disabled Veterans (unfortunately not yet available in official print; very important survey).

MATUSSEK, P., et al. *Die Konzentrationslagerhaft und ihre Folger*, Berlin, Göttingen, Heidelberg, 1971.

MEERLOO, J.A.M. 'Pavlovian strategy as a weapon of menticide', *American Journal of Psychiatry*, 110, 809-13, 1954.

MILGRAM, S. 'Some conditions of obedience and disobedience to authority', *Human Relations*, 18, 57-74, 1965.

NIREMBERSKI, M. 'Psychological investigation of a group of internees at Belsen Camp', *Journal of Mental Science*, 92, 60-74, 1946.

RUSK, H.A. 'Aftermath of torture', *New York Times*, 7 July 1968.

SANTUCCI, P.S. & WINOKER, G. 'Brainwashing as a factor in psychiatric illness', *Archives of Neurology and Psychiatry*, 74, 11-16, 1955.

SARGANT, W. *Battle for the Mind*, London, 1957.

SCHEIN, E.H. 'Man against man: brainwashing', *Corrective Psychiatry and Journal of Social Therapy*, 8, 2, 90-7, 1962.
SCHILLING, P. *Brasil: Seis anos de dictadura y torturas*, Quadernos de marcha No. 37, Montevideo, 1970.
SEDMAN, G. 'Brainwashing and sensory deprivation as factors in the production of psychiatrie states: the relation between such states and schizophrenia', *Confinia Psychiatrica*, 4, 28-44, 1961.
SHALLICE, T. 'The Ulster depth interrogation techniques and their relation to sensory deprivation research', *Cognition*, 1973.
SHURLEY, J.T. 'Stress and adaptation as related to sensory/perceptual isolation research', *Military Medical*, 131, 254-8, 1966.
SOLOMON, P. et al. (eds) *Sensory Deprivation*, Cambridge, Mass., 1961.
STROM, A. *Norwegian Concentration Camp Survivors*, Oslo, 1973.
SWANK, R.L. 'Combat exhaustion', *Journal of Nervous and Mental Disorders*, 109, 475, 1949.
SWANK, R.L. & MARCHAND, E. 'Combat neurosis: development of combat exhaustion', *A.M.A. Archives of Neurology and Psychiatry*, 55, 236-47, 1946.
U.S. GOVERNMENT, *POW: The Fight Continues After the Battle, Report of the Secretary of Defence's Advisory Committee on Prisoners of War*, Washington D.C., 1955.
VIETNAM VETERANS AGAINST THE WAR, *The Winter Soldier Investigation*, New York, 1972.
WADE, N. 'Technology in Ulster: rubber bullets hit home, brainwashing backfires', *Science*, 176, 1102-5, 1972.
WEXLER, D., MENDELSON, J., LEIDERMAN, H.L. & SOLOMON, P. 'Sensory deprivation', *Archives of Neurology and Psychiatry*, Chicago, 79, 225-233, 1958.
WINNEK, H.Z. 'Further comments concerning problems of late psychopathological effects of Nazi persecution and their therapy', *Ann. Psychiat.*, 5, 1-6, 1967.
WOLF, S. & RIPLEY, H.S. 'Reactions among Allied prisoners subjected to three years of imprisonment and torture by the Japanese', *American Journal of Psychiatry*, 104, 180-93, 1947.
ZUBEK, J.P. (ed.) *Sensory Deprivation: Fifteen Years of Research* New York, 1969.
ZUCKERMAN, M. 'Perceptual isolation as a stress situation: a review', *Archives of General Psychiatry*, 11, 255-76, 1964.
ZUCKERMAN, M. et al. 'Experimental and subject factors determining responses to sensory deprivation, social isolation and confinement', *Journal of Abnormal Psychology*, 73, 183-94, 1966.